Happy Father's Day

A Treasury of

AMERICAN BALLADS

Gay, Naughty, and Classic

A Treasury of

AMERICAN BALLADS

Gay, Naughty, and Classic

Edited with an Introduction and Notes
by
CHARLES O'BRIEN KENNEDY

Illustrated by
BARYE PHILLIPS

THE McBRIDE COMPANY

NEW YORK

In fond memory of my departed friends

FRANK R. HEUSTIS,

ARTHUR HOPKINS,

LOUIS WOLHEIM,

JOHN BARRYMORE,

EUGENE O'NEILL

Foreword

THE PROBLEMS of a ballad compiler, like those of a lover, make every other form of human travail seem meaningless.

By way of explanation, let me tell you that the compiler of this work had been an actor for over fifty years, until the theatre began to recede from him. Now, what to do? The answer came while I was recuperating from an operation and an editor with a soul came to my bedside. After many expressions of sympathy, his voice took on a steely note as he broached the subject of my compiling a small book of ballads for his firm. Much as I hated to cut short my enjoyable convalescence, I realized that a new and interesting field was opening up for me; that I was being promoted from a mere collector to a compiler. Before long I was struggling in the slough of indecision as to the difference between a ballad and a poem. At last I arrived at an elastic formula. viz: "One writes a poem to the girl he loves, but one writes a ballad about her."

From childhood I have been more or less blessed with a retentive memory and immediately little snatches of poems, songs, and ballads were popping out from the hidden recesses of my mind. With them came the labor of tracking down the full texts from which they sprung in order to classify them properly. I must say in all modesty that industry triumphed and the result was a successful pocket book of ballads, Published as a Fawcett Red Seal book and entitled **American Ballads: Naughty, Ribald, and Classic.**

But I could not stop there; something like a virus possessed me, urging me to search for more material. I started quizzing my fellow members of The Lambs and got many good leads. I corresponded with historical societies all over the country. Each night found me digging in the catacombs at the New York Public Library. All in all, I must have looked through five to six hundred books, not to mention old newspapers and magazines. My store of treasure was piling up. Now, what to do with it? At this juncture my present publishers invited me to compile a large book, one which would emphasize American history from before the Revolution down to the present time.

Here my old actor's instinct started envisioning a book rich in dramatic values; a book patterned after the old de-luxe vaudeville show, with an eye to quality and infinite variety. The kindly new editor agreed and the work was on.

All pieces dealing with historical events have been arranged chronologically; the others according to the times in which their authors lived. Sometimes one ballad controverts another and they are placed back to back to forestall any suspicion of partisanship.

In the pre-mechanical age, when there was neither radio nor television, people put down their feelings on paper for the edification of their families and friends and for future generations. Every public event brought forth its quota of such writings, telling of battles, rebellions, assassinations, whiskey, tobacco, politicians, clergymen, desperadoes, and Irishmen. Some wrote in a tragic mood, some in a comic. All these together have served to afford us a valid Americana in the form of balladry.

No doubt you will occasionally look up from the page and say: "That's not the way I heard it." Please bear in mind that there are several versions of most ballads, particularly those which have been set to music; but my purpose has been to trace them all down to their original sources to insure historical integrity. You may wonder why some old favorites have been excluded. I felt that since you already know these you will find it exciting to read some which have not seen the light of day for many generations. Added to those you know, these will increase your repertoire. If we made a book of all the ballads which you and I love, the result would be too bulky for comfort. Perhaps more will come later on.

Before closing, I must express my gratitude to William C. Lengel and Richard Carroll of Fawcett Publications, Inc. for their fatherly solicitude and assistance. It was they who dragged me out of my luxurious sickbed and made me a compiler.

CHARLES O'BRIEN KENNEDY

New York

September, 1954

A Treasury of

AMERICAN BALLADS

Gay, Naughty, and Classic

Contents

✤ XIII ✤

❦ XIV ❦

❧ XV ❧

❧ XVII *❧*

Five Kernels of Corn

By Hezekiah Butterworth

In 1622 the people of Plymouth, Mass. were suffering from a shortage of food. This ballad shows how they met the situation with sanity and fortitude.

'Twas the year of the famine in Plymouth of old,
The ice and the snow from the thatched roofs had
    rolled;
Through the warm purple skies steered the geese o'er
    the seas,
And the woodpeckers tapped in the clocks of the trees;
And the boughs on the slopes to the south winds lay
    bare,
And dreaming of summer, the buds swelled in the air.
The pale Pilgrims welcomed each reddening morn;
There were left but for rations Five Kernels of Corn.
    Five Kernels of Corn!
    Five Kernels of Corn!
But to Bradford a feast were Five Kernels of Corn!

"Five Kernels of Corn! Five Kernels of Corn!
Ye people, be glad for Five Kernels of Corn!"
So Bradford cried out on bleak Burial Hill,

And the thin women stood in their doors, white and
  still.
"Lo, the harbor of Plymouth rolls bright in the spring,
The maples grow red, and wood robins sing,
The west wind is blowing, and fading the snow,
And the pleasant pines sing, and the arbutuses blow.
  Five Kernels of Corn!
  Five Kernels of Corn!
To each one be given Five Kernels of Corn!"

O Bradford of Austerfield haste on thy way.
The west winds are blowing o'er Provincetown Bay,
The white avens bloom, but the pine domes are chill,
And new graves have furrowed Precisioners' Hill!
"Give thanks, all ye people, the warm skies have come,
The hilltops are sunny, and green grows the holm,
And the trumpets of wind, and the white March is
  gone,
And ye still have left you Five Kernels of Corn.
  Five Kernels of Corn!
  Five Kernels of Corn!
Ye have for Thanksgiving Five Kernels of Corn!

"The raven's gift eat and be humble and pray,
A new light is breaking, and Truth leads your way;
One taper a thousand shall kindle: rejoice
That to you has been given the wilderness voice!"
O Bradford of Austerfield, daring the wave,
And safe through the sounding blasts leading the
  brave,
Of deeds such as thine was the free nation born,
And the festal world sings the "Five Kernels of
  Corn!"
  Five Kernels of Corn!
  Five Kernels of Corn!
The nation gives thanks for Five Kernels of Corn!
To the Thanksgiving Feast bring Five Kernels of
  Corn!

Meat Out of the Eater

By Michael Wigglesworth

This is an excerpt from a long work by this Malden, Mass. preacher and friend of Cotton Mather. He believed that unbaptized infants were assigned to the "easiest room in hell." His book was first published in 1689.

Much honey turns to gall
And Choleric Excess;
And too-too-much Prosperity
Breeds Pride and Wantonness;
Afflictions purge them out,
Like bitter aloe,
Which though unpleasant to the taste,
Far wholesomer may be.
Full Diet, dainty Fare,
With Idleness and Ease
Heap up bad Humours and Contract
Many a foul disease,
To Soul and Body too,
Dang'rous and troublesome,
Which must be purged out in time
With some *Catholicum.*
Strong wines make weak heads *giddy,*
Procuring drunkenness;
Long peace and plenty likewise breed
Intemperance and excess.
We soon are surfeited
With strong delicious matter;
And therefore God who *knows our frame*
Mingleth our wine with water.

The Downfall of Piracy

BY BENJAMIN FRANKLIN

Benjamin Franklin, who caught lightning in a bottle, who wrote "Poor Richard's Almanac," and who was one of America's greatest statesmen, also loved and wrote ballads. We remembered this one from our youth. Robert Teach, the pirate, was known as "Blackbeard". This happened in 1718.

Will you hear of a bloody Battle,
    Lately fought upon the Seas?
It will make your Ears to rattle,
    And your Admiration cease;
Have you heard of *Teach* the Rover,
    And his Knavery on the Main;
How of Gold he was a Lover,
    How he lov'd all ill-got Gain?

When the Act of Grace appeared,
    Captain *Teach,* with all his Men,
Unto *Carolina* steered,
    Where they kindly us'd him then;
There he marry'd to a Lady,
    And gave her five hundred Pound,
But to her he prov'd unsteady,
    For he soon march'd off the Ground.

And returned, as I tell you,
  To his Robbery as before,
Burning, sinking Ships of value,
  Filling them with Purple Gore;
When he was at *Carolina,*
  There the Governor did send
To the Governor of *Virginia,*
  That he might assistance lend.

Then the Man-of-War's Commander,
  Two small Sloops he fitted out,
Fifty Men he put on board, Sir,
  Who resolv'd to stand it out;
The Lieutenant he commanded
  Both the Sloops, and you shall hear
How, before he landed,
  He suppress'd them without fear.

Valiant *Maynard* as he sailed,
  Soon the Pirate did espy,
With his Trumpet he then hailed,
  And to him did reply:
Captain *Teach* is our Commander,
  Maynard said, he is the Man
Whom I am resolv'd to hang, Sir,
  Let him do the best he can.

Teach replyed unto *Maynard,*
  You no Quarter here shall see,
But be hang'd on the Mainyard,
  You and all your Company;
Maynard, said, I none desire
  Of such Knaves as thee and thine,
None I'll give, *Teach* then replyed,
  My Boys, give me a Glass of Wine.

He took the Glass, and drank Damnation
    Unto *Maynard* and his Crew;
To himself and Generation,
    Then the Glass away he threw;
Brave *Maynard* was resolv'd to have him,
    Tho' he'd Cannons nine or ten;
Teach a broadside quickly gave him,
    Killing sixteen valiant Men.

Maynard boarded him, and to it
    They fell with Sword and Pistol too;
They had Courage, and did show it,
    Killing of the Pirate's Crew.
Teach and *Maynard* on the Quarter,
    Fought it out most manfully,
Maynard's Sword did cut him shorter,
    Losing his head, he there did die.

Every Sailor fought while he, Sir,
    Power had to wield the Sword,
Not a Coward could you see, Sir,
    Fear was driven from aboard;
Wounded Men on both Sides fell, Sir,
    'T was a doleful Sight to see,
Nothing could their Courage quell, Sir,
    O, they fought courageously.

When the bloody Fight was over,
    We're informed by a Letter writ,
Teach's Head was made a Cover,
    To the Jack Staff of the Ship;
Thus they sailed to *Virginia,*
    And when they the Story told,
How they kill'd the Pirates many,
    They'd Applause from young and old.

To the King's Most Excellent Majesty

By Phillis Wheatley

About 1761 this colored girl, aged eight, was brought from Africa and sold into slavery to a wealthy Boston Tory family. She was our first negro poetess.

Your subjects hope, dread Sire—
The crown upon your brows may flourish long,
And that your arm may in your God be strong!
O, may your sceptre num'rous nations sway,
And all with love and readiness obey!
But how shall we the *British King* reward?
Rule thou in peace, our father and our lord!
Midst the remembrance of thy favors past,
The meanest peasants most admire the last.
May *George,* beloved by all the nations round,
Live with heav'n's choicest constant blessings
    crown'd!
Great God, direct and guard him from on high,
And from his head let ev'ry evil fly!
And may each clime with equal gladness see
A monarch's smile can set his subjects free.

Unhappy Boston

By Paul Revere

We already know of this author's horsemanship; but this was written after the Boston Massacre (1770) in which some men were killed by the British soldiers. John Adams defended the soldiers and they were acquitted. "C . . . ts" means "Courts."

Unhappy Boston! see thy sons deplore
Thy hallowed walks besmear'd with guiltless gore.

While faithless Preston and his savage bands,
With murderous rancor stretch their bloody hands;
Like fierce barbarians grinning o'er their prey,
Approve the carnage and enjoy the day.
If scalding drops, from rage, from anguish wrung,
If speechless sorrows lab'ring for tongue,
Or if a weeping world can aught appease
The plaintive ghosts of victims such as these;
The patriot's copious tears for each are shed,
A glorious tribute which embalms the dead.
But know, Fate summons to that awful goal,
Where justice strips the murderer of his soul:
Should venal C——ts, the scandal of the land,
Snatch the relentless villain from her hand,
Keen execrations on this plate inscrib'd
Shall reach a judge who never can be bribed.

The Battle of the Kegs

By FRANCIS HOPKINSON

The British, seeing some kegs floating down the Delaware River, and suspecting some Yankee trick, opened fire on the kegs from ship and shore and destroyed them. Sir William Howe sent word to George III of a great victory. Hopkinson was a signer of the Declaration of Independence and helped design the American flag.

Gallants attend and hear a friend,
Trill forth harmonious ditty,
Strange things I'll tell which late befel
In Philadelphia City.

'Twas early day, as the poets say,
Just when the sun was rising,
A soldier stood on a log of wood,
And saw a thing surprising.

⁂ 8 ⁂

As in a maze he stood to gaze,
The truth can't be denied, sir,
He spied a score of kegs or more,
Come floating down the tide, sir.

A sailor too in jerkin blue,
This strange appearance viewing,
First damned his eyes, in great surprise,
Then said, "Some mischief's brewing.

"These kegs I'm told, the rebels hold,
Packed up like pickled herring:
And they come down t' attack the town,
In this new way of ferrying."

The soldier flew, the sailor too,
And scar'd almost to death, sir,
Wore out their shoes, to spread the news,
And ran till out of breath, sir.

Now up and down throughout the town,
Most frantic scenes were acted,
And some ran here, and others there,
Like men almost distracted.

Some "fire" cried, while some denied,
But said the earth had quaked;
The girls and boys, with hideous noise,
Ran thro' the streets half naked.

Sir William, he, snug as a flea,
Lay all this time a-snoring,
Nor dreamed of harm as he lay warm,
In bed with Mrs. L——g.

Now in a fright, he starts upright,
Awak'd by such a clatter;
He rubs both eyes, and boldly cries,
"For God's sake, what's the matter?"

At his bed-side he then espy'd,
Sir Erskine at command, sir,
Upon one foot he had one boot,
And the other in his hand, sir.

"Arise, arise," Sir Erskine cries,
"The rebels—more's the pity
Without a boat are all afloat,
And rang'd before the city.

"The motley crew, in vessels new,
With Satan for their guide, sir,
Pack'd up in bags, or wooden kegs,
Come driving down the tide, sir.

"Therefore prepare for bloody war,
These kegs must all be routed,
Or surely we despised shall be,
And British courage doubted."

The royal band, now ready stand
All ranged in dread array, sir,
With stomach stout to see it out,
And make a bloody day, sir.

The cannons roar from shore to shore,
The small arms make a rattle;
Since war began I'm sure no man
E'er saw so strange a battle.

The rebel dales, the rebel vales,
With rebel trees surrounded;
The distant woods, the hills and floods,
With rebel echoes sounded.

The fish below swam to and fro,
Attack'd from ev'ry quarter;
"Why sure," thought they, "the devil's to pay,
'Mongst folks above the water."

The keg, 'tis said, tho' strongly made,
Of rebel stave and hoop, sir,
Could not oppose their powerful foes,
The conq'ring British troops, sir.

From morn to night these men of might
Displayed amazing courage;
And when the sun was fairly down,
Retired to sup their porridge.

An hundred men with each a pen,
Or more, upon my word, sir,
It is most true would be too few,
Their valour to record, sir.

Such feats did they perform that day,
Against those wicked kegs, sir,
That years to come, if they get home,
They'll make their boasts and brags, sir.

Liberty Tree

BY THOMAS PAINE

Evidently the author of "The Rights of Man" and "The Crisis" knew the power of the ballad to stir up the most people. The first Liberty Tree was planted in Boston in 1765.

In a chariot of light from the regions of the day,
The Goddess of Liberty came;
Ten thousand celestials directed the way,
And hither conducted the dame.
A fair budding branch from the gardens above,
Where millions agree,
She brought in her hand as a pledge of her love,
And the plant she named *Liberty Tree.*
The celestial exotic struck deep in the ground,
Like a native it flourish'd and bore;

The fame of its fruit drew the nations around,
To seek out the peaceable shore.
Unmindful of names or distinctions they came,
For freemen like brothers agree;
With one spirit endued, they on friendship pursued,
And their temple was *Liberty Tree*.
Beneath this fair tree, like the patriarchs of old,
Their bread in contentment they ate
Unvex'd with the trouble of silver and gold,
The cares of the grand and the great.
With timber and tar they Old England suppli'd,
And supported her pow'r on the sea;
Her battles they fought, without getting a groat,
For the honor of *Liberty Tree*.
But hear ye, O*h* Swains, 'tis a tale most profane,
How all the tyrannical powers,
Kings, Commons and Lords, are uniting amain,
To cut down this guardian of ours;
From the East to the West blow the trumpets to arms,
Thro' the land let the sound of it flee,
Let the far and the near, all unite with a cheer,
In defence of the *Liberty Tree*.

Chester

By WILLIAM BILLINGS

As popular during the Revolution as "Over There" was to become later on. This half-blind cripple was the first American composer. Note, he' claims New England as the residence of the Deity.

Let tyrants shake their iron rod,
And slavery clank her galling chains.
We fear them not, we trust in God,
New England's God forever reigns.
Howe and Burgoyne and Clinton, too,
With Prescott and Cornwallis join'd,
Together plot our overthrow,

In one Infernal league combin'd.
When God inspired us for the fight,
Their ranks were broke, their lines were forc'd,
Their Ships were Sheltered in our sight,
Or swiftly driven from our coast.
The Foe comes out with haughty Stride,
Our troops advance with martial noise,
Their Vet'rans flee before our Youth,
And gen'rals yield to beardless boys.
What grateful Off'ring can we bring,
What shall we render to the Lord?
Loud Hallelujahs let us Sing,
And praise his name in ev'ry chord.

Burrowing Yankees

ANONYMOUS

This ballad from the Halifax, Nova Scotia Journal of 1776 clearly shows the state of mind of the Loyalists who fled there when the Revolution broke out. Little can be said for their sense of prophecy.

Ye Yankees who, mole-like, still throw up the earth,
And like them, to your follies are blind from your
 birth;
Attempt not to hold British troops at defiance,
True British, with whom you pretend an alliance.
Mistake not; such blood ne'er run in your veins,
'Tis no more than the dregs, the lees, or the drains:
Ye affect to talk big of your hourly attacks;
Come on! and I'll warrant, we'll soon see your backs.
Such threats of bravadoes serve only to warm
The true British hearts, you ne'er can alarm;
The Lion once roused, will strike such a terror,
Shall show you, poor fools, your presumption and
 error.
And the time will soon come when your whole rebel
 race

Will be drove from the lands, nor dare show your face:
Here's a health to great *George,* may he fully determine
To root from the earth all such insolent vermin.

A Fragment

BY ROBERT BURNS

*This fragment from a longer ballad was written in 1763 and clearly
shows that "Bobby" Burns was a supporter of the American Revolution.*

When Guilford good our pilot stood,
And did our helm thraw, man,
A night at tea, began a plea,
Within America, man;
Then up they gat the maskin'-pat,
And in the sea did jaw, man;
And did nae less, in full Congress,
Then quite refuse our law, man.
Then through the lakes Montgomery takes,
I wat he was na slaw, man;
Down Lowrie's burn he took a turn,
And Carleton did ca', man.
But yet, what-reck, he, at Québec,
Montgomery-like did fa, man,
Wi's sword in hand, before his band,
Amang his enemies: a', man.
Poor Tommy Gage, within a cage,
Was kept at Boston ha', man;
Till Willie Howe took o'er the knowe
For Philadelphia, man;
Wi' sword and gun he thought a sin
Guid Christian blood to draw, man:
But in New York, wi' knife and fork,
Sir-loin he hackèd sma', man.
Burgoyne gaed up, like spur and whip,
Till Fraser brave did fa', man;

Then lost his way, ae misty day,
In Saratoga shaw, man.
Cornwallis fought as lang's he dought,
And did the buckskins claw, man;
But Clinton's glaive frae rust to save,
He hung it to the wa', man.

A Gentleman of Exeter

ANONYMOUS

This is an old Vermont ballad. One can imagine Ethan Allen and his Green Mountain Boys singing this as they rode off to capture Ticonderoga.

A gentleman of Exeter,
He had but one only daughter dear.
When she was scarce sixteen years of age
Was courted by young lords and squires.

But none of them her mind could move.
At length a sea captain he did prove
To be the master of her heart.
She often says, "We ne'er will part."

A piece of gold he broke in two
Saying, "Love, I'll give this to you,
May the Lord's revengeance from above
Light on the man that slights true love."

"I wish the very same," says she,
"And if I ever prove false to you,
My body never might find no grave,
My soul no resting place might have."

The day before he sailed to sea
Unto his love he this did say,
"Remember me whilst I am gone?
It will comfort me if I'm left alone."

He had scarce been gone one month to sea
When that wicked creature she
Was courted by another man
And yielded him her heart and hand.

When hearing how her mind was bent,
A letter then to her he sent,
She came to him with scornful frown
Saying, "What winds brought you to town?"

Tears choked his speech. Nothing he could say.
Then from his arms she flew away.
She left him there to mourn alone.
Her heart was colder than a stone.

Early next morning as soon as 'twas light,
Another letter he did write,
And straight directed to his dear
And these are the lines, which you will hear.

"You wretched creature of womankind,
What peace or comfort can you find
That so unconstant you have been?
How can you answer for all your sin?"

She took the letter with a scoff
And read it through, profanely lost,
Then in her pocket put the same,
Back to her company again.

It was on the very day he died
That she was made another's bride;
With joy and mirth the day was passed
But mark what sorrow came at last.

Day being past, night coming on,
Says she, "My dear, 'tis first to bed let me prepare
And then if you do wish to come
My maid will light you to the room."

As being said, it was agreed
And they had just got into bed.
The maid took leave and turned downstairs—
'Twas just this moment, his ghost appears.

"You purched creature of womankind,
'Twas for your very sake I died.
Not all the love that I could give—
How can you now expect to live?

"Not all your screeches can you save;
This mortal body I must have,
To sleep with me this night in clay."
And then he took her straight away.

Her father cries, "She is undone."
Her husband then distracted run.
Come all fair maids, both young and old,
Don't break your vows for the sake of gold.

Loyalist Song

By Joseph Stansbury

Stansbury, who was linked with Arnold's conspiracy, wrote this for a Loyalist banquet in 1781. Time proved him a bad prophet.

Friends, push round the bottle and let us be drinking
While Washington up in his mountains is slinking.
Good faith, if he's wise he'll not leave them behind
    him,
For he knows he's safe nowheres where Britons can
    find him.
When he and Fayette talk of taking this city,
Their vaunting moves only our mirth and our pity.
But tho' near our lines they're too cautious to tarry,
What courage they show when a hen-roost to harry!
Who can wonder that Poultry and Oxen and Swine
Seek shelter in York from such Valour divine,

While Washington's jaws and the Frenchman's are
    aching
The spoil they have lost to be boiling and baking.
Let Clinton and Arnold bring both to subjection,
And send us more Geese here to seek our protection.
Their flesh and their feathers shall meet a kind greet-
    ing:
A fat Rebel Turkey is excellent eating:
A Lamb fat as butter, and white as a Chicken—
These sorts of tame Rebels are excellent picking.
Today a wild Rebel has smoked on the Table:
You've cut him and slic'd him as long as you're able.
He bounded like Congo, and bade you defiance;
And placed in his running his greatest reliance.
But Fate overtook him and brought him before ye,
To shew how Rebellion will wind up *her* story.
Then cheer up, my lads: if the Prospect grows
    rougher,
Remember from whence, and for whom 'tis, you
    suffer:
From whom Mild laws, and too happy Condition,
Have puffed up with pride and inflamed with Sedition:
For George, whose reluctance to punish Offenders
Has strengthened the hands of these upstart Pre-
    tenders.

A Political Litany

By Philip Freneau

This poet of the Revolution premises his ballad thusly: "Deliver us, O Lord, not only from British dependence, but also:"

From a junta that labor with absolute power,
Whose schemes disappointed have made them look
    sour,
From lords of the Council who fight against freedom,

Who still follow on where delusion would lead them.
From the group at St. James, who slight our petitions,
And fools that are waiting for further submissions—
From a nation whose manners are rough and severe,
From scoundrels and rascals,—do keep us all clear
From pirates sent out by command of the king
To murder and plunder, but never to swing.
From Wallace and Greaves, and Vipers and Roses,
Whom, if heaven pleases, we'll give bloody noses.
From the valiant Dunmore, with his crew of banditti,
Who plunder Virginians at Williamsburg city,
From hot-headed Montague, mighty to swear,
The fat little man with the pretty white hair.
From bishops in Britain whose butchers are grown,
From slaves that would die for a smile from the
    throne,
From assemblies that vote against Congress proceed-
    ings,
(Who now see the fruit of their stupid misleadings.)
From Tryon the mighty, who flies from our city,
And swelled with importance disbands the committee:
(But since he is pleased to proclaim us his foes,
What the devil care we where the devil he goes!)
From the caitiff, Lord North, who would bind us in
    chains,
From the royal king Log, with his toothfull of brains,
Who dreams, and is certain (when taking a nap)
He has conquered our lands, as they lay on his map.
From a kingdom that bullies, and hectors, and swears,
We send up to heaven our wishes and prayers,
That we, disunited, may freemen be still,
And Britain go on—to be damned if she will.

✦ ✦ ✦

Hale in the Bush

ANONYMOUS

Among the patriots of the world no one ranks higher than our own Nathan Hale who, at the age of twenty-one, was hanged by the British. His last words were, "I only regret that I have but one life to lose for my country."

The breezes went steadily through the tall pines,
Asaying "Oh! Hu-ush!" asaying "Oh! Hu-ush!"
As stilly stole by a bold legion of horse,
For Hale in the bush, for Hale in the bush.

"Keep still!" said the thrush, as she nestled her
    young
In a nest by the road, in a nest by the road;
"For the tyrants are near, and with them appear
What bodes us no good, what bodes us no good."

The brave captain heard it, and thought of his home
In a cot by the brook, in a cot by the brook;
With mother and sisters and memories dear,
He so gladly forsook, he so gladly forsook.

Cooling shades of the night were coming apace,
The tatoo had beat, the tatoo had beat;
The noble one sprang from his dark lurking place
To make his retreat, to make his retreat.

He warily trod on the dry rustling leaves
As he passed through the wood, as he passed through
    the wood,
And silently gained his rude launch on the shore,
As she played with the flood, as she played with the
    flood.

The guards of the camp on that dark dreary night,
Had a murderous will, had a murderous will;
They took him and bore him afar from the shore,
To a hut on the hill, to a hut on the hill.

No mother was there, nor a friend who could cheer,
In that little stone cell, in that little stone cell;
But he trusted in love from his Father above—
In his heart all was well, in his heart all was well.

An ominous owl with his solemn bass voice
Sat moaning hard by, sat moaning hard by;
"The tyrant's proud minions most gladly rejoice,
For he must soon die, for he must soon die."

The brave fellow told them, no thing he restrained—
The cruel gen'ral; the cruel gen'ral!
His errand from camp, of the ends to be gained,
And said that was all, and said that was all.

They took him and bound him and bore him away,
Down the hill's grassy side, down the hill's grassy
    side.
'Twas there the base hirelings, in royal array,
His cause did deride, his cause did deride.

Five minutes were given, short moments, no more,
For him to repent, for him to repent.
He prayed for his mother—he asked not another—
To heaven he went, to heaven he went.

The faith of a martyr the tragedy showed,
As he trod the last stage, as he trod the last stage.
The British still shudder at gallant Hale's blood,
As his words do presage, as his words do presage.

"Thou pale king of terrors, thou life's gloomy foe,
Go frighten the slave, go frighten the slave;
Tell tyrants, to you their allegiance they owe—
No fears for the brave, no fears for the brave."

André's Request to Washington

BY NATHANIEL PARKER WILLIS

In the years since the Revolution, Major André, executed British spy, has become a romantic and sympathetic figure.

It is not the fear of death
That damps my brow,
It is not for another breath
I ask thee now;
I can die with a lip unstirr'd
And a quiet heart—
Let this prayer be heard
Ere I depart.

I can give up my mother's look—
My sister's kiss;
I can think of love—yet brook
A death like this!
I can give up young fame
I burn'd to win—
All—but the spotless name
I glory in.

Thine is the power to give,
Thine to deny,
Joy for the hour I live—
Calmness to die.
By all the brave should cherish,
By my dying breath,
I ask that I may perish
By a soldier's death!

✦　✦　✦

The Battle of Eutaw

By William Gilmore Simms

In the ante-bellum days anyone who wrote for a living was held in low esteem by the elite of Charleston, S.C., but a respectable merchant or professional man might woo the muse with approval. One of these, William Gilmore Simms, was a lawyer, but we doubt if his legal triumphs ever outshone "The Battle of Eutaw." The battle was fought in 1781.

Hark! 'tis the voice of the mountain,
    And it speaks to our heart in its pride,
As it tells of the bearing of heroes
    Who compassed its summits and died!
How they gathered to strife as the eagles,
    When the foeman had clambered the height!
How, with scent keen and eager as beagles,
    They hunted him down for the fight.

Hark! through the gorge of the valley,
    'Tis the bugle that tells of the foe;
Our own quickly sounds for the rally,
    And we snatch down the rifle and go.
As the hunter who hears of the panther,
    Each arms him and leaps to his steed,
Rides forth through the desolate antre,
    With his knife and his rifle at need.

From a thousand deep gorges they gather,
    From the cot lowly perched by the rill,
The cabin half hid in the heather,
    'Neath the crag which the eagle keeps still;
Each lonely at first in his roaming,
    Till the vale to the sight opens fair,
And he sees the low cot through the gloaming,
    When his bugle gives tongue to the air.

Thus a thousand brave hunters assemble
  For the hunt of the insolent foe,
And soon shall his myrmidons tremble
  'Neath the shock of the thunderbolt's blow.
Down the lone heights now wind they together,
  As the mountain-brooks flow to the vale,
And now, as they group on the heather,
  The keen scout delivers his tale:

"The British—the Tories are on us,
  And now is the moment to prove
To the women whose virtues have won us,
  That our virtues are worthy their love!
They have swept the vast valleys below us
  With fire, to the hills from the sea;
And here would they seek to o'erthrow us
  In a realm which our eagle makes free!"

No war-council suffered to trifle
  With the hours devote to the deed;
Swift followed the grasp of the rifle,
  Swift followed the bound to the steed;
And soon, to the eyes of our yeomen,
  All panting with rage at the sight,
Gleamed the long wavy tents of the foeman,
  As he lay in his camp on the height.

Grim dashed they away as they bounded,
  The hunters to hem in the prey,
And, with Deckard's long rifles surrounded,
  Then the British rose fast to the fray;
And never with arms of more vigor
  Did their bayonets press through the strife,
Where, with every swift pull of the trigger,
  The sharpshooters dashed out a life!

'Twas the meeting of eagles and lions;
  'Twas the rushing of tempests and waves;

Insolent triumph 'gainst patriot defiance,
  Born freemen 'gainst sycophant slaves;
Scotch Ferguson sounding his whistle,
  As from danger to danger he flies,
Feels the moral that lies in Scotch thistle,
  With its "touch me who dare!" and he dies!

An hour, and the battle is over;
  The eagles are rending the prey;
The serpents seek flight into cover,
  But the terror still stands in the way:
More dreadful than doom that on treason
  Avenges the wrongs of the state;
And the oak-tree for many a season
  Bears fruit for vultures of fate!

Barbara Allen

ANONYMOUS

*This is considered to be one of the oldest American ballads. Its origin
is probably English.*

In scarlet town, where I was born,
  There was a fair maid dwellin',
Made every youth cry *Well-a-way!*
  Her name was Barbara Allen.

All in the merry month of May
  When green buds they were swellin',
Young Jemmy Grove on his death-bed lay,
  For love of Barbara Allen.

He sent his man in to her then,
  To the town where she was dwellin',
"O haste and come to my master dear,
  If your name be Barbara Allen."

So slowly, slowly rose she up,
    And slowly she came nigh him,
And when she drew the curtain by—
    "Young man, I think you're dyin'."

"O it's I'm sick and very very sick,
    And it's all for Barbara Allen."
"O the better for me ye'se never be,
    Tho' your heart's blood were a-spillin'!

"O dinna ye mind, young man," says she,
    "When the red wine ye were fillin',
That ye made the healths go round and round,
    And slighted Barbara Allen?"

He turn'd his face unto the wall,
    And death was with him dealin':
"Adieu, adieu, my dear friends all,
    And be kind to Barbara Allen!"

As she was walking o'er the fields,
    She heard the dead-bell knellin';
And every jow the dead-bell gave
    Cried "Woe to Barbara Allen."

"O mother, mother, make my bed,
    O make it saft and narrow:
My love has died for me today,
    I'll die for him tomorrow.

"Farewell," she said, "ye virgins all,
    And shun the fault I fell in;
Henceforth take warning by the fall
    Of cruel Barbara Allen."

✦ ✦ ✦

The Smooth Divine

By Timothy Dwight

This educator, clergyman, and grandfather of a President of Yale must have had some knowledge of his subject matter.

There smiled the smooth divine, unused to wound
The sinner's heart with hell's alarming sound.
No terrors on his gentle soul attend;
No grating truths the nicest ear offend,
That strange new-birth, that methodistic grace,
Nor in his heart nor sermons found a place.
Plato's fine tales he clumsily retold,
Trite, fireside, moral seesaws, dull as old;
His Christ and Bible placed at good remove,
Guilt hell-deserving, and forgiving love.
'Twas best, he said, mankind should cease to sin:
Good fame required it; so did peace within.
Their honors, well he knew, would ne'er be driven;
But hope they still would please to go to Heaven.
Each week he paid his visitation dues;
Coaxed, jested, laughed, rehearsed the private news;
Smoked with each goody, thought her cheese excelled;
Her pipe he lighted, and her baby held.
Or placed in some great town, with lacquered shoes,
Trim wig, and trimmer gown, and glistening hose,
He bowed, talked politics, learned manners mild;
Most meekly questioned, and most smoothly smiled;
At rich men's jests laughed loud, their stories praised;
Their wives' new patterns gazed, and gazed, and
      gazed;
Most daintily on pampered turkeys dined;
Nor shrunk with fasting, nor with study pined:
Yet from their churches saw his brethren driven,

Who thundered truth, and spoke the voice of heaven.
Chilled trembling guilt, in Satan's headlong path,
Charmed the feet back, and roused the ear of death.
"Let fools," he cried, "starve on, while prudent I
Snug in my nest shall live, and snug shall die."

The Coxcomb's Judgment

BY PETER MARKOE

Some of us know how we shudder when praised by the wrong kind of people.

Despising gain, intent on fame,
A painter drew the Cyprian dame:
But fearful of some latent fault,
The counsel of a critic sought.
The connisseur with candour blam'd
Each blemish, and each beauty nam'd.
The painter listened with disdain;
(For painters are like poets, vain)
But whilst his labour he defended,
A coxcomb thus the contest ended.
"Artist! he cries," thy finished piece
"Excels the boast of Rome or Greece.
"In every happy stroke we trace
"Superior skill and matchless grace
"Yon jetty tresses seem to deck
"With added white the polished neck.
"The cheek with new blown roses vies;
"What lightning flashes from the eyes!
"How smoothly swell the globes of love!
"The snowy bosom seems to move."
Confus'd, abash'd the painter stood;
No more the piece with pleasure view'd;
But sneering, thus the fool addressed;
"Your taste, sir, is by all confessed;

"Some doubts, I own, remain'd before;
"Your judgment makes me doubt no more."
He ceas'd, and with a furious stroke
The labour'd piece to atoms broke;
Then fretting to his home repaired.
The critic smiled; the coxcomb stared.
A coxcomb's taste contempt must raise;
His praise is shame; his censure praise.

The Monkey

Who shaved himself and his friends

BY DAVID HUMPHREYS

*Frifeur's barber shop in York, Pa. was the scene of these strange doings.
Authors, please note the moral at the end.*

A man who owned a barber's shop
At York, and shaved full many a fop,
A monkey kept for their amusement;
He made no other kind of use on't—
This monkey took great observation,
Was wonderful at imitation,
All that he saw the barber do
He mimicked straight, and did it too.
It chanced in shop, the dog and cat,
While Frifeur dines, demurely fat,
Jacko found nought to play the knave in,
So thought he'd try his hand at shaving.
Around the shop in haste he rushes,
And gets the razors, soap and brushes;
Now Puss he fixed (no muscle miss stirs)
And lathered well her beard and whiskers,
Then gave a gash, as he began—
The cat cried "waugh!" and off she ran.
Next Towser's beard he tried his skill in,

Though Towser seemed somewhat unwilling:
As badly here again suceeding,
The dog runs howling round and bleeding.
Nor yet was tired our rougish elf,
He'd seen the barber shave himself;
So by the glass, upon the table,
He rubbed with soap his visage sable,
Then with left hand holds smooth his jaw,—
The razor, in the dexter paw;
Around he flourishes and flashes,
Till his own face is seamed with gashes.
His cheeks dispatched—his visage thin,
He cocked to shave beneath his chin;
Drew razor swift as he could pull it,
And cut from ear to ear, his gullet.

MORAL

Who cannot write, yet handle pens,
Are apt to hurt themselves and friends.
Though others use them well, yet fools
Should never meddle with edge tools.

Echo

By THEODORE DWIGHT

In this ballad a "Hartford Wit" shows us two ways of describing a thunderstorm. This is a segment of a long ballad.

On Tuesday last great Sol, with piercing eye,
Pursued his journey thro' the vaulted sky,
And in his car effulgent rolled his way
Four hours beyond the burning zone of day;
When lo! a cloud o'ershadowed all the plain,
From countless pours perspired a *liquid* rain,
While from its cracks and lightnings made a peep,
And chit-chat thunders rock'd our fears asleep.
But soon the vapoury fog dispers'd in air,

And left the azure blue-eyed concave bare:
Even to the last drop of hope, which dripping skies
Gave for the moment to our straining eyes,
Like *Boston Rum,* from Heaven's *junk bottles* broke,
Lost all the corks and vanished into smoke.
But swift from worlds unknown, a fresh supply
Of vapour dimmed the great horizon's eye;
The crazy clouds, by shifting zephers driven,
Wafted their courses through the high-arch'd heaven,
Till pil'd aloft in one stupendous heap,
The seen and unseen worlds grew dark, and Nature
    'gan to weep.
Attendant lightnings stream'd their tales afar,
And social thunders wak'd ethereal war,
From dark deep sockets brought their treasur'd store,
Embattled elements increas'd the roar—
Red crinkling fires expended all their force,
And tumbling rumblings steer'd their headlong
    course.
Those guarded frames by thunder poles secur'd,
Tho' wrapp'd in sheets of flame, those sheets endured,
O'er their broad roofs the fiery torrents roll'd,
And every shingle seemed of burning gold.
Majestic thunders, with disploding roar,
And sudden crashing, bounced along the shore
Till, lost in other lands, the whispering sound
Fled from our ears and fainted on the ground.
Rain's house on high its window sashes op'd,
And out a cataract impetuous hopp'd,
While the grand scene by far more grand appear'd
With lightnings never seen and thunders never heard.
More salutory showers have not been known,
To wash dame Nature's dirty homespun gown—
For several weeks the good old Joan's been seen,
With filth bespatter'd like a lazy quean.
The husbandman fast travelling to despair,

Laid down his hoe and took his rocking chair,
While his fat wife, the well and cistern dried,
Her mop grown useless hung it up and cry'd.
The rain-bows fair that Iris brought along,
Pick'd from the choicest of her colour'd throng;
The first-born decked in pristine hues of light,
In all its native glories glowing bright,
The next adorn'd with less refulgent rays,
By borrowing lustre from it's brother's blaze;
Shone a bright reflex of these colours gay
That deck'd with light creation's primal day,
When infant Nature lisp'd her earliest notes,
And *younker Adam* crept in petticoats:
And to the people to reflection given,
"The sons of Boston, the elect of heaven,"
Presented Mercy's Angel smiling fair,
Irradiate splendors frizzled in his hair,
Uncorking demi-johns, and pouring down
Heaven's liquid blessings on the gaping town.

* * * * * *

    N.B. At Cambridge town, the self-same day
        A barn was burnt well-filled with hay.
        Some say the lightning turned it red,
        Some say the thunder struck it dead,
        Some say it made the cattle stare,
        And some it kill'd the aged mare:
        But we expect the truth to learn
        From Mr. Wythe, who own'd the barn.

● ● ●

The Mob-Call, or the Charter of Sedition

By St. John Honeywood

In 1786 Captain Daniel Shays and fellow Revolutionary soldiers re-
belled because they were not paid and their homes were being seized for
debt. Shays' Rebellion was put down and the men were sentenced to
death but subsequently pardoned, much to the disgust of this author.

Huzza, my Jo Bunkers, no taxes we'll pay;
Here's a pardon for Wheeler, Shays, Parsons and
    Day:
Put green boughs in your hats and renew the old
    cause,
Stop courts in each county, and bully the laws;
Constitutions and oaths, sir, we mind not a rush;
Such trifles must yield to us lads of the bush;
New laws and new charters our books shall display,
Composed by Conventions and Counsellor Grey.
Since Boston and Salem so haughty have grown,
We'll make them to know we can let them alone.
Of Glasgow or Pelham we'll make a sea-port,
And there we'll assemble our General Court;
Our Governor, now, boys, shall turn out to work,
And live like ourselves on molasses and pork;
In Adams or Greenwich he'll live like a peer
On three hundred pounds, paper money, per year.
Grand jurors, and sheriffs and lawyers we'll spurn.
As judges we'll all take the bench in our turn,
And sit the whole term without pension or fee,
Nor Cushing nor Sewal look graver than we.
Our wigs, though they're rusty, are decent enough;
Our aprons, though black, are of durable stuff;
Arrayed in such gear, the laws we'll explain,
That poor people no more shall have cause to com-
    plain.

To Congress and impost we'll plead a release;
The French we can beat half-a-dozen apiece;
We want not their guineas, their arms, or alliance;
And as for the Dutchmen, we bid them defiance.
When huzza, my Jo Bunkers! No taxes we'll pay!
Here's a pardon for Wheeler, Shays, Parsons and Day;
Put green boughs in your hats, and renew the old
   cause;
Stop the Courts in each county and bully the laws.

The Whiskey Rebellion

BY HUGH HENRY BRACKENRIDGE

The farmers of Western Pennsylvania could find but a scant market for their grain and turned to making whiskey. The Government decided to tax them, hence the Whiskey Rebellion. These lines are an excerpt from a longer ballad.

What profits it to have knocked down
The great Cornwallis and Burgoyne
If in the meantime, money-less,
Your agriculture languishes?

It is the fault of those at helm
That these distresses overwhelm,
For if just measures were pursued
Our Government would do us good;
And mischiefs that are come to pass
Be remedied by proper laws.
But those you send are loggerheads
And might as well be in their beds;
Or if they have a little share
Of sense and industry to spare,
They lay it out for their own use
And personal interest introduce.

Will, The Maniac

By Washington Allston

The author of this fine ballad was also a distinguished painter; his masterpiece, "Belshazzar's Feast", hangs in the Boston Athenaeum.

Hark! what wild sound is on the breeze?
'Tis Will, at evening fall
Who sings to yonder waving trees,
That shade his prison-wall.
Poor Will was once the gayest swain
At village dance was seen;
No freer heart of wicked stain
E'er tripped the moonlight green.
His flock was all his humble pride,
A finer ne'er was shorn;
And only when a lambkin dies
Had Will a cause to mourn.
But now poor William's brain is turned,
He knows no more his flock;
For when I asked "If them he mourned,"
He mocked the village clock.
No, William does not mourn his fold,
Though tenantless and drear;
Some day a love he never told
Did crush his heart with fear.
And she, 'tis said, for whom he pined
Was heiress of the land,
A lovely lady, pure of mind,
Of open heart and hand.
And others tell, as *how* he strove
To win the noble fair,
Who, scornful, jeered his simple love,
And left him in despair.
Will wandered then among the rocks
Through all the livelong day,

And oft would creep where bursting shocks
Had rent the earth away.
He loved to delve the darksome dell,
Where never pierced a ray,
There to the waiting night-bird tell
"How love was turned to clay."
And oft upon yon craggy mount,
Where threatening cliffs hang high,
Have I observed him stop to count
With fixless stare the sky.
Then to himself, in murmurs low,
Repeating as he wound
Along the mountain's woody brow,
Till lost was every sound.
But soon he went so wild astray,
His kindred ached to see;
And now, secluded from the day,
In younder cell is he.

Pills

By THOMAS GREEN FESSENDEN

Writing under the nom de plume "Peter Pepper Box," this New Hampshire satirist blasts Thomas Jefferson and Congress for trying to destroy the nation. How modern it reads!

A state physician most profound
That ever trod Columbian ground;
Compared with whom, old Doctor Caustick
Is but a crabbed, care-crazed Gnostic;
Whose council when we're threatened harm is
Worth more than forty standing armies;
Combining in his single sconce
A dozen Congresses at once;
Who without vanity or boast
His smallest finger is a host,

The keystone of our social arch,
Has, after long and deep research,
With much more grace and condescension,
Than suits his modesty to mention,
Come forward, in these times tremendous,
To sooth, in spirit and defend us.
I fear our great and far-famed nation,
Is in an awful situation;
That dame Columbia, free and brave,
Has one foot fairly in her grave;
Yes, she is gasping for her breath,
While certain journeymen of Death,
At Washington have been at work,
To send her packing in a jerk,
And her unburied corpse expose
To glut the maws of Gallic crows!
Remorseless rogues! whose proper station
Should be that sort of elevation,
With which Jack Ketch, Esquire, delights,
In honoring his favorites;
This question answer, if you can,
If murdering a single man,
By "even-handed justice" bring
A wretched criminal to swing,
What ought to be the reparation
For murdering a mighty nation?

✦ ✦ ✦

Anecdote

By Issac Story

*Possibly the first story every told about two Irishmen by an American
balladist, writing under the name of "Peter Quince."*

Escap'd from fretful Neptune's billowy maw,
Two honest, ignorant, Irish tars were found,
Strolling across the common burial ground,
Unheeding custom's rights, or sacred law.
Thro' the red gate, in musing mood, they past;
First humming, then a new quid taking,
As if to keep their joints from shaking,
While they beheld, along their road,
The docks in which old wrecks were stow'd,
When they upon death's ledge are cast
O'er many a tomb they stretch'd their tarry limbs
With wonder-gazing eye to spell
Under which heap, condemn'd to dwell,
Lay poor Bob's body, and his mess-mate Jim's.
These two, from weath'ring many a sea-girt shoal,
From guiding many a crazy, leaky bark,
Had life's thread snap'd by sickness, or by shark,
And were sad huddl'd in some dismal hole.
Such was the tale these wat'ry pilgrims heard,
Who having leisure, came to seek the spot;
To know as how and where themselves may rot,
Should Captain Death of sudden give the word.
Groping along, from grave to grave, one spy'd,
In characters extremely big and clear,
These words, "I am not dead, but sleeping here."
With which he to his spelling brother cry'd—
"Now, Jack! I'd scorn to lie about such things;
For when I'm dead, I'll own it by the kings."

The Fall of Tecumseh

ANONYMOUS

In 1811 the Shawnees under their Chief Tecumseh were defeated by General Harrison while defending their homes against the encroachments of the whites.

What heavy-hoofed coursers the wilderness roam,
    To the war-blast indignantly tramping?
Their mouths are all white, as if frosted with foam,
    The steel bit impatiently champing.

'Tis the hand of the mighty that grasps the rein.
    Conducting the free and the fearless.
Ah! See them rush forward, with wild disdain,
    Through paths unfrequented and cheerless.

From the mountains had echoed the charge of death,
    Announcing that chivalrous sally;
The savage was heard, with untrembling breath,
    To pour his response from the valley.

One moment, and nought but the bugle was heard,
    And nought but the war-whoop given;
The next, and the sky seemed convulsively stirred,
    As if by the lightning riven.

The din of the steed, and the sabred stroke,
    The blood-stifled gasp of the dying,
Were screened by the curling sulphur-smoke,
    That upward went wildly flying.

In the mist that hung over the field of blood,
    The chief of the horsemen contended;
His rowels were bathed in purple flood,
    That fast from his charger descended.

That steed reeled, and fell, in the van of the fight.
    But the rider repressed not his daring,

Till met by a savage, whose rank and might
　Were shown by the plume he was wearing.

The moment was fearful; a mightier foe
　Had ne'er swung the battle-axe o'er him;
But hope nerved his arm for a desperate blow,
　And Tecumseh fell prostrate before him.

O ne'er may the nations again be cursed
　With the conflict so dark and appalling!—
Foe grappled with foe, till the life-blood burst
　From their agonized bosoms in falling.

Gloom, silence, and solitude rest on the spot
　Where the hopes of the red man perished;
But the fame of the hero who fell shall not,
　By the virtuous, cease to be cherished.

He fought, in defence of his kindred and king,
　With a spirit most loving and loyal.
And long shall the Indian warrior sing
　The deeds of Tecumseh the royal.

The lightning of intellect flashed from his eye,
　In his arm slept the force of the thunder,
But the bolt passed the suppliant harmlessly by,
　And left the freed captive to wonder.

Above, near the path of the pilgrim, he sleeps,
　With a rudely built tumulus o'er him;
And the bright-bosomed Thames, in his majesty,
　sweeps,
　By the mound where his followers bore him.

✦　✦　✦

An Elegy

By Robert Stevenson Coffin

Thus "The Boston Bard" writes about a cow, assassinated by dastardly British sailors during the War of 1812. Down with them!

Ill-fated Cow! my muse thy faith shall sing,
And to thy grave a dewy wreath I bring;
A wreath from fragrant grass and clover wove—
Such grass and clover as thou once did love.
Short was thy life, oh, heifer sleek and fair!
What cruel wretches those rude sailors were,
Who could, without a single sigh or tear,
Cut thy long, gristly throat from ear to ear!
What time those sailors mount to furl the sail,
Then may they hear thee bellowing in the gale,
And see thee grind thy teeth with vengeful ire,
As when thou didst upon the sand expire.
Oh, may they long thy glaring eyeballs meet—
Thy body robed in death's huge winding-sheet;
And may the wind, hoarse whistling through thy
        bones,
Sound in their ears worse than thy dying groans.
Yes, luckless heifer! may thy horned shade
Those wretches' every path through life invade;
And when they fain would drink their grog on shore,
Whisk thou thy tail, and knock their glasses o'er.
And now, lamented shade! I'll say, adieu!
But still with sweetest grass thy grave I'll strew;
Hoping that when death sets *my* spirit free,
Some friend, at least, will *paw* the earth on *me*.

Perry's Victory

BY JOHN NEAL

On September 10, 1813, Perry sent his famous message, "We have met the enemy and they are ours." This was the bloodiest naval battle ever fought on inland waters.

Columbia appear! to thy mountains ascend,
And pour thy bold hymn to the winds and the woods.
Columbia appear!—O'er thy tempest-harp bend,
And far, to all nations, its trumpet-song send:
Let thy cliff echoes wake, with their sun-nourished
     broods,
And chant to the deserts, the skies and the floods;
       And bid them remember
       The tenth of September,
When our eagle came down from her home in the sky,
And the souls of our ancients were marshalled on
     high.
Columbia appear!—Let thy warriors behold,
Their flag—like a firmament bend o'er thy head—
The wide—rainbow flag—with its star-clustered fold!
Let the knell of dark Battle, beneath it, be tolled;
While the anthem of peace shall be pealed for the
     dead,
And rude waters heave, on whose bosom they bled:
       O they will remember
       The tenth of September,

When their souls were let loose in a temple of flame,
And wide Erie shook at the trumpets of Fame!
Columbia appear!—Let thy cloud-minstrels wake,
As they march on the storm—all the grandeur of song,
Till the far mountains nod, and the motionless lake
Shall be mantled in froth—and its monarch shall
    quake
On his green, oozy throne, as their harping comes
    strong,
With the chime of the winds that are bursting along;
    For he will remember
    The tenth of September,
When he saw his dominions all covered with foam,
And heard the loud war in his echoless home.
Columbia appear!—Be thine olive displayed!
O cheer, with thy smile, all the land and the tide!
Be the anthem we hear, not the song that was made
When the victims of slaughter stood forth, all arrayed
In blood-dripping garments—and shouted—and died:
    But, let us remember
    The tenth of September,
When the dark waves of Erie were brightened to day;
And the flames of the battle were quenched in their
    spray.

Jackson

By Jason R. Orton

Of all American heroes one of the most outstanding is "Old Hickory"
Andrew Jackson, the hero of the battle of New Orleans in 1815.

Man of the honest heart and iron will!
Cold is thy form and dim thine eagle eye;
Earth bids thee a good-night, and tower and hill
Wave their black flags upon the solemn sky.
The booming guns and pealing anthems, high,
Hallow thy exit to the realms of light.

The cot, the palace, heave alike and sigh,
And, sorrowing, tell thy deeds and honors bright—
A mighty nation weeps at bidding thee good-night!
Thou wast a star of glory to thy friends;
Thou wast a scourge of terror to thy foes;
As the soft sunshine with the torrent blends,
Blended thy might purpose and repose.
For thou wast all alive to human woes,
The loving husband and the gentle sire;
And as the sods upon thy mortal close,
Fame lights her altar with unwonted fire,
And gives thee to our hearts, thy paeans to the lyre.
Man of the age! thy voice of humble prayer,
Which called down blessings on thine enemy—
Thy battle cry, which terrified the air,
And woke of old the land of chivalry
Are mute; and yet their echoes will not die;
For thou hast left thine impress on the world.
Thy name shall light the nations, as they try
The issues of the future, and is hurled
Man's last defiance forth, and his last flag unfurled.

Root Hog or Die

ANONYMOUS

I'll tell you a story that happened long ago,
When the English came to America, I s'pose you all
    know,
They couldn't whip the Yankees, I'll tell you the rea-
    son why,
Uncle Sam made 'em sing Root Hog or Die.

John Bull sent to Boston, as you shall plainly see,
Forty large ships loaded clear up with tea,

The Yankees wouldn't pay the tea tax, I'll tell you the
    reason why,
The Yankee boys made 'em sing Root Hog or Die.

They first met our armies on the top of Bunker Hill,
When it came to fighting I guess they got their fill,
The Yankee boys chased them off, I'll tell you the
    reason why,
The Yankee boys made 'em sing Root Hog or Die.

Then they met our Washington at Yorktown,
There the Yankees mowed 'em down like grass from
    the ground,
Old Cornwallis gave up his sword, I'll tell you the
    reason why,
General Washington made 'em sing Run Hog or Die.

Then they came to Baltimore forty years ago,
They tried to take North Point, but found it wouldn't
    go.
The Baltimoreans chased 'em off, I'll tell you the rea-
    son why,
The Yankee boys made 'em sing Root Hog or Die.

Then they marched their armies down to New Orleans,
That was the place, I think, that Jackson gave 'em
    beans,
They couldn't take our Cotton Bales, I'll tell you the
    reason why,
General Jackson made 'em sing Root Hog or Die.

Now Johnny Bull has been kicking up a fuss,
He'd better keep quiet or he'll surely make it worse,
We're bound to have Cuba, I'll tell you the reason
    why,
For Uncle Sam will make 'em sing Root Hog or Die.

The Erie Canal

ANONYMOUS

When Governor Clinton started the construction of the Erie Canal, in 1817, he was subjected to the usual derision of the mossbacks. They didn't believe it would ever be completed. "If I can live till Clinton's ditch is done I'll die content" was their cynical comment. Many ballads have been written about the canal, but I choose this one as the best.

I've got a mule, her name is Sal,
Fifteen miles on the Erie Canal—
She's a good ol' worker an' a good ol' pal,
Fifteen miles on the Erie Canal.
We've hauled some barges in our day,
Fill'd with lumber, coal and hay,
And we know ev'ry inch of the way
From Albany to Buffalo.

CHORUS

Low bridge, ev'rybody down!
Low bridge, for we're comin' to a town!
And you'll always know your neighbor,
You'll always know your pal,
If you've ever navigated on the Erie Canal.

We better get along on our way, ol' gal,
Fifteen miles on the Erie Canal—
'Cause you bet your life I'd never part with Sal,
Fifteen miles on the Erie Canal.
Git up there, mule, here comes a lock,
We'll make Rome 'bout six o'clock—
One more trip an' back we'll go—
Right back to Buffalo.

✦ ✦ ✦

Virginia Springs

BY FRANCIS SCOTT KEY

Once the pun was considered a high form of devastating wit, hence its use here by the author of "The Star Spangled Banner."

A word of advice about matters and things
May be useful to those that visit the Springs;
So list' to the muse as she kindly sings
All for your good, ye folks at the Springs.

I purpose to tell you of all the fine things
That are here to be seen at these Sulphur Springs;
First there's a bell in the morning that rings
To awaken the other belles at the Springs;
And the belles fix their ribbands and tie up their
    strings
And look very beautiful here at the Springs;
And then they all fly as if they had wings
To eat the hot cakes that abound at the Springs.

There's an insect or two called a flea, that here stings
The skins of the people who stay at the Springs;
There's a broom and a half here for nobody brings
Such articles here to sweep out the Springs;
There's a maid and a half, too, for one of them swings
Rather much to one side, for she's lame at the Springs;
There's mint in great plenty for juleps and slings,
When the water's too cold or too weak at the Springs.

There's bawling all day—but the ball at night clings
To most of my fancy of all at the Springs—
To conclude, though some things here might e'en do
    for kings,
If you wish to fare well, say farewell to the Springs.

✄ 47 ✄

King Philip

By M'Donald Clarke

This ballad was written in 1883, and its author was called "The Mad Poet." His eccentric fancy is evident in this tribute to a great Indian chief.

I stood upon the Battle Hill—
The midnight was around me—and
Amid the darkness—all was still
Far up and down the land.
Yet I saw, thro' wall-like clouds, in piles,
The broad circumference of a thousand miles.

Within that circle slowly came
The ghosts of Centuries wild and proud,
That might blanch the burning cheek of Fame,
Each in its bloody shroud.
And while I gazed at them—they knelt—
My heart feels now—as it never felt.

Until that awful moment rose
Before my spirit—lone, and grand,
When I beheld my father's foes,
The Gods of this illustrious land,
Kneel down before me, with a look
That few in this world e'er could brook.
Within the mighty circle came
The Great—of the departed days,
When there was pride—ay, pride in Fame,—
When she blushed at things *we* praise,—
When Glory's brow was without a frown,—
The poetic baboon wore no crown.

When men dared firmly to look at Truth,
And stand uncovered in the sun,
When Lust sucked not the veins of youth,

But blood like lightning through them run,
When wealth was thought to consist
In a noble mind and a naked fist.
When the loveliest, dearest girls were those,
Who'd the brightest eye, and the biggest waist.
When feet peep'd out from homespun clothes,
Were not in squeezing shoes encased,
When Philip was their Prince—because
He could take care of the—most squaws.

Osceola Signing the Treaty

By Mary Elizabeth Hewitt

During the Seminole War (1835-37) Chief Osceola was captured through a violation of a flag of truce and died in prison. The American public was severely critical of General Jesop's treacherous act.

Stern in the white man's council hall,
Amid the red chiefs of the wood,
While fearless flashed his eye on all,
The warrior Osceola stood—
And fast the words that keenly stung,
Like arrows bounded from his tongue!
"Brothers!" he said, "and ye are come
To sign the white man's treaty here—
To yield to him our forest home,
And he will give us lands and deer,
Beyond the western prairie flowers,
For these broad hunting grounds of ours.
The paleface is a singing bird!
Hungry and crafty as a kite—
And ye his cunning song have heard
Till, like his cheek, your hearts are white!
Till for his fire-drink and his gold
Your fathers' bones their sons have sold.
And ye, the strong and pale of face,
Have bought the Indian's hunting ground—

Bought his time-honored burial place
With little gold and many a wound—
Yea—bought his right with hand of mail!
And with your blood-hounds on the trail,
You drive him from the everglades,
Beyond the Mississippi's flow;
And, with your rifles and your blades,
You hunt him like a buffalo—
Till turns he, goaded, maddened, back,
To strike the foe upon his track!
Let the white chieftains pause, and hear
The answer of the Seminole:—
The red man is a foe to fear—
He will not sign your faithless scroll,
Nor yield to you the lands you prize—
The war-belt on your pathway lies!"
Leapt forth the glaive beneath his hand,
As from the bent bow leaps the shaft,
And fierce he drove the tempered brand
Through board and parchment, to the haft—
"And thus," he said, with eye of flame—
"*Thus* Osceola signs your claim!"

The Men of the Alamo

By James Jeffrey Roche

What names came to my mind the day long ago I stood in the Alamo! Bowie, Crockett, Barrett Travis, brave men all, going to their death against overwhelming odds in 1836. Here is a chapter that will adorn the pages of American history forever.

To Houston at Gonzales town, ride, Ranger, for your
life,
Nor stop to say good-bye to-day to home, or child, or
wife;
But pass the word from ranch to ranch, to every Texan
sword,

That fifty hundred Mexicans have crossed the Nueces
  ford,
With Castrillon and perjured Cos, Sesma and Almonte,
And Santa Anna ravenous for vengeance and for prey!
They smite the land with fire and sword; the grass
  shall never grow
Where northward sweeps that locust herd on San
  Antonio!
Now who will bar the foeman's path, to gain a breath-
  ing space,
Till Houston and his scattered men shall meet him
  face to face?
Who holds his life as less than naught when home and
  honor call,
And counts the guerdon full and fair for liberty to fall?
Oh, who but Barrett Travis, the bravest of them all!
With seven score of riflemen to play the rancher's
  game,
And feed a counter-fire to halt the sweeping prairie
  flame;
For Bowie of the broken blade is there to cheer them
  on,
With Evans of Concepcion, who conquered Castrillon,
And o'er their heads the Long Star flag defiant floats
  on high,
And no man thinks of yielding, and no man fears to
  die.

But ere the siege is held a week a cry is heard without,
A clash or arms, a rifle peal, the Ranger's ringing
  shout,
And two-and-thirty beardless boys have bravely hewed
  their way
To die with Travis if they must, to conquer if they
  may.
Was ever valor held so cheap in Glory's mart before
In all the days of chivalry, in all the deeds of war?

But once again the foeman gaze in wonderment and
   fear
To see a stranger break their lines and hear the Texans
   cheer.
God! how they cheered to welcome him, those spent
   and starving men!
For Davy Crockett by their side was worth an army
   then.
The wounded ones forgot their wounds; the dying
   drew a breath
To hail the king of border men, then turned to laugh
   at death.
For all knew Davy Crockett, blithe and generous as
   bold,
And strong and rugged as the quartz that hides its
   heart of gold.
His simple creed for word or deed true as the bullet
   sped,
And rung the target straight: "Be sure you're right,
   then go ahead!"

And were they right who fought the fight for Texas
   by his side?
They questioned not; they faltered not; they only
   fought and died.
Who hath an enemy like these, God's mercy slay him
   straight!—
A thousand Mexicans lay dead outside the convent
   gate,
And half a thousand more must die before the fortress
   falls,
And still the tide of war beats high around the
   leaguered walls.
At last the bloody breach is won; the weakened lines
   give way;
The wolves are swarming in the court; the lions stand
   at bay.

The leader meets them at the breach, and wins the
    soldier's prize;
A foeman's bosom sheathes his sword when gallant
    Travis dies.
Now let the victor feast at will until his crest be red—
We may not know what raptures fill the vulture with
    the dead.
Let Santa Anna's valiant sword right bravely hew and
    hack
The senseless corse; its hands are cold; they will not
    strike him back.
Let Bowie die, but 'ware the hand that wields his
    deadly knife;
Four went to slay and one comes back, so dear he sells
    his life.
And last of all let Crockett fall, too proud to sue for
    grace,
So grand in death the butcher dared not look upon his
    face.

But far on San Jacinto's field the Texan toils are set,
And Alamo's dread memory the Texan steel shall
    whet.
And Fame shall tell their deeds who fell till all the
    years be run.
"Thermopylae left one alive—the Alamo left none."

The Wants of Man

BY JOHN QUINCY ADAMS

John and John Quincy Adams, father and son, both served as President,
the only instance in our history. John Quincy was also Minister to Ger-
many, Russia, and Great Britain, Secretary of State, then President.
After he failed of re-election, he served many years in the House. Be-
sides being an advocate of free speech and human rights, he was a
scholar and a poet.

    "Man wants but little here below,
    Nor wants that little long,"

'Tis not with me exactly so,
But 'tis said so in the song.
My wants are many and, if told,
Would muster many a score;
And were each wish a mint of gold
I still should long for more.

What first I want is daily bread
And canvas-back—and wine—
And all the realms of nature spread
Before me when I dine.
Four courses scarcely can provide
My appetite to quell;
With four choice cooks from France beside
To dress my dinner well.

What next I want at princely cost
Is elegant attire:
Black sable furs for winter's frost
And silks for summer's fire,
And cashmere shawls and Brussels lace
My bosom's front to deck—
And diamond rings my hands to grace,
And rubies for my neck.

I want (who does not want?) a wife,
Affectionate and fair;
To solace all the woes of life,
And all its joys to share,
Of temper sweet, of yielding will,
Of firm, yet placid mind—
With all my faults to love me still
With sentiment refined.

And as Time's car incessant runs,
And Fortune fills my store,
I want of daughters and of sons

From eight to half a score.
I want (alas! shall mortal dare
Such bliss on earth to crave?)
That all the girls be chaste and fair
The boys all wise and brave.

I want a warm and faithful friend
To cheer the adverse hour;
Who ne'er to flatter will descend,
Nor bend the knee to power—
A friend to chide me when I'm wrong,
My inmost soul to see;
And that my friendship prove as strong
For him as his for me.

I want the seals of power and place,
The ensigns of command;
Charged by the People's unbought grace
To rule my native land.
Nor crown nor scepter would I ask
But from my country's will,
By day, by night, to ply the task
Her cup of bliss to fill.

I want the voice of honest praise
To follow me behind,
And to be thought in future days
The friend of human kind;
That after ages, as they rise,
Exulting may proclaim
In choral union in the skies
Their blessings on my name.

These are the Wants of Mortal Man,
I cannot want them long,
For life itself is but a span,
And earthly bliss—a song.
My last great Want—absorbing all—

Is, when beneath the sod,
And summoned to my final call,
The Mercy of my God.

Tippecanoe and Tyler, Too

By ALEXANDER COFFMAN ROSS

Presidential campaign song for William Henry Harrison when he de-
feated Martin Van Buren in 1840. He died after a month in office and
was succeeded by John Tyler.

Oh! what has caused this great commotion, motion,
  motion
Our country through?
It is the ball that's rolling on,
For Tippecanoe and Tyler too.

CHORUS

For Tippecanoe and Tyler too,
And with them we'll beat little Van, Van, Van,
Van, oh! he's a used up man!
And with them, we'll beat little Van.

Like the working of the might waters, waters, waters,
On it will go;
And its course will clear the way
For Tippecanoe and Tyler too. — *Chorus*

The Bay State boys turned out in thousands, thou-
  sands, thousands,
Not long ago;
And at Bunker Hill, they set their seals
For Tippecanoe and Tyler too. — *Chorus*

Now you hear the Van-jacks talking, talking, talking,
They look quite blue,

For all the world seems turning round
For Tippecanoe and Tyler too. — *Chorus*

Let them talk about hard cider, cider, cider,
And Log Cabin too.
It will only help to speed the ball
For Tippecanoe and Tyler too. — *Chorus*

His latch-string hangs outside the door, door, door
And never is pulled in,
For it always was the custom of
Tippecanoe and Tyler too. — *Chorus*

See the spoilsmen and leg treasurers, treasurers, treas-
    urers,
All in a stew,
For well they know they stand no chance
With Tippecanoe and Tyler too. — *Chorus*

Little Marty's days are numbered, numbered, num-
    bered,
And out he must go.
For in his place we'll put the good
Old Tippecanoe and Tyler too. — *Chorus*

Liberation

BY POPULUS

Thomas Wilson Dorr was sentenced for life for instigating the Dorr Rebellion. The verdict was set aside by popular demand and the reforms Dorr advocated were adopted and became law. This poem is taken from The Providence Journal, *March 3, 1843.*

Messers Printers, we are coming,
Mark the coons' departing grin,
While they read this dreadful warning,
Mene tekel Upharsin.
Look out old Durham, we are coming,

Your base apostasy you'll rue,
Our Democratic flag is waving,
The coon skin must cover you.
Harken, Byron, we are coming,
Your mantle soon will furless be,
You always have been good at turning,
But now, dear sir, you're up a tree.
Henry, darling, we are coming,
Vicar you'll be no more of Bray,
April will trim you out in mourning,
Every dog must have his day.
Little Josey, we are coming.
Why did you join the coon skin clan?
Quit them, Josey, show your cunning,
Else you are a used up man.
Stephen, mark it, we are coming,
Make out your bills and pay yourself,
The Democratic tide is flowing,
High 'twill land you on the shelf.
Little Whiglets, we are coming,
Doff your caps and stop your noise,
Never learned, but ever learning,
Learn this, we're not beat by boys.
Tyrants! Algerines! we are coming,
Brightly burns the patriot fire,
Upwards high the blaze is streaming,
Fear and tremble and retire.
Robbers! Burglars! we are coming,
Order we bring with us and law,
You had better now be running
Ere you feel the halter draw.
Courage! Mechanics! we are coming,
Proscription soon will be proscribed,
Freedom—Liberty—returning
All your wants will be supplied.
Cheer up, Farmers, we are coming,

Your land from taxes shall be free.
Those who've been after fiddles running,
Now must pay the fiddlers' fee.
Ladies, smile on us, we are coming,
Your closets shall be searched no more,
Down the stairs the intruder trembling
Shall find egress at the back door.
Listen, Democrats, we are coming,
Heard you not that deafening shout.
Coon skins rattling, bands rumbling,
Log cabins too turned inside out.
Friends of Equal Rights, we are coming,
Our sovereign will must be obeyed,
By equal laws in triumph reigning
Shall Rhode Island's plague be stayed.
Patriot prisoner, we are coming,
Your prison doors shall open wide,
Exiles to their homes returning
Friends shall meet on every side.
Let every land rejoice, we are coming,
Down the tyrant shall be humbled,
Success the patriot's efforts crowning,
Shall cheer, ransom and bless the world.

The Kidnapping of Lieutenant General Joseph Smith

By Eliza R. Snow Smith

This Mormon author accompanied her people on their heroic trek to the West. This ballad celebrated Smith's release after an illegal arrest in 1842, but he was killed by a mob in 1844.

Like bloodhounds fiercely prowling,
With pistols ready drawn,

With oaths like tempests howling,
These kidnappers come on.
He bared his breast before them;
But as they hurried near,
A fearfulness came o'er them—
It was a coward's fear.
Well might their dark souls wither
When he their courage dared—
Their pity fled, O whither,
When he his bosom bared?
"Death has to me no terrors,"
He said, "I hate a life
So subject to the horrors
Of your ungodly strife."
What means your savage conduct?
Have you a lawful writ?
To any *legal* process
I cheerfully submit."
"Here," said these lawless ruffians,
"Is our authority,"
And drew their pistols nearer
With rude ferocity.
With more than savage wildness—
Like hungry beasts of prey,
They bore, in all his mildness,
The man of God away!
With brutish haste they tore him
From her he loves so well;
And far away they bore him,
With scarce a word farewell.
Their hearts are seats where blindness
O'er foul corruption reigns,
The milk of human kindness
Flows not within their veins.
Their conduct was unworthy
The meanest race of men:

'Twould better fit a tiger
Emerging from its den.
Missouri! O Missouri,
You thus prolong your shame,
By sending such as Reynolds
Abroad to bear your name.
Could Jackson County furnish
No tamer thing than he?
Must legal office burnish
Such wild barbarity?
Go search the rudest forests,
The panther and the bear
As well would grace your suffrage—
As well *deserve* a share.
Then might the heartless Wilson,
Thy shame, O Illinois!
Become confederate with them,
And teach them to destroy.
So much ferocious nature
Should join the brutish clan;
And not disgrace the features
That claim to be of man.
But hear it, O Missouri,
Once more the prophet's free—
Your ill-directed fury
Brings forth a jubilee.

Ballad

By Abraham Lincoln

Perhaps you share my conviction that a great statesman must have a song in his heart. Take this untitled ballad written by Lincoln in 1846 at the age of thirty-seven. Judging from his letters, he wrote many more that were destroyed, with other Lincolniana, by people who should never have been born.

My childhood's home I see again,
  And sadden with the view;
And still, as memory crowds my brain,
  There's pleasure in it too.

O Memory! thou midway world
  'Twixt earth and paradise,
Where things decayed and loved ones lost
  In dreamy shadows rise,

And, freed from all that's earthly vile,
  Seem hallowed, pure and bright,
Like scenes in some enchanted isle
  All bathed in liquid light.

As dusky mountains please the eye
  When twilight chases day;
As bugle-notes that passing by,
  In distance die away;

As leaving some grand waterfall,
  We, lingering, list its roar—
So memory will hallow all
  We've known but know no more.

Near twenty years have passed away
  Since here I bid farewell
To woods and fields, and scenes of play,
  And playmates loved so well.

Where many were, but few remain
  Of old familiar things;
But seeing them to mind again
  The lost and absent brings.

The friends I left that parting day,
  How changed, as time has sped!
Young childhood grown, strong manhood gray;
  And half of all are dead.

I hear the loved survivors tell
  How nought from death could save,
Till every sound appears a knell,
  And every spot a grave.

I range the fields with pensive tread,
  And pace the hollow rooms,
And feel (companion of the dead)
  I'm living in the tombs.

Ole Joel Golden

ANONYMOUS

*Sung by the Christy Minstrels in 1848. It was Christy who popularized
the immortal songs of Stephen Foster throughout America and Europe.*

One Sunday when the sun was hot
I'd take a nap ob sleep I thought,
I hung my coat on a fence to dry,
As old Joel Golden cam along by
D'ye see him den?
See him when?
When he stole my knife and basker too.

Ole Joel's cousin, Lindy Sal,
I used to court when she was a gal
But it am my real and true belief
Dat de whole biling am a thief.
D'ye see him den?
See him when?
When he stole my knife and basker too.

Ole Joel Golden went to plough,
And put his gear on the muley cow,
De cow 'gin a beller, and off she run,

And the mule died laughin' to see de fun.
D'ye see him den?
See him when?
When he didn't know the mule from a muley cow.

Ole Joel Golden lived on the coast,
Where culled folks live on herrings most;
De herring bones choke him ten times a minute,
And that's the way he got dat squint.
D'ye see him den?
See him when?
When de herring bones choke him and make him
    squint.

Ole Joel's wife and my wife together,
Went to town to sell chicken fedder.
"O buy my fedders," said Ole Yaller Sal.
"O come buy fedders of dis yaller gal."
D'ye see him den?
See him when?
When they bought deir fedders of Ole Yaller Sal.

A lizzard in de sun, a-sottin' on a rail,
His head went a-bobbin' and wiggle went his tail;
"O come along 'lang", de lizzard say,
"I'm hungry, bug, so don't stay away."
D'ye see him den?
See him when?
When his head went a-bobbin' and wiggle went his tail.

✦ ✦ ✦

Oh, My Darling
Clementine

Anonymous

This ballad is in the mood of Stephen Foster and has been attributed to him. I have never found the true author.

In a cavern, in a canyon,
Excavating for a mine,
Dwelt a miner, 'Forty-Niner,
And his daughter Clementine.

CHORUS

Oh, my darling, oh, my darling,
Oh, my darling Clementine,
You are lost and gone forever,
Dreadful sorry, Clementine.

Light she was and like a fairy,
And her shoes were number nine;
Herring boxes, without topses,
Sandals were for Clementine. — *Chorus*

Drove she ducklings to the water,
Every morning just at nine;
Hit her foot against a splinter,
Fell into the foaming brine. — *Chorus*

Ruby lips above the water,
Blowing bubbles soft and fine;
Alas for me! I was no swimmer,
So I lost my Clementine. — *Chorus*

In a churchyard, near the canyon,
Where the myrtle doth entwine,
There grow roses and other posies,
Fertilized by Clementine. — *Chorus*

Then the miner, 'Forty-Niner,
Soon began to peak and pine,
Thought he oughter jine his daughter,
Now he's with his Clementine. — *Chorus*

In my dreams she still doth haunt me,
Robed in garments soaked in brine,
Though in life I used to hug her,
Now she's dead, I'll draw the line. — *Chorus*

Pastoral Love Ditty

BY JOSEPH DENNIE

*This Boston editor, essayist and poet was known as "The American
Addison".*

Where the Schuylkill o'er his rocky bed
Roars, like a bull in battle,
In neat log-cabin lives a maid
Who tends her father's cattle;
With every form of charm and face,
Young, handsome, gay and witty,

She weekly rides with wond'rous grace!
With butter to the city.

Her churns and pails, scoured white as snow,
Are placed upon a dresser,
And pewter plates in many a row,
Where you can see your face, Sir;
She'll raise the haycock on the mead,
Or toss it out, so pretty;
Or. mounted on old Gray, will speed
With butter to the city.

To see her panting o'er her churn,
With charms so flushed and glowing,
Would make a hermit's bosom burn,
His frozen blood set flowing;
But all the lads their art have tried,
In vain to move her pity;
She jeers, then mounts old Gray, to ride
With butter to the city.

Ah me! though us'd to stir my stumps,
My cart I scarce can follow,
While sharing in his master's dumps,
Not Dobbin minds my *Hollo!*
O! could I make this lass my bride,
Culd I but marry Kitty,
Together in my cart, we'd ride
With butter to the city.

The Oregon Trail

ANONYMOUS

Away down yonder in the Wahee Mountains,
Where folks don't know about books nor countin's,
There lived a Zeke, a old galoot,

And all he knew was how to shoot.
He had a girl and he would always tell 'er
Not to monkey with a city feller;
The city feller came without fail
And old Zeke shot him on the Oregon Trail.

On the Oregon Trail, that's where he shot 'im;
On the Oregon Trail, they came down and got 'im.
The city feller came without fail
And old Zeke shot 'im on the Oregon Trail.

Hezekiah had a lovely daughter,
Never did a thing she hadn't oughter,
She married Zeke and they went alone
Up in the mountains and built a home.
It wasn't long until the stork came flying,
Brought a kid that was always crying.
The poor stork died he grew so frail—
Couldn't stand it on the Oregon Trail.

On the Oregon Trail, that's where they killed 'im.
On the Oregon Trail a tomb they built 'im.
They dug his grave and on it wrote:
"This poor bird was the family goat."
He carried kids until his back was broke on the Oregon
    Trail.

Zachary Taylor

ANONYMOUS

The War with Mexico (1846-1848) was unpopular both with the army and the public. It served, however, to make General Zachary Taylor President of the United States. It looks as if every soldier in the army had a hand in writing this ballad.

Zachary Taylor was a brave old feller,
Brigadier-General, A, Number One.

He fought twenty thousand Mexicanos;
Four thousand he killed, the rest they "cut and run."

Arista was the first that he gave "fits" to,
Just this side of the Rio Grand-ee;
Resasca de Palma and Palo Alto
Proved to the Mexicanos they couldn't come to tea.

Matamoras he disturbed with American thunder,
He knocked their houses and soldiers down;
And when the inhabitants had knocked under
He struck up "Yankee Doodle" and marched into
town.

Camargo was the place where he next went to;
The individuals there received him well;
They wheeled up their flour and their vegetables,
And other "fixin's" they had a mind to sell.

To Monterey then he turned his attention,
And ousted 'leven thousand, every mother's son;
When the Yankee nation came for to hear it,
They very much applauded what he had done.

To Saltillo town he introduced himself,
And marched right in and made himself at home,
Until he heard the valiant Santa Anna,
To that place had a mind to come.

Twelve miles old Rough and Ready traveled out to
meet him,
At Buena Vista Pass they had a bloody fight;
Santa Anna and his army had a touch of Yankee
mettle
That showed them "the Elephant" just about right.

In the thickest of the fight old Zachary appeared,
And shot flew about him as hot as any hail,
And the only injury that he received there
Was a compound fracture of his brown coat tail.

Long live old Zachary and his brave army!
Three time three! Now give them a shout!
To punish all foes whenever they are "sassy,"
Yankee Volunteers are always about.

Love and Battle

ANONYMOUS

*Perhaps young Lieutenants U.S. Grant, Robert E. Lee, William T.
Sherman, Thomas J. Jackson, Jefferson Davis, et. al. joined in on this
between battles in Mexico.*

A soldier wooed a peerless maid,
Soft love his bosom swelling
As they on the mountain strayed,
His tender tale was telling;
When, across the distant vale
They heard the war drums rattle,
The trump far-sounding in the gale
Called him from love to battle.

The soldier looked a long adieu,
His breast with ardor glowing,
And she with sobs sad, soft, and true,
Beheld her lover going.
"Fare thee well," the soldier cried,
"Again the war drums rattle,"
A fervent prayer to Heaven she sighed
To bring him back from battle.

The soldier fell among the slain
Upon the bed of glory;
And, from another favored swain
She heard the fatal story.
"I thought," she said, " 'twould be his last
When I heard the war drums rattle;
Had he stayed here he'd not been shot,
So never go to battle."

None Can Love

Like An

Irishman

By Collins

This ballad came from Ireland to become part of our Americana among the singing pioneers of Illinois. We have it on the word of Dennis Hanks that it was a favorite among the Lincolns and the Hankses. Dennis was Abraham Lincoln's cousin and should know.

The turban'd Turk who scorns the world,
May strut about with his whiskers curled,
Keep a hundred wives under lock and key
For nobody else but himself to see;
Yet long may he pray with his Alcoran
Before he can love like an Irishman.

The gay Monsieur, a slave no more,
The solemn Don, the soft Signor,
The Dutch Mynheer, so full of pride,
The Russian, Prussian, Swede beside—
They all may do whate'er they can,
But they'll never love like an Irishman.

The London folks themselves beguile,
And think they please in a capital style:
Yet let them ask, as they cross the street,
Of any young virgin they happen to meet,
And I know she'll say, from behind her fan,
That there's none can love like an Irishman.

Oh! Susanna

By Stephen Foster

I come from Alabama
    Wid my banjo on my knee,
I'm g'wan to Lousiana,
    My true love for to see;
It rained all night the day I left,
    The weather it was dry,
The sun so hot I froze to death;
    Susanna, don't you cry.

CHORUS

Oh! Susanna,
    Don't you cry for me,
I come from Alabama
    Wid my banjo on my knee.

I jumped aboard de telegraph
    And trabbled down de ribber,
De lectric fluid magnified,
    And killed five hundred nigger;

De bullgine bust, de horse run off,
    I really thought I'd die;
I shut my eyes to hold my breath,
    Susanna, don't you cry. — *Chorus*

I had a dream de udder night,
    When eberyting was still;
I thought I saw Susanna,
    A coming down de hill;
De buckwheat-cake was in her mouth,
    De tear was in her eye,
Say I, I'm coming from de South,
    Susanna, don't you cry. — *Chorus*

Oh! when I gets to New Orleans
  I'll look all round and round,
And when I find Susanna
  I'll fall right on de ground;
But if I do not find her,
  Dis darkey'll surely die,
And when I'm dead and buried,
  Susanna, don't you cry. — *Chorus*

The Main-Truck: or,
The Leap for Life

BY GEORGE POPE MORRIS

This is the authentic original version of this ballad taken from Morris's book of poems published in 1853. This is based on a true incident.

Old Ironsides at anchor lay,
In the harbor of Mahon;
A dead calm rested on the bay—
The waves to sleep had gone,
When little Jack, the Captain's son,
With gallant hardihood,
Climbed shroud and spar—and then upon
The main-truck rose and stood.
A shudder ran through every vein—
All eyes were turned on high!
There stood the boy, with dizzy brain,
Between the earth and sky!
No hold had he above—below,
Alone he stood in air!
At that far height none dared to go—
No aid could reach him there.
We gazed—but not a man could speak!—
With horror all aghast

In groups, with pallid brow and cheek,
We watched the quivering mast.
The atmosphere grew thick and hot,
And of a lurid hue,
As riveted unto the spot,
Stood officers and crew.
The father came on deck!—he gasped,
"O God, Thy will be done!"
Then suddenly a rifle grasped,
And aimed it at his son!
"Jump, far out, boy! into the wave!
Jump or I fire!" he said:
"That only chance your life can save!
Jump—jump, boy!"—he obeyed.
He sank—he rose—he lived—he moved—
He for the ship struck out!
On board we hailed the lad beloved
With many a manly shout.
His father drew, in silent joy,
Those wet arms around his neck,
Then folded to his heart the boy,
And fainted on the deck!

Domestic Happiness

By Fitz-Greene Halleck

Halleck was secretary to John Jacob Astor and a friend of Washington Irving.

"Beside the nuptial curtain bright,"
The Bard of Eden sings,
"Young Love his constant lamp will light,
And wave his purple wings."
But raindrops from the clouds of care
May bid the lamp be dim,

And the boy Love will pout and swear
'Tis then no place for him.
So mused the lovely Mrs. Dash;
'Tis wrong to mention names;
When for her sure husband's cash
She urged in vain her claims.
"I want a little money, dear,
For Vandervoort and Flandin,
Their bill, which now has run a year,
Tomorrow mean to hand in."
"More?" cried the husband, half asleep,
"You'll drive me to despair;"
The lady was too proud to weep
And too polite to swear.
She bit her lip for very spite,
He felt a storm was brewing,
And dreamed of nothing else all night,
But brokers, banks, and ruin.
He thought her pretty once, but dreams
Have sure a wondrous power,
For to his eye the lady seems
Quite altered since that hour;
And Love, who on their bridal eve
Had promised long to stay,
Forgot his promise, took French leave,
And bore his lamp away.

To Persecuted Foreigners

BY PENINA MOISE

This stirring ballad was written by the first known Jewish-American authoress at the age of 23. She lived in Charleston S. C.

Fly from the soil whose devastating creed,
Outraging faith, makes human victims bleed.
Welcome! where every Muse has reared a shrine,

The respect of wild Freedom to refine.
Upon our chieftain's brow no crown appears;
No gems are mingled with his silver hairs.
Enough that laurels bloom amid its snows,
Enriched with these, the sage all else foregoes,
If thou art one of the oppressed race,
Whose name's a proverb, and whose lot's disgrace,
Brave the Atlantic—Hope's broad anchor weigh.
A Western Sun will gild your future day.
Zeal is not blind in this our temp'rate soil;
She has no scourge to make the soul recoil
Her darkness vanished when our stars did flash;
Her red arm, grasped by reason, dropt the lash.
Our Union, Liberty and Peace imparts,
Stampt on our standards, graven on our hearts;
The first, from crushed Ambition's ruin rose,
The last, in Victory's field spontaneous grows.
Rise, then, elastic from Oppression's tread,
Come and repose in Plenty's flowery bed.
Oh! not as Strangers shall your welcome be,
Come to the homes and bosoms of the free.

✦ ✦ ✦

John Henry

ANONYMOUS

The story of John Henry is to the Southern Railroad men what the story of Paul Bunyan is to the lumbermen of the north woods.

When John Henry was a little fellow,
  You could hold him in the palm of your hand,
He said to his pa, ''When I grow up
  I'm gonna be a steel-driving man.
    Gonna be a steel-driving man.''

When John Henry was a little baby,
  Setting on his mammy's knee,
He said ''The Big Bend Tunnel on the C. & O. Road
  Is gonna be the death of me,
    Gonna be the death of me.''

One day his captain told him,
  How he had bet a man
That John Henry would beat his steam drill down,
  Cause John Henry was the best in the land,
    John Henry was the best in the land.

John Henry kissed his hammer,
　White man turned on steam,
Shaker held John Henry's trusty steel,
　Was the biggest race the world had ever seen,
　　Lord, biggest race the world ever seen.

John Henry on the right side,
　The steam drill on the left,
"Before I'll let your steam drill beat me down,
　I'll hammer my fool self to death,
　　Hammer my fool self to death."

Captain heard a mighty rumbling,
　Said "The mountain must be caving in,"
John Henry said to the Captain,
　"It's my hammer swinging in de wind,
　　My hammer swinging in de wind."

John Henry said to his shaker,
　"Shaker, you'd better pray;
For if ever I miss this piece of steel,
　Tomorrow'll be your burial day,
　　Tomorrow'll be your burial day."

John Henry said to his captain,
　"Before I ever leave town,
Gimme a twelve-pound hammer wid a whale-bone han-
　　dle,
　And I'll hammer dat steam driver down,
　　I'll hammer dat steam drill on down."

John Henry said to his captain,
　"A man ain't nothin' but a man,
But before I'll let dat steam drill beat me down
　I'll die wid my hammer in my hand,
　　Die wid my hammer in my hand."

The man that invented the steam drill
　He thought he was mighty fine,

John Henry drove down fourteen feet,
  While the steam drill only made nine,
  Steam drill only made nine.

"Oh, lookaway over yonder, captain,
  You can't see like me,"
He gave a long and loud and lonesome cry,
  "Lawd, a hammer be the death of me,
  A hammer be the death of me!"

John Henry hammering on the mountain
  As the whistle blew for half-past two,
The last words his captain heard him say,
  "I've done hammered my insides in two,
  Lawd, I've hammered my insides in two."

The hammer that John Henry swung
  It weighed over twelve pound,
He broke a rib in his left hand side
  And his intrels fell on the ground,
  And his intrels fell on the ground.

John Henry, O, John Henry,
  His blood is running red,
Fell right down with his hammer to the ground
  Said, "I beat him to the bottom but I'm dead,
  Lawd, beat him to the bottom but I'm dead."

When John Henry was laying there dying,
  The people all by his side,
The very last words they heard him say,
  "Give me a cool drink of water 'fore I die,
  Cool drink of water 'fore I die."

John Henry had a little woman,
  The dress she wore was red,
She went down the track, and she never looked back,
  Going where her man fell dead,
  Going where her man fell dead.

They carried him down by the river,
    And buried him in the sand,
And everybody that passed that way,
    Said, "There lies that steel-driving man,
        There lies a steel-driving man."

They took John Henry to the river,
    And buried him in the sand,
And every locomotive come a-roaring by,
    Says, "There lies that steel-drivin' man,
        Lawd, there lies a steel-driving man."

Some say he came from Georgia,
    And some from Alabam,
But its wrote on the rock at the Big Bend Tunnel,
    That he was an East Virginia man,
        Lord, Lord, an East Virginia man.

War

BY CHIEF JOSEPH OF THE NEZ PERCÉ TRIBE

Even Indian chiefs were not immune to the divine afflatus, as is evidenced by this ballad of lament by Chief Joseph of the Nez Percé tribe. This was written after his defeat in 1877.

Hear me, my warriors; my heart is sick and sad.
Our chiefs are killed,
The old men are all dead.
It is cold, and we have no blankets;
The little children are freezing to death.
Hear me, my warriors; my heart is sick and sad.
From where the sun now stands I will fight no more
    forever!

Rail No More, Ye Learned Asses

ANONYMOUS

I say down with these pundits who would deny us honest toilers our moments of eloquence and song.

Rail no more, ye learned asses,
'Gainst the joys the bowl supplies;
Sound its depth, and fill your glasses,
Wisdom at the bottom lies:
Fill them higher still, and higher,
Shallow drafts perplex the brain;
Sipping quenches all our fire,
Bumpers light it up again.

Draw the scene for wit and pleasure,
Enter jollity and joy:
We for thinking have no leisure,
Many mirth is our employ:
Since in life there's nothing certain,
We'll the present hour engage;
And when death shall drop the curtain,
With applause we'll leave the stage.

The Loaves and the Fishes

BY AUGUSTUS BALDWIN LONGSTREET

This Georgia clergyman and editor wrote his humorous verse under the name of "Bob Short."

What a pity it is in our passage thro' life
To find so much jarring, contention and strife.
How snug we might sail thro' life's ruffled sea,

If mankind to each other as brethren would be:
But the reason is plain, there is scarce one but wishes
A scrambling to get at the loaves and the fishes.

The lawyer, who strives with his unblushing face,
Your sense to mislead by puzzling the case.
The doctor, who studies to make out a bill
By drenching his patient with bolus and pill
As sure as a gun, you will find that each wishes
A scrambling to get at the loaves and the fishes.

The preacher, who makes it his study and care
To plunge all his auditors into despair,
The patriot, who rants and talks very loud,
Has something to say to humor the crowd,
Full nine times in ten, you will find that each wishes
A scrambling to get at the loaves and the fishes.

The tailor, who cheats you behind and before,
And instead of three yards will charge you for more;
The us'rer, who, when that money is lent,
Receives more than what is a legal per cent;
You may plainly discover that each of them wishes
A scrambling to get at the loaves and the fishes.

In short then we find in our passage thro' life,
Self-int'rest occasions most jarring and strife;
'Tis a folly egregious then riches to mind,
As we very well know we must leave them behind:
Yet by all 'tis admitted there's scarce one but wishes
A scrambling to get at the loaves and the fishes.

Content in our state gives zest to the mind,
The greatest of blessings on earth we can find;
'Twill soothe all our sorrows, our cares lull to rest,
And render us happy in time to be blest;
Be gone, ye *Time menders,* as you must have your
    wishes,
A scrambling to get at the loaves and the fishes.

Curiosity

By Charles Sprague

*These are excerpts from a long ballad, written when the author was
quite young. After he became a prosperous Boston banker he ceased to
write things like this.*

Turn to the Press—its teeming sheets survey,
Big with the wonders of each passing day;
Births, deaths and weddings, forgeries, fires and
    wrecks,
Harangues and hailstorms, brawls and broken necks;
Where half-fledged bards of feeble pinions seek
An immortality of near a week;
Where cruel eulogists the dead restore
In maudlin praise to martyr them once more;
Where ruffian slanderers wreak their coward spite,
And need no venomed danger while they write:
There, (with a quill so noisy and so vain,
We almost hear the goose it clothed complain,)
Where each hack scribe, as hate or interest burns,
Toad and toad-eater, stains the page by turns;
Enacts virtue, usurps the critic's chair,
Lauds a mock Guido, or a mouthing player;
Viceroys it o'er the realms of prose and rhyme,
Now puffs pert "Pelham", now "The Course Of
    Time";
And, though ere Christmas both may be forgot,
Vows this beats Milton and Sir Walter Scott:
With Samson's vigor feels his nerves expand,
To overthrow the nobles of the land;
Soils the green garlands that for Otis bloom,
And plants a brier even on Cabot's tomb;
As turn the party coppers, heads or tails,
And now this faction and now that prevails,
Applauds today what yesterday he cursed,

Lampoons the wisest and extols the worst;
While hard to tell, so coarse a daub he lays,
Which sullies most, the slander or the praise.

'Tis this sustains that coarse, licentious tribe
Of tenth-rate type-men, gaping for a bribe;
That reptile race, with all that's good at strife,
Who trail their slime through every walk of life;
Stains the white tablet where a great man's name
Stands proudly chiseled by the hand of Fame,
Nor round the sacred fireside fear to crawl,
But drop their venom there, and poison all.

'Tis Curiosity—though in the round
No one poor dupe the calumny has found,
Still shall it live, and still new slanders breed;
What though we ne'er believe,—we buy and read.

The Two Windmills

By Samuel Griswold Goodrich

Born in Connecticut. Pen name, "Peter Parley". Let this be a lesson to all owners of windmills.

Two neighbors living on a hill
Had each—side by side—a mill.
The one was Jones,—a thrifty wight—
Whose mill in every wind went right.
The storm and tempest vainly spent
Their rage upon it—round it went!
E'en when the summer breeze was light,
The whirling wings performed their flight;
And hence a village saying rose—
"As sure as Jones's mill, it goes."

Not so with neighbor Smith's, close by,
Full half the time it would not ply:

Save only when the wind was west,
Still as a post it stood at rest.
By every tempest it was battered,
By every thunderbolt 'twas shattered;
Through many a rent the rain did filter;
And, fair or foul, 'twas out of kilter;
And thus the saying came at last—
"Smith's mill is made for folks that fast."

Now, who can read this riddle right?
Two mills are standing on the height—
One whirling brisk, whate'er the weather,
The other idle, weeks together!
Come, gentle readers, lend thine ear,
And thou the simple truth shall hear;
And mark,—for here the moral lurks,—
Smith held to faith, but not to works;
While Jones believed in both, and so,
By faith and practice made it go!

Smith prayed, and straight sent in his bill,
Expecting Heaven to tend his mill;
And grumbled sore, whene'er he found
That wheels ungreased will not go round.

Not so with Jones—for, though as prayerful,
To grease his wheels he e'er was careful,
And healed, with ready stitch, each rent
That ruthless time or tempest sent;
And thus, by works, his faith expressed,
Good neighbor Jones by Heaven was blessed.

❖ ❖ ❖

The Charms of Tobacco

By Philip Pendleton Cooke

*Instead of listening to sinister cigarette-pluggers over the radio, let us
slaves of the weed read this and make firm resolutions.*

Ill-hap betide thee, baneful weed,
Of nerves unstrung the fruitful seed.
Thy very name I hate to read:
          Tobacco.
For thee the outcast negro moil
Stains with his blood a stranger soil,
Worn down with unremitting toil:
          Tobacco.
Small paper tube of virgin white,
Whose graceful curve attracts the sight,
I mourn thy fortune while I write:
          Tobacco.
Thy bole a fetid cloud exhales,
While wafted in pernicious gales,
To blunt the senses never fails:
          Tobacco.

More potent still, the rank segar,
Which slowly kills without a scar,
Waging a dark insidious war:
                    Tobacco.

Tobacco

BY JOHN FINLEY

*Since much has been written on the evils of tobacco, it is only fair that
we include this ballad in its favor.*

Thou much abused and slandered plant!
Poor victim of the vilest cant!
Hast thou no champion extant,
                    Tobacco?
Are all thy lovers "on the fence,"
O'erawed by ultra temperance,
That none will stand to thy defense,
                    Tobacco?
No, there is one who knows thy worth,
Who deemed thee, almost from its birth,
The greatest luxury on earth,
                    Tobacco.
Let Antis lecture till they sweat,
And parlor dames scold, fume, and fret;
Give me thy luscious juices yet,
                    Tobacco.
When satiate from the board we rise,
And sensual enjoyment flies,
We draw on thee for fresh supplies,
                    Tobacco.
'Tis then with quid or Spanish Nine,
For taste and flavor superfine,
Thy relish is almost divine,
                    Tobacco.

To soothe and calm the trouble mind—
For half the ills of humankind—
A panacea thee we find,
   Tobacco.
For sight and taste some thousands spend
On foolish fancies without end,
But grudge a "bit" for man's best friend,
   Tobacco.
Great solace of life's humble ranks!
Thou fillest many dreary blanks,
For which accept our grateful thanks,
   Tobacco.
Should unrelenting fate decree
My comforts one by one to flee,
Divorce me last of all from thee,
   Tobacco.

Salem

By Edmund Clarence Stedman

The man who wrote this was one of those rare combinations—a stock-broker and a poet.

Soe, Mistress Anne, faire neighbor myne,
How rides a witch when night-winds blowe?
Folks say that you are none too goode

To join the crewe in Salem woode,
When one you wot of gives the signe:
Right well, methinks, the pathe you knowe.

In meeting-house I watched you well,
Whilst godly Mister Parris prayed:
Your folded hands laye on your booke;
But Richard answered with a looke
That fain would tempt him into hell,
Where, Mistress Anne, your place is made.

You looke into my Richard's eyes
With wicked glances shamelesse growne:
I found about his wrist a hair,
And guesse what fingers tyd it there!
He shall not lightly be your prize—
Your Master first shall take his owne.

'Tis not in nature he should be
(Who loved me so when Spring was green)
A childe to hang upon your gowne!
He loved me well in Salem towne
Until this wanton witcherie
His heart and myne crept dark between.

Last Sabbath night, the gossips saye,
Your goodman missed you from his side.
He had no strength to move, until
Agen, as if in slumber still,
Beside him at the dawn you laye.
Tell, nowe, what meanwhile did betide?

Dame Anne, mye hate goe with you fleete
As drifts the Bay fogg overhead—
Or over yonder hill-top, where
There is a tree ripe fruit shall bear
When, neighbor myne, your wicked feet
The stones of Gallows Hill shall tread.

The Court of Berlin

By Henry T. Stanton

Besides giving us a fine ballad, this Cincinnati author has given us something to take to our hearts.

King Frederick of Prussia grew nervous and ill
When pacing his chambers one day,
Because of the sound of a crazy old mill
That clattered so over the way.
"Ho, miller!" cried he, "What sum shall you take
In lieu of that wretched old shell?
It angers my brain, and it keeps me awake"—
Said the miller, "I want not to sell."
"But you must," said the King—in a passion for
    once—
"But I won't" said the man in a heat.
"Gods! this to my face? Ye are daft or a dunce—
We can raze your old mill to the street."
"Aye, true, my good sire, if such be your mood,"
Then answered the man with a grin;
"But never you'll move it a tenth of a rood
As long as there's law in Berlin."
"Good, good," said the King—for the answer was
    grand,
As opposing the Law to the Crown—
"We bow to the Court, and the mill it shall stand,
Though even the palace come down."

Even This Shall Pass Away

By Theodore Tilton

Once in Persia reigned a king,
Who upon his signet ring

'Graved a maxim true and wise,
Which, if held before the eyes,
Gave him counsel at a glance,
Fit for every change and chance.
Solemn words, and these were they:
"Even this shall pass away."

Trains of camels through the sand
Brought him gems from Samarcand;
Fleets of galleys through the seas
Brought him pearls to match with these.
But he counted not his gain
Treasures of the mine and main;
"What is wealth?" the king would say;
"Even this shall pass away."

In the revels of the court
At the zenith of the sport,
When the palms of all his guests
Burned, with clapping at his jests,
He, amid his figs and wine,
Cried! "Oh, loving friends of mine!
Pleasure comes, but not to stay;
Even this shall pass away."

Fighting on a furious field,
Once a javelin pierced his shield.
Soldiers with a loud lament
Bore him bleeding to his tent;
Groaning from his tortured side,
"Pain is hard to bear," he cried,
"But with patience, day by day—
Even this shall pass away."

Towering in the public square,
Twenty cubits in the air,
Rose his statue carved in stone.
Then the king, disguised, unknown,

Stood before his sculptured name,
Musing meekly, "What is fame?
Fame is but a slow decay—
Even this shall pass away."

Struck with palsy, sere and old,
Waiting at the gates of gold,
Said he, with his dying breath:
"Life is done, but what is death?"
Then in answer to the king
Fell a sunbeam on his ring,
Showing by a heavenly ray—
"Even this shall pass away."

The World's Way

BY THOMAS BAILEY ALDRICH

This ballad teaches us, "If at first you do succeed, don't try again."

At Haroun's court it chanced, upon a time,
An Arab poet made this pleasant rhyme:
"The new moon is a horseshoe, wrought of God,
Wherewith the Sultan's stallion shall be shod."
On hearing this, the Sultan smiled, and gave
The man a gold-piece. *Sing again, O Slave!*
Above his lute the happy singer bent,
And turned another gracious compliment.
And, as before, the smiling Sultan gave
The man a sehan. *Sing again, O Slave.*
Again the verse came, fluent as a rill
That wanders, silver-footed, down a hill.
The Sultan, listening, nodded as before,
Still gave the gold, and still demanded more.
The nimble fancy that had climbed so high
Grew weary with its climbing by and by:

Strange discords rose; the sense went quite amiss;
The singer's rhymes refused to meet and kiss:
Invention flagged, the lute had got unstrung,
And twice he sang the song already sung.
The Sultan, furious, called a mute and said,
O Musta, straightway whip me off his head!
Poets! not in Arabia alone
You get beheaded when your skill is gone.

From Life

BY SARAH KNOWLES BOLTON

*Sometimes a rich man fancies himself an authority on other people's
conduct, and sometimes it backfires on him.*

The rich man sat in his costly store,
After the work of the day was done,
Thinking and planning with eager heart
How more gold could be won.
Twilight softened the city's din,
Lessened the crowds along the street,
Shaded the face of a pale young girl,
Who passed with hurrying feet.
A timid knock at the merchant's door:
"Come in!" with a cold, ill-natured grace.
"I read that you needed help," she said,
"And could I fill the place?"
"You seem too young and your hands too white;
You have worked before today, you said.
Has your life been right and free from stain?
No sin upon your head?"
"I am well and strong for my every task,
You shall find me honest, and just, and true;
The past is buried with me and God:
And can I serve for you?"

"A woman must be above reproach,
No matter what she has power to be!"
And he turned the door on the trembling girl
Into the human sea.
The years went by, and the merchant's child,
Grown to womanhood fair and sweet,
Trusted and nursed with her virgin soul
A viper at her feet.
The rich man, broken in heart and home,
Thought of the girl he had turned away:
"I wish she might come again," he said,
"For my heart is kind today."

The Deacon's Masterpiece,
or The Wonderful
"One-Hoss Shay"

By Oliver Wendell Holmes

In which Doctor Holmes comments humorously on the decaying orthodoxies in a certain church of that time.

Have you heard of the wonderful one-hoss shay,
That was built in such a logical way
It ran a hundred years to a day,
And then, of a sudden, it—ah, but stay,
I'll tell you what happened without delay,
Scaring the parson into fits,
Frightening people out of their wits,—
Have you ever heard of that, I say?

Seventeen hundred and fifty-five.
Georgius Secundus was then alive,—
Snuffy old drone from the German hive.
That was the year when Lisbon-town
Saw the earth open and gulp her down,
And Braddock's army was done so brown,
Left without a scalp to its crown.
It was on the terrible Earthquake-day
That the Deacon finished the one-hoss shay.

Now in building of chaises, I tell you what,
There is always *somewhere* a weakest spot,—
In hub, tire, felloe, in spring or thill,
In panel, or crossbar, or floor, or sill,
In screw, bolt, thoroughbrace,—lurking still,
Find it somewhere you must and will,—
Above or below, or within or without,—
And that's the reason, beyond a doubt,
That a chaise *breaks down,* but doesn't *wear out.*

But the Deacon swore (as Deacons do,
With an "I dew vum," or an "I tell *yeou,*")
He would build one shay to beat the taown
'N' the keounty 'n' all the kentry raoun';
It should be so built that it *couldn'* break daown:
—"Fur," said the Deacon, " 't's mighty plain
Thut the weakes' place mus' stan' the strain;
'N' the way t' fix it, uz I maintain,

Is only jest
T' make that place uz strong uz the rest.''

So the Deacon inquired of the village folk
Where he could find the strongest oak,
That couldn't be split nor bent nor broke,—
That was for spokes and floor and sills;
He sent for lancewood to make the thills;
The crossbars were ash, from the straightest trees,
The panels of white-wood, that cuts like cheese,
But lasts like iron for things like these;
The hubs of logs from the "Settler's Ellum,''—
Last of its timber,—they couldn't sell 'em,
Never an axe had seen their chips,
And the wedges flew from between their lips,
Their blunt ends frizzled like celery-tips;
Step and prop-iron, bolt and screw,
Spring, tire, axle, and linchpin, too,
Steel of the finest, bright and blue;
Thoroughbrace bison-skin, thick and wide.
Boot, top, dasher, from tough old hide
Found in the pit when the tanner died.
That was the way he "put her through."—
"There!" said the Deacon, "naow she'll dew!"

Do! I tell you, I rather guess
She was a wonder, and nothing less!
Colts grew horses, beards turned gray,
Deacon and Deaconess dropped away,
Children and grandchildren—where were they?
But there stood the stout old one-hoss shay
As fresh as on Lisbon Earthquake-day!
EIGHTEEN HUNDRED;—it came and found
The Deacon's masterpiece strong and sound.
Eighteen hundred increased by ten;—
"Hahnsum kerridge" they called it then.
Eighteen hundred and twenty came;—

Running as usual; much the same.
Thirty and forty at last arrive,
And then come fifty, and FIFTY-FIVE.

Little of all we value here
Wakes on the morn of its hundredth year
Without both feeling and looking queer.
In fact, there's nothing that keeps its youth,
So far as I know, but a tree and truth.
(This is a moral that runs at large;
Take it.—You're welcome.—No extra charge.)
FIRST OF NOVEMBER,—the Earthquake-day—
There are traces of age in the one-hoss shay,
A general flavor of mild decay,
But nothing local, as one may say,
There couldn't be,—for the Deacon's art
Had made it so like in every part
That there wasn't a chance for one to start.
For the wheels were just as strong as the thills,
And the floor was just as strong as the sills,
And the panels just as strong as the floor,
And the whiffle-tree neither less nor more,
And the back cross-bar as strong as the fore,
And spring and axle and hub *encore.*
And yet, *as a whole,* it is past a doubt
In another hour it will be *worn out!*

First of November, 'Fifty-five!
This morning the parson takes a drive.
Now, small boys, get out of the way!
Here comes the wonderful one-hoss shay,
Drawn by a rat-tailed, ewe-necked bay.
"Huddup!" said the parson.—Off went they.

The parson was working his Sunday's text,—
Had got to *fifthly,* and stopped perplexed
At what the—Moses—was coming next.
All at once the horse stood still,

Close by the meet'n'-house on the hill.
—First a shiver, and then a thrill,
Then something decidely like a spill,—
And the parson was sitting upon a rock,
At half past nine by the meet'n'-house clock,—
Just the hour of the Earthquake's shock!
—What do you think the parson found,
When he got up and stared around?
The poor old chaise in a heap or mound,
As if it had been to the mill and ground!

You see, of course, if you're not a dunce,
How it went to pieces all at once,—
All at once, and nothing first,—
Just as bubbles do when they burst.

End of the wonderful one-hoss shay.
Logic is logic. That's all I say.

Strange

BY EDWARD ROWLAND SILL

This ironic ballad is from an author born in Windsor, Connecticut. He was a schoolteacher and professor in various colleges.

He died at night. Next day they came
To weep and praise him: sudden fame
These suddenly warm comrades gave.
They called him pure, they called him brave;
One praised his heart, and one his brain;
All said, "You'll seek his like in vain,—"
Gentle, and strong, and good: none saw
In all his character a flaw.

At noon he wakened from his trance,
Mended, was well! they looked askance;
Took his hand coldly; loved him not,

Though they had wept him; quite forgot
His virtues; lent an easy ear
To slanderous tongues; professed a fear
He was not what he seemed to be;
Thanked God they were not such as he;
Gave to his hunger stones for bread;
And made him, living, wish him dead.

The Shattered Idol

By WILL CARLETON

*According to the author of "Over The Hill to the Poor-House," this
really happened. Many of us have had similar experiences.*

On the mountains I was walking,
Where enchanted records say,
From diffuse domestic talking,
Rip Van Winkle fled away.
Then in dreamy mood I pondered
'Mid the verdant valley deep,
Where that rough immortal wandered
To unprecedented sleep.
Then a storm displayed its molars,
And a growl of thunder came,
Till I fancied that the bowlers
Had commenced another game;
But that couch of pen creative
I was anxious to espy;
So I asked a friendly native,
"Where did Rip Van Winkle lie?"
Then the dear old man diverted
Some tobacco from its sheath,
And a goodly bit inserted
In a trap of yellow teeth,
And with sneering that could go where

Better proof would be denied,
He responded, "It wasn't nowhere:
'Twas another man that lied!"
"But," said I, "it *must* be found here!"
(With a pleading tone and look;)
"They describe it all around here—
I have read it in a book.
That so many do not doubt it
Makes its likelihood appear;
They have asked me all about it,
Many thousand miles from here,
Round the world, with smiles repeated,
Is that mortal's precious hap,
Who for twenty years was treated
To a straight, delicious nap."
"But you see," he said—with twinkles
In his eyes direct and clear—
"I'd ha' known of the Van Winkles,
Ef they ever settled here;
An' my father an' his father—
Don't it look upon its face
They'd be apt to mention, rather,
Such a very sing'lar case?
An' now does it stand to reason
That a live 'un could remain
Through the naggin' winter season
An' the drenching summer rain?
Wouldn't the wolves be apt to scent him,
An' the wildcats suck his breath?
There'd be nothin' to prevent him
Takin' quite a sudden death.
Or, if animals didn't mind him—wal—
There'd some city feller find him
Spoonin' round here with his gal.
No—that yarn won't pay expenses:
It's too open to be smart;
An' a person in his senses

Ought to've known it from the start."
Not particularly flattered,
I felt called upon to say,
"Here's another idol shattered!"
And pursued my weary way.

The Girl at the Crossing

By EDGAR FAWCETT

This author was a popular novelist, playwright and versifier of his day.

She was just sixteen, that night as she stood
In her ragged dress and her dusty hood.
She had swept the crossing the same old way
You have seen the beggars do, any day,
With first a rush to the passer's side
Then a dash ahead, and the broom well plied,
And then, as she gained the curb, you know,
The ancient professional moan of woe.
But now she is tired; the night grows late:
She leaves the crossing with laggard gait.
And as she passes the street lamp's glare,
You catch the sheen of her unkempt hair,
Falling to meet with its tangled flow,
The two great weary black eyes below.
She goes from the haunts of the rich and sleek

To dull-lit regions of murk and reek;
And under a lamp that flickers frail,
In the sudden breath of the autumn gale,
Pausing, she searched her dress, to drag
From its pocket a dingy twisted rag,—
Her pennies, earned through the long day, all
Lumped into this unsightly ball.
With a feeble smile she counts them o'er,
And is slipping them out of sight once more,
When a hand from the dimness, quick and bold,
Tears the rag from her careless hold.
She cries out sharply. A form shoots fleet,
Yards beyond, through the vague void street.
She stands in the doorway; she does not stir;
While her drunken father scowls at her.
He has wondered long that she still should stay,
For he craved her earnings to drink away.
With trembling voice, in her words uncouth,
She tells him simply the simple truth.
He lifts his hand while his dull eyes glow,
And strikes her down with a brutal blow.

* * * * * *

You may see her now, any night that's fair,
In a certain street, by a certain square—
See her well, if you wait for a little while,
In her silken dress, with her brazen smile!

The Carpenter

By George Houghton

I hope all fellows, like you and me, who never liked to work, will take this ballad to heart.

I'm sad, I'm sad, for the joy I had
Is wrecked like a craft in mid-sea;
It's strange, but suddenly youth's fond hope

Seems lost forever to me.
Oho! how slow the shavings go;
But let me do what I can—
For man, for man was meant for labor,
And labor was meant for man.
I'm glad, I'm glad, for the grief I had
Has blown like a cloud away;
My heart, my plane, let us laugh together,
For night has bloomed into day.
Hi, hi! how spry the shavings fly!
I'll work as well as I can,—
For man, for man was meant for labor,
And labor was meant for man.
O, weary the hour that ushers toil,
And heavy the moan of the plane,
When labor is not the labor of love,
And can never be again.
Oho! how slow the shavings go;
But let us do what we can,—
For man, for man was meant for labor,
And labor was meant for man.
But light is endeavor that hath a heart;
O. sweet those sunshiny days,
When every bird-call carols of hope,
And joy speaks a thousand ways.
Hi, hi! how spry the shavings fly!
I'll work as well as I can,—
For man, for man was meant for labor,
And labor was meant for man.

Litoria! Litoria!

Anonymous

We can imagine John C. Calhoun, Class of 1804. and William H. Taft, Class of 1878, sitting with other merry Yale fellows, singing this with gusto.

Yale College is a jolly home,
Swe-de-le-we-dum-dum,

We love it still wherever we roam,
Swe-de-le-we-dum-dum.
The very songs we used to sing,
Swe-de-le-we-tehi-hi-ra-sa,
'Mid memories echoes long shall ring,
Swe-de-le-we-dum-dum.

CHORUS

Litoria! Litoria! Swe-de-le-we-hi-ra-sa,
Litoria! Litoria! Swe-de-le-we-dum-dum.

As Freshmen first we came to Yale,
Examinations made us pale;
But when we reach our Senior year,
Of such things we have lost our fear.

As Sophomores we have a task—
'Tis best performed by torch and mask,
For Euclid dead the students weep,
And bury him while the Tutors sleep.

In Junior years we take our ease—
We smoke our pipes and sing our glees;
When college life begins to swoon,
It drinks new life from the Wooden Spoon.

In Senior year we act our parts
In making love and winning hearts,
The saddest tale we have to tell,
Is when we bid our friends farewell.

And then into the world we come,
We've made good friends and studied some:
And till the sun and moon shall pale,
We'll love and reverence Mother Yale.

✦ ✦ ✦

Peanut Song

ANONYMOUS

The philosophy of this ballad makes us believe that young Oliver Wendell Holmes, afterwards Justice, must have joined in heartily when they sang it at Harvard.

The man who hath plenty of peanuts
And giveth his neighbor none,
He shan't have any of my peanuts
When his peanuts are gone.

CHORUS

When his peanuts are gone,
When his peanuts are gone;
He shan't have any of my peanuts,
When his peanuts are gone.

The man who hath plenty of good oranges
And giveth his neighbor none,
He shan't have any of my good oranges
When his good oranges are gone. (When his good
oranges, etc.)

The man who hath plenty of soft, sweet soda crackers
And giveth his neighbor none,
He shan't have any of my soft, sweet soda crackers
When his soft, sweet soda crackers are gone. (When
his soft, etc.)

The man who hath plenty of red, ripe strawberry
shortcake
And giveth his neighbor none,
He shan't have any of my red, ripe strawberry short-
cake
When his red, ripe strawberry shortcake is gone.
(When his red, etc.)

The man who hath any salt junk
And giveth his neighbor none,
He shan't have any of my salt junk
When his salt junk is gone. (When his salt, etc.)

The man who has any spondulacs
And giveth his neighbor none,
He shan't have any of my spondulacs
When his spondulacs are gone. (When his spondulacs,
    etc.)

Young Roger

ANONYMOUS

*As a loyal Bostonian I resent this but, as a conscientious compiler, I
am forced to include it.*

Young Roger he courted me for a whole year,
He sigh'd and made such a moan,
That I loved him, yet dared not to tell him, through
    fear,
So I vowed that I would die alone.

He said, and he swore, if I'd be his bride,
Would bring me to fine Boston town.
I should see the dance hall and the playhouse beside,
But I still said I would lie alone.

Away then he went to a dance at the fair,
Where I saw him give Sue a green gown;
I wish'd from my heart that I had not gone there,
And hoped that she might lie alone.

I redden'd and sigh'd, I danced and I cried,
And my heart sent forth many a groan;
To get him away all my arts they were tried,
For I now thought I'd not lie alone.

T'other evening he came to my cot with a smile,
And asked if I kinder had grown;
I told him no longer his hopes I'd beguile,
Nor would I lie longer alone.

To Boston we came, to the playhouse I've been,
And then the dance hall was I shown;
Such dressing, such dancing, such sights have I seen,
That I'm glad I no more lie alone.

Annie Breen

ANONYMOUS

Come all ye men of Arkansas, a tale to you I'll sing,
Of Annie Breen from old Kaintuck who made the
   forest ring.
For sweeter gal and sweeter voice no man did ever
   know,
And well she loved a straight-limbed lad whose name
   was Texas Joe.

To meetin' she and Joe they went, and oh, her eyes
   did shine,
To see him full of manly strength, so clear and tall
   and fine.
To be his wife and helping hand she wanted as her
   fate,
But sad the story that befell as now I will relate.

One morn when birds were singin' an' the lilacs were
   abloom,
There came unto the little town and there he took a
   room,
An evil-hearted city man who said he'd made his
   stake,
And then it was that the serpent in the Paradise did
   wake.

At meetin' after prayers were said, sweet Ann sang
    clear and fine.
The stranger said upon his knees, ''That girl she must
    be mine.''
So arm in arm they both walked home and wandered
    up and down,
Which caused the neighbors, who loved Ann, to shake
    their heads and frown.

He entered in and brought a stain on Annie Breen's
    fair life.
He told her that he loved the girl, would take her for
    his wife.
When Joe got wind how matters stood his heart was
    like a stone,
With ne'er a word of parting he went off to Texas
    alone.

Before a year in shallow grave lay Annie and her
    child,
But when the tidings reached brave Joe's ears that
    lad went almost wild.
He saddled up and cantered hard, and rode both long
    and fast
And in Fort Smith he found the man who'd ruined
    Ann at last.

Then words were spoke and shots were fired and Joe
    fell on the floor,
He said, ''In spite of all that's been I love my Ann the
    more.''
His face was white as driven snow, his breath came
    gasping low,
He said, ''My soul is clean and to my Maker it must
    go.''

Before he closed his dimming eye he said, "My work's
    not done,"
And turning on his aching side he drew his faithful
    gun.
"You've done your mischief, stranger, but from life
    you've got to part."
His finger pressed the trigger and he shot him through
    the heart.

Kentucky Moonshiner

ANONYMOUS

*Among the romantic figures of early America are the moonshiners of
Kentucky. They made their own laws and lived by their own code.
What more need be said of any race of men?*

I've been a moonshiner for seventeen long years,
I've spent all my money for whiskey and beers.
I'll go to some holler, I'll pull up my still,
I'll make you a gallon for a two-dollar bill.

I'll go to some grocery and drink with my friends,
No woman to follow to see what I spends.
God bless those pretty women, I wish they were mine,
Their breath smells as sweet as the dew on the vine.

I'll eat when I'm hungry and drink when I'm dry,
If moonshine don't kill me, I'll live till I die.
God bless those moonshiners, I wish they were mine,
Their breath smells as sweet as the good old moon-
    shine.

✦ ✦ ✦

New England's Annoyances

ANONYMOUS

Recommended to those who enjoy a recital of the annoyances of pioneer life.

New England's annoyances, you that would know
  them,
Pray ponder these verses which briefly do show them.

The place where we live is a wilderness wood,
Where grass is much wanting that's fruitful and good
Our mountains and hills and our valleys below
Being commonly covered with ice and with snow:
And when the northwest wind with violence blows,
Then every man pulls his cap over his nose:
But if any's so hardy and will it withstand,
He forfeits a finger, a foot or a hand.

But when the spring opens, we then take the hoe,
And make the ground ready to plant and to sow;
Our corn being planted and seed being sown,
The worms destroy much before it is grown;
And when it is growing some spoil there is made
By birds and by squirrels that pluck up the blade;
And when it comes to full corn on the ear,
It is often destroyed by racoon and by deer.

And now do our garments begin to grow thin,
And wool is much wanted to card and to spin;
If we can get a garment to cover without,
Our other in-garments are clout upon clout:
Our clothes we brought with us are apt to be torn,
They need to be clouted soon after they're worn;
But clouting our garments they hinder us nothing,
Clouts double are warmer than single whole clothing.

If fresh meat is wanting we fill up our dish,
We have carrots and pumpkins and turnips and fish:
And is there a mind for a delicate dish,
We repair to the clam banks and there we catch fish.
Instead of pottage and puddings and custards and
    pies,
Our pumpkins and parsnips are common supplies;
We have pumpkins at morning and pumpkins at noon,
If it was not for pumpkins we should be undone.

Now while some are going let others be coming,
For while liquor's burning it must have a scumming;
But I will not blame them, for birds of a feather,
By seeking their fellows, are flocking together.
But you whom the Lord intends hither to bring,
Forsake not the honey for fear of the sting,
But bring both a quiet and contented mind,
And all needful blessings you surely will find.

Learn the Songs of Victory

Collected and arranged by Frances Densmore

The warlike Sioux Indians had their balladists as well as their war-
riors, and, though their victories are things of the past, their ballads
remain part of our American heritage.

With the warriors he is gone
In the war canoe.
This is what he said:
"You must learn to sing only the songs of victory.
Do not weep for him who goes to war,
It is what every man must do."

Reprinted by courtesy of The Smithsonian Institution Bureau of
American Ethnology.

In the dawn and in the evening,
In my tepee alone,
I can hear him say:
"Thou must learn to sing only songs of victory."
I can see his face though far away
And grieve as a woman may do.

In the starlight and the moonlight,
When the tepees are dark,
By the water's edge I am standing there,
Looking into the misty night.
Then the songs of victory I sing
As I watch for the war canoes.

All the daytime in the village,
As I labor at my task,
I am list'ning for the shout that tells
That the warriors come again.
Then, ah, then, for you my song shall be
In the hour of victory.

Old Dan Tucker

By Dan D. Emmet

I come to town de udder night,
I hear de noise, den saw de sight,
De watchmen dey were runnin' roun,
Cryin' Old Dan Tucker's come to town,
  Git out ob de way! *(Banjo)*
  Git out ob de way! *(Banjo)*
Git out ob de way, old Dan Tucker,
You're too late to come to your supper.

Tucker is a nice old man,
He used to ride our darby ram,
He sent him whizzin' down de hill,

If he hadn't got up—he'd laid dar still.
     Git out ob de way! *etc.*

Sheep an de hog walkin' in de pastur
Sheep sez: "hog, can't ye go a little faster?
Hush! hush honey! hear de wolf howlin!
Ah, ah, de lawd—old bull dog growlin,"
     Git out ob de way! *etc.*

Jaybird in de martin's nest,
To sabe he soul he got no rest,
Ole Tucker run in de fox's den,
Out come de young ones—nine or ten.
     Git out ob de way! *etc.*

Tucker on de wood pile—can't count 'lebben,
Put in a fedder bed—him gwine to hebben,
His nose so flat, his face so full,
De top ob his head like a bog ob wool.
     Git out ob de way! *etc.*

Tucker went round hickory steeple,
Dar he met some colored people.
Some was black and some was blacker,
Some was de color ob brown tobacur.
     Git out ob de way! *etc.*

High-hold on de holler tree.
He poke his bill in for to see,
De lizzard cotch 'im by de snout,
He call old Tucker to pull 'im out.
     Git out ob de way! *etc.*

Tucker he had cash a plenty,
Dressed to death—his old trunk empty,
To kiss de gals he thot was useless,
'Cept he kissed wid a sway-back-looseness.
     Git out ob de way! *etc.*

Here's my razor in good order,
Magnum bonum—jis hab bought 'er,
Sheep shell de oats, old Tucker shell de corn
I'll shabe you all when de water gets warm.
　　　Git out ob de way!　*etc.*

I went to meetin' de udder day,
To hear old Tucker preach and pray,
Dey all got drunk, but me alone,
I make old Tucker walk jaw-bone,
　　　Git out ob de way!　　　*(Banjo)*
　　　Git out ob de way!　　　*(Banjo)*
Git out ob de way, you harden'd sinner,
You're too late to come to your dinner.

Bluetail Fly

Anonymous

When Ah was young Ah used tuh wait
　On Massa an' hand him duh plate,
Pass down duh bottle when he felt dry
　An' shoo away duh bluetail fly.

Jim crack corn, Ah don't care,
Ole Massa's gone away.

After dinnah Massa sleep,
　An' bid me a sharp eye tuh keep,
An' when he gwaine tuh shut his eye,
　He tell me watch duh bluetail fly.—*Chorus*

When he ride duh afternoon,
　Ah follow with a hick'ry broom,
Duh pony bein' like tuh shy
　When bit by duh bluetail fly.—*Chorus*

One day he ride aroun' duh farm,
　Duh flies so numerous dey do swarm,
One chance tuh bite him on duh thigh
　Before Ah bash duh bluetail fly.—*Chorus*

Duh pony run an' jump an' pitch
　An' tumble Massa in duh ditch.
He died an' duh jury find out why,
　Duh verdic' am duh bluetail fly.—*Chorus*

Dey lay him under duh 'simmon tree,
　An' readin' dere yuh still may see.
"Beneath dis stone Ah'm forced tuh lie,
　All by duh means o' duh bluetail fly."—*Chorus*

Big Rock Candy Mountains

ANONYMOUS

One evening, as the sun went down,
And the jungle fires were burning,
Down the tracks came a hobo humming,

And he said, "Boys, I'm not turning.
I'm headed for a land that's far away
Beside the crystal fountains,—
I'll see you all this coming fall
In the Big Rock Candy Mountains.

"In the Big Rock Candy Mountains
There's a land that's fair and bright,
Where the handouts grow on bushes—
And you sleep out ev'ry night,
Where the box cars are all empty
And the sun shines ev'ry day,
Oh, the birds and the bees and the cigarette trees,—
The rock rye springs where the whang doodle sings
In the Big Rock Candy Mountains.

"In the Big Rock Candy Mountains
You never change your socks,
And the little streams of al-ky-ho
Come trickling down the rocks!
The shacks all have to tip their hats
And the railroad bulls are blind,
There's a lake of stew and of whiskey, too,
And you can paddle all around in a big canoe
In the Big Rock Candy Mountains."

Old MacDonald Had a Farm

ANONYMOUS

Old MacDonald had a farm,
E-I-E-I-O!
And on this farm he had some chicks,
E-I-E-I-O!
With a chick, chick here and a chick, chick there,

Here a chick, there a chick,
Everywhere a chick
Old MacDonald had a farm.
E-I-E-I-O!

And on this farm he had some ducks,
E-I-E-I-O!
With a quack, quack here, and a quack, quack there,
Here a quack, there a quack,
Everywhere a quack.
Old MacDonald had a farm,
E-I-E-I-O!

And on this farm he had turkeys,
E-I-E-I-O!
With a gobble, gobble here and a gobble, gobble there,
Here a gobble, there a gobble,
Everywhere a gobble.
Old MacDonald had a farm,
E-I-E-I-O!

And on this farm he had some pigs,
E-I-E-I-O!
With a hoink, hoink here and a hoink, hoink there,
Here a hoink, there a hoink,
Everywhere a hoink.
Old MacDonald had a farm,
E-I-E-I-O!

And on this farm he had a horse,
E-I-E-I-O!
With a he-haw here, and he-haw there,
Here a he, there a haw,
Everywhere a haw.
Old MacDonald had a farm.
E-I-E-I-O!

And on this farm he had a cow,
E-I-E-I-O!
With a moo moo here, and a moo moo there,
Here a moo, there a moo,
Everywhere a moo.
Old MacDonald had a farm,
E-I-E-I-O!

And on this farm he had a dog,
E-I-E-I-O!
With a bow wow here, and a bow wow there,
Here a bow, there a wow,
Everywhere a wow.
Old MacDonald had a farm,
E-I-E-I-O!

The Sweat of the Poor and the Blood of the Brave

By Park Benjamin

Based on the saying of Joseph Napoleon Bonaparte: "God is, in last analysis, the sweat of the poor and the blood of the brave."

Waste treasure like water, ye noble and great!
Spend the wealth of the world to increase your estate;
Pile up your temples of marble, and raise
Columns and domes that the people may gaze
And wonder at beauty, so gorgeously shown
By subjects more rich than a king on his throne.
Languish and squander—for why should ye save
"The sweat of the poor and the blood of the brave"?

Pour wine into goblets, all crusted with gems—
Wear pearls on your collars and pearls on your hems;
Let diamonds in splendid profusion outvie

The myriad stars of a tropical sky!
Though from the night of the fathomless mine
These may be dug at your banquet to shine,
Little care ye for the chains of the slave
"The sweat of the poor and the blood of the brave."

Behold at your gates stand the feeble and old,
Let them burn in the sunshine and freeze in the cold—
Let them starve, though a morsel, a drop will impart
New vigor and warmth to the limb and the heart:
You taste not their anguish, you feel not their pain,
Your heads are not bare to the winds and the rain—
Must wretches like these of your charity crave
"The sweat of the poor and the blood of the brave"?

An army goes out in the morn's early light,
Ten thousand gay soldiers equipped for the fight;
An army comes home at the closing of day;
Oh, where are your banners, their goodly array?
Ye widows and orphans bewail not so loud—
Your groans may embitter the feast of the proud;
To win for *their* store—did the wild battle rave—
"The sweat of the poor and the blood of the brave."

Gold! Gold in all ages the curse of mankind,
Thy fetters are forged for the soul and the mind:
The limbs may be fast as the wings of a bird
And the mind be the slave of a look and a word.
To gain thee, men barter eternity's crown,
Yield honor, affection and lasting renown,
And mingle like foam with Life's swift-rushing wave,
"The sweat of the poor and the blood of the brave."

Annabel Lee

By EDGAR ALLAN POE

Edgar Allan Poe has been accused of being somewhat artificial in some of his poems, but in this ballad of Annabel Lee, written after the death of his young wife, he is as warm and tender and suffering as his own fateful life.

It was many and many a year ago,
    In a kingdom by the sea,
That a maiden there lived whom you may know
    By the name of Annabel Lee;
And this maiden she lived with no other thought
    Than to love and be loved by me.

I was a child and she was a child,
    In this kingdom by the sea;
But we loved with a love that was more than love—
    I and my Annabel Lee—
With a love that the winged seraphs of heaven
    Coveted her and me.

And this was the reason that, long ago,
    In this kingdom by the sea,
A wind blew out of a cloud, chilling
    My beautiful Annabel Lee;
So that her high-born kinsmen came
    And bore her away from me,
To shut her up in a sepulchre
    In this kingdom by the sea.

The angels, not half so happy in heaven,
    Went envying her and me—
Yes! that was the reason (as all men know,
    In this kingdom by the sea)
That the wind came out of the cloud by night.
    Chilling and killing my Annabel Lee.

But our love it was stronger by far than the love
  Of those who were older than we—
  Of many far wiser than we;
And neither the angels in heaven above,
  Nor the demons down under the sea,
Can ever dissever my soul from the soul
  Of the beautiful Annabel Lee:

For the moon never beams without bringing me
    dreams
  Of the beautiful Annabel Lee;
And the stars never rise but I feel the bright eyes
  Of the beautiful Annabel Lee;
And so, all the night-tide, I lie down by the side
Of my darling—my darling—my life and my bride,
  In the sepulchre there by the sea,
  In her tomb by the sounding sea.

Bos'n Hill

BY JOHN ALBEE

This weird ballad is based on an old New Castle, New Hampshire legend.

The wind blows wild on Bos'n Hill,
Far off is heard the ocean's rote;
Low overhead the gulls scream shrill,
And homeward scuds each little boat.
Then the dead Bos'n wakes in glee
To hear the storm-king's song;
And from the top of a mast-pine tree
He blows his whistle loud and long.
The village sailors hear the call,
Lips pale and eyes grow dim;
Well know they, though he pipes them all,

He means but one shall answer him.
He pipes the dead up from their graves,
Whose bones the tansy hides;
He pipes the dead beneath the waves,
They hear and cleave the rising tides.
But sailors know when next they sail;
Beyond the Hilltop's view,
There's one amongst them shall not fail
To join the Bos'n's crew.

Old Grimes

By Albert Gorton Greene

*Let your mind drift back to childhood and remember Mother singing
this while working hard in the kitchen.*

Old Grimes is dead, that good old man
    We never shall see more;
He used to wear a long black coat
    All button'd down before.

His heart was open as the day,
    His feelings all were true;
His hair was some inclined to gray—
    He wore it in a queue.

Whene'er he heard the voice of pain,
    His breast with pity burn'd;
The large, round head upon his cane
    From ivory was turn'd.

Kind words he ever had for all;
    He knew no base design:
His eyes were dark and rather small,
    His nose was aquiline.

He lived at peace with all mankind,
  In friendship he was true;
His coat had pocket-holes behind,
  His pantaloons were blue.

Unharm'd, the sin which earth pollutes
  He pass'd securely o'er,
And never wore a pair of boots
  For thirty years or more.

But good old Grimes is now at rest,
  Nor fears misfortune's frown:
He wore a double-breasted vest—
  The stripes ran up and down.

He modest merit sought to find,
  And pay it its dessert:
He had no malice in his mind,
  No ruffles on his shirt.

His neighbors he did not abuse—
  Was sociable and gay:
He wore large buckles on his shoes,
  And changed them every day.

His knowledge hid from public gaze,
  He did not bring to view,
Nor made a noise town-meeting days,
  As many people do.

His worldly goods he never threw
  In trust to fortune's chances,
But lived (as all his brothers do)
  In easy circumstances.

Thus undisturb'd by anxious cares,
  His peaceful moments ran;
And everybody said he was
  A fine old gentleman.

The Fine Arkansas Gentleman

By ALBERT PIKE

This poet, Sanskrit scholar and journalist, was born in Boston but moved to Arkansas and became a General in the Confederate forces commanding an army of Indians at the Battle of Pea Ridge. He lost.

Now all good fellows, listen, and a story I will tell
Of a mighty clever gentleman who lives extremely
    well
In the western part of Arkansas, close to the Indian
    line,
Where he gets drunk once a week on whisky, and im-
    mediately sobers himself completely on the very
    best of wine;
  A fine Arkansas gentleman,
  Close to the Choctaw Line.

This fine Arkansas gentleman has a mighty fine estate
Of five or six thousand acres or more of land, that will
    be worth a great deal some day or other if he
    don't kill himself too soon, and will only condes-
    cent to wait;
And four or five dozen negroes that would rather
    work than not,
And such quantities of horses and cattle, and pigs,
    and other poultry, that he never pretends to know
    how many he has got.
  This fine Arkansas gentleman,
  Close to the Choctaw Line.

This fine Arkansas gentleman has built a splendid
    house
On the edge of a big prairie, extremely well populated
    with deer and hares, and grouse;
And when he wants to feed his friends he has nothing
    more to do

Than to leave the pot-lid off, and the decently behaved
   birds fly straight into the pot, knowing he'll shoot
   them if they don't; and he has a splendid stew.
   This fine Arkansas gentleman,
   Close to the Choctaw Line.

This fine Arkansas gentleman makes several hundred
   bales,
Unless from drought or work, a bad stand, or some
   other damned contingency, his crop is short or
   fails;
And when it's picked, and ginned, and baled, he puts
   it on a boat,
And gets aboard himself likewise, and charters the
   bar, and has a devil of a spree, while down to New
   Orleans he and his cotton float.
   A fine Arkansas gentleman,
   Close to the Choctaw Line.

And when he gets to New Orleans he sacks a clothing
   store
And puts up at the City Hotel, the St. Louis, the St.
   Charles, the Veranda, and all the other hotels in
   the city, if he succeeds in finding any more;
Then he draws upon his merchant, and goes about and
   treats
Every man from Kentucky, and Arkansas, and Ala-
   bama, and Virginia, and the Choctaw Nation, and
   every other damned vagabond he meets.
   A fine Arkansas gentleman,
   Close to the Choctaw Line.

The last time he was down there, when he thought of
   going back,
After staying fifteen days, more or less, he discovered
   that by lending and by spending, and being a prey
   in general to gamblers, hackmen, loafers, brokers

hoosiers, tailors, servants, and many other individuals, white and black,
He distributed his assets, and got rid of all his means,
And had nothing left to show for them, barring two or three headaches, an invincible thirst, and an extremely general and promiscuous acquaintance in the aforesaid New Orleans.
A fine Arkansas gentleman,
Close to the Choctaw Line.

Now, how this gentleman got home is neither here nor there,
But I've been credibly informed that he swore worse than forty-five pirates, and finally combed his hair;
And after he got safely home, they say he took an oath
That he'd never bet a cent again at any game of cards, and, moreover, for want of decent advisers, he forswore whisky and women both;
A fine Arkansas gentleman,
Close to the Choctaw Line.

This fine Arkansas gentleman went strong for Pierce and King,
And so came to Washington to get a nice fat office, or some other equally comfortable thing;
But like him from Jerusalem that went to Jericho,
He fell among thieves again, and could not win a bet whether he coppered it or not, so his cash was bound to go—
A fine Arkansas gentleman,
Close to the Choctaw Line.

So when his moneys all were gone, he took unto his bed,
And Dr. Reyburn physicked him, and the chamber-

maid, who had a great affection for him, with her
    arms held up his head;
And all his friends came weeping round, and bidding
    him adieu,
And two or three dozen preachers, whom he didn't
    know at all, and didn't care a damn if he didn't,
    came praying for him too;
  A fine Arkansas gentleman,
  Close to the Choctaw Line.

They closed his eyes and laid him out all ready for the
    tomb,
And merely to console themselves they opened the
    biggest kind of faro right there in his own room;
But when he heard the checks, he flung the linen off
    his face,
And sung out, just precisely as he used to do when he
    was alive, "Prindle, don't turn! Hold on! I've got
    twenty on the kind, and a copper on the ace!"
  A fine Arkansas gentleman,
  Close to the Choctaw Line.

The Hermit of East Rock

By John Turvil Adams

*When passing through New Haven, Connecticut, look out the train
window and see the locale of this ballad.*

Lo! now the sun seems taking leave of earth,
Is not yon crag a glorious spectacle!
Mark, with what emulating glow, his beams
Flame o'er its reddish perpendicular wall,
While, with chastened radiance, they repose
On the green coronal that girts its brow.

It is a pleasant spot, and oftentimes,
At this delicious season, doth the foot
Of Curiosity explore its haunts,
And, gazing from its top, the entranced soul
Drinks draughts of quiet pleasure from the scene.
I do remember an old man, that once,
For some years in that crag made his abode,
And hence was named, "The Hermit of East Rock."
It was a wretched cabin—such, indeed,
As one would think, no being e'er could choose;
Constructed of rough stones and clay between,
With sticks transversely laid above, to bear
Its superincumbent roof of humble straw:
And there he lived, without companions, save
The birds, that looked upon him as a friend,
And also a few sheep which he had taught
To draw a little cart, wherein he placed
What his own feebleness refused to bear.
I know not that he ever left that place
Of loneliness, unless imperious want
Drove him away, and then he might be seen,
With slow and melancholy steps, beside
His dwarfish team, seeking the neighboring town.
He never asked alms, but patiently
Would wait, until some pitying hand bestowed
Its charitable dole, and then, as sad
As when he came, he would return again,
To pine away in hopeless misery.
A gentle heart could hardly look at him,
Without some throbs of tender sorrowfulness;
For, through the rags in which he was disguised,
One might perceive the relic of a form
That once was noble, and a countenance,
O'er which a manly beauty lingered yet:
And many were the speculations framed
Respecting his estrangement from the world;

But they were only visions of romance:
The secret of his grief is in his grave.
A party of gay visitants of the rock
Found him one day, extended in his hut,
Apparently in deep and quiet sleep;
But they were quickly undeceived, and knew
The sorrows of the wretched man were o'er.
His spirit had departed, and alone,
As he had lived, so did he die, alone.

A Frontier Incident

BY CHARLES FENNO HOFFMAN

*Read this one about a brave New York State maiden who liquidated
an Indian chief who interrupted the family prayers.*

The Indian whoop is heard without,
Within the Indian arrow lies;
There's horror in that fiendish shout,
There's death where'er that arrow flies.
Two trembling women there alone,
Alone to guard a feeble child;

What shield, O God! is round them thrown
Amid that scene of peril wild?
Thy Book upon the table there
Reveals at once from whence could flow
The strength to dash aside despair,
The meekness to abide the blow.
Already, half resigned, she kneels,
And half imploring kneels to Mother,
While angelic courage steels
The gentle nature of the other.
They thunder on the oaken door,
They pierce the air with furious yell,
And soon that plume upon the floor
May grace some painted warrior well.
Oh, why cannot one stalwart arm
But wield the brand that hangeth by?
And snatch the noble girl from harm,
Who heedeth not the hellish cry?
A shot! the savage leader falls—
The maiden's eye which aimed the gun—
That eye, whose deadly aim appals
Is tearful when its task is done.
He falls—and straight with baffled cries,
His tribesmen fly in wild dismay;
And now, beneath the evening skies,
That household may in safety pray.

Roy Bean

ANONYMOUS

*Judge Roy Bean was a fabulous Texan in a state abounding with fab-
ulous characters. He was known as "the law west of the Pecos." This
ballad gives a glimpse of his versatility, and proves him to have been
indeed a law unto himself.*

Cowboys, come and hear a story of Roy Bean in all his
　　glory,
"All the law West of the Pecos," was his line:
You must let our ponies take us, to a town on Lower
　　Pecos
Where the High Bridge spans the canon thin and fine.

He was born one day near Toyah where he learned to
　　be a lawyer
And a teacher and a barber for his fare,
He was cook and old shoe mender, sometimes preacher
　　and bar-tender:
It cost two bits to have him cut your hair.

He was certain sure a hustler and considerable a rust-
　　ler
And at mixing up an egg nog he was grand.
He was lively, he was merry, he could drink a Tom and
　　Jerry,
On occasion at a round-up took a hand.

You may find the story funny, but once he had no
　　money
Which for him was not so very strange and rare,
And he went to help Pap Wyndid but he got so absent-
　　minded,
Then he put his RB brand on old Pap's steer.

Now Pap was right smart angry so Roy Bean went
　　down to Langtry
Where he opened up an office and a store.
There he'd sell you drinks or buttons or another ranch-
　　er's muttons,
Though the latter made the other feller sore.

Once there came from Austin city a young dude re-
　　puted witty,
Out of Bean he thought he'd quickly take a rise:

And he got frisky as he up and called for whiskey
And he said to Bean, "Now hurry, damn your eyes."

On the counter threw ten dollars and it very quickly
    follers
That the bar-keep took full nine and gave back one,
Then the stranger give a holler as he viewed his single
    dollar,
And at that commenced the merriment and fun.

For the dude he slammed the table just as hard as he
    was able,
That the price of whiskey was too high he swore.
Said Roy Bean, "Cause of your fussin' and your most
    outrageous cussin'
You are fined the other dollar by the law.

"On this place I own a lease, sir, I'm the justice of the
    peace, sir,
And the Law west of the Pecos all is here,
For you've acted very badly," then the stranger went
    off sadly
While down his cheek there rolled a bitter tear.

Then one day they found a dead man who had been in
    life a Red man
So it's doubtless he was nothing else than bad.
Called on Bean to view the body, so he took a drink of
    toddy,
Then he listed all the things the dead man had.

Now the find it was quite rare, oh, for he'd been a
    "cocinero"
And his pay day hadn't been so far away,
He'd a bran' new fine white Stetson and a dandy Smith
    and Wesson
And a bag of forty dollars jingled gay.

Said Roy Bean, "You'll learn a lesson for I see a Smith
    and Wesson
And to carry implements of war is wrong,
So I fine you forty dollar," and the man gave ne'er a
    holler
Which concludes this very interesting song.

The Poor Voter on Election Day

BY JOHN GREENLEAF WHITTIER

*Although by birth a peaceful Quaker, Whittier had some decided
opinions and one of these is forcibly expressed in this ballad.*

The proudest now is but my peer,
The highest not more high;
Today, of all the weary year,
A king of men am I.
Today alike are great and small,
The nameless and the known;
My palace is the people's hall,
The ballot box my throne!

Who serves today upon the list
Beside the served shall stand;
Alike the brown and wrinkled fist,
The gloved and dainty hand!
The rich is level with the poor,
The weak is strong today;
The sleekest broadcloth counts no more
Than homespun frock of gray.

Today let pomp and vain pretense
My stubborn right abide;
I set a plain man's common sense
Against the pedant's pride.
Today shall simple manhood try

The strength of gold and land,
The wide world has not wealth to buy
The power in my right hand!

While there's a grief to seek redress,
Or balance to adjust,
Where weighs our living manhood less
Than Mammon's vilest dust—
While there's a right to need my vote,
A wrong to sweep away,
Up! clouted knee and ragged coat!
A man's a man today!

The Rumseller Recognized

BY LYDIA BAXTER

Certain unregenerates I know would have said to the rum-seller, "Mix me up just one more for the road."

Stretched on a hard and tattered bed,
No pillow bore his aching head,
While thus he dreamed his life away,
The ever-fearful, madd'ning dreams
That haunt the drunkard's burning brain
With pallid ghost and fiery fiends,
Appeared with all their frightful train.
The voice of her, his tender wife,
His heart once filled with throbs of joy;
And dearer, too, than his own life,
Once stood his darling, prattling boy.
But now, alas, no soothing tone
Can reach that hopeless, sinking heart;
With tearless eye and sadd'ning moan,
His spirit must from hence depart.
But stop—the voice of one that filled

For him so oft the fatal cup,
Has through his dying spirit thrilled,
And broke his heavy slumber up:
And, "Dost thou know me, then," he said,
And neared his paltry, shaking cot—
"Know thee!" the dying man replied,
"Know thee! ah, Sir, why know thee not?
And these, *my wife* and *weeping child*
Will know thee, too, when I am dead!"
Said he—and raved in accents wild,
Then lifeless sank upon his bed.

Crossed Swords

BY THOMAS WENTWORTH HIGGINSON

*This Massachusetts author was an Abolitionist, soldier, friend of Emily
Dickinson, and a backer of John Brown's raid.*

My grandsire fought for England, sword in hand;
My other grandsire joined in high debate,
To free a nation and to mould a State!
Within my blood the two commingled stand,
Yielding this heart, still true to its own land,
A mingled heritage of love and hate.
The peevish pens of London cannot prate
So coarsely, but I feel the eternal band
That binds me, England, to thy low-hung shore,
Thy dainty turf, smooth stream, and gentle hill,
So alien from our spaces vast and wild.
Were England dying, at her cannon's roar,
I think my grandsire's sword would stir and thrill,
Though when this land lay bleeding, England smiled.

John Brown

BY EUGENE FITCH WARE

*This author, prominent in the late '80s and the early '90s, wrote under
the nom de plume of "Ironquill."*

States are not great
Except as men make them;
Men are not great except they do and dare.
But states, like men,
Have destinies that take them—
That bear them on, not knowing why or where.

The WHY repels
The philosophic searcher—
The WHY and WHERE all questionings defy.
Until we find,
Far back in youthful nurture,
Prophetic facts that constitute the WHY.

All merit comes
From braving the unequal;
All glory comes from daring to begin.
Fame loves the State
That, reckless of the sequel,
Fights long and well, whether to lose or win.

Than in our State
No illustration apter
Is seen or found of faith and hope and will.
Take up her story;
Every leaf and chapter
Contains a record that conveys a thrill.

And there is one
Whose faith, whose fight, whose failing,
Fame shall placard upon the walls of time.
He dared begin—

Despite the unavailing,
He dared begin when failure was a crime.

When over Africa
Some future cycle
Shall sweep the lake-crammed uplands with its surge;
When, as with a trumpet
Of Archangel Michael,
Culture shall bid a colored race emerge;

When busy cities
There, in constellations,
Shall gleam with spires and palaces and domes,
With marts wherein
Is heard the noise of nations;
With summer groves surrounding stately homes—

There, future orators
To cultured freemen
Shall tell of valor, and recount with praise,
Stories of Kansas
And the Lacedaemon—
Cradles of freedom, then of ancient days.

From boulevards
O'erlooking both Nyanzaz,
The statured bronze shall glitter in the sun,
With rugged lettering;
   JOHN BROWN OF KANSAS
    HE DARED BEGIN,
     HE LOST,
   BUT, LOSING, WON.

True Courage

BY WILLIAM LLOYD GARRISON

*This is characteristic of a man whose motto was: "I am in earnest;
I will not equivocate; I will not excuse; I will not retreat a single
inch; and I will be heard!"*

I boast no courage on the battle-field,
Where hostile troops immix in horrid fray;
For Love or Fame I can no weapon wield,
With burning lust an enemy to slay;—
But test my spirit at the blazing stake,
For advocacy of the Rights of Man,
And Truth—Or on the wheel my body break;
Let persecution place me 'neath its ban;
Insult, defame, proscribe my humble name.
Yea, put a dagger to my naked breast;
If I recoil in terror from the flame,
Or recreant prove when Peril rears its crest,
To save a limb, or shun the public scorn—
Then write me down for aye, weakest of Woman Born.

Abraham Lincoln —
The Mohammed of the
Modern Hegira

ANONYMOUS

This is meant to satirize Lincoln's precautions against a plot to assassinate him while he was on his way to his first inauguration. It is taken from The New Orleans Crescent, *March 5th, 1861.*

At midnight in the Keystone State,
Old Abe was *dreaming* of the hour
When Southern rebels, soon or late,
Should tremble at his power;
In *dreams* "Old Fuss and Feathers" bore
The trophies of the conqueror;
In dreams his song of triumph heard,
Then waved the Union banner, stirred
O'er Southers forts by Southern gales,
And planted down his foot as firm

As when he split the rails.
An hour pressed on—Old Abe awoke
To sounds that made him pale;
Not triumph this, nor friendly joke—
"To flight—they wait—by rail—by rail!"
He woke to list, 'midst sobs and tears,
A tale of horror and of fears—
And death to be *his* lot—
For lurking near the morning train,
Plug Uglies wait in might and main,
With dirk and pistol shot!
"Fly ere the morning's sun arise;
"Fly from the foe that waiting lies,
"Fly 'neath this *all*-concealing guise,
To Scott and Washington!"
They begged like men inspired by dread,
They told their tale of murder grim—
They conquered—and Old Abr'ham fled,
Trembling at every limb.
His *wife* and other comrades watch
The gliding train, his form to catch,
And felt *his* danger past;
But when the morning sun arose,
They dared the rail and all his foes,
Yet *safe* arrived at last!
And thus our hero, by his flight,
Has won the White House on the Fourth,
And by *rail-splitting* and his height
Will rule the North with all his might,
Negroes and whites henceforth.
And learn from this the truth sublime—
"That *he* who runs away"
Saves life and limb, whie gaining time,
"To fight another day."

Jefferson D.

By HENRY SYLVESTER CORNWELL

Written by a Charlestown, N. H. physician during the national crisis variously called "The War of The Rebellion", "The Civil War", "The Late Unpleasantness" and "The War Between the States".

You're a traitor convicted, you know very well!
       Jefferson D., Jefferson D.!
You thought it a capital thing to rebel.
       Jefferson D.!
  But there's one thing I'll say:
  You'll discover some day,
When you see a stout cotton cord hang from a tree,
There's an accident happened you didn't foresee,
       Jefferson D.!
What shall be found on historys' page?
       Jefferson D., Jefferson D.!
When the student explores the Republican age!
       Jefferson D.!
  He will find, as is meet,
  That at Judas's feet
You sit in your shame, with the impotent plea,
That you hated the land and the law of the free,
       Jefferson D.!
What do you see in your visions of night,
       Jefferson D., Jefferson D.?
Does the spectacle furnish you any delight,
       Jefferson D.?
  Do you feel, in disgrace,
  The black cap o'er your face,
While the tremor creeps down from your heart to your
  knee.
And freedom, insulted, approves the decree,
       Jefferson D.?

Oh! long have we pleaded, till pleading is vain,
Jefferson D., Jefferson D.!
Your hands are imbued with the blood of the slain,
Jefferson D.!
And at last, for the right,
We arise in our might,
A people united, resistless and free,
And declare that rebellion no longer shall be!
Jefferson D.!

Wait for the Wagons

ANONYMOUS

A hundred thousand Northmen,
In glittering war array,
Shout, "Onward now to Richmond!
We'll brook no more delay;
Why give the traitors time and means
To fortify the way
With stolen guns, in ambuscades?
Oh! answer us, we pray."

CHORUS OF CHIEFTAINS

You must wait for the wagons,
The real army wagons,
The fat contract wagons,
Bought in the red-tape way.

Now, if for army wagons,
Not for compromise you wait,
Just ask them of the farmers
Of any Union state;
And if you need ten thousand,
Sound, sound, though second-hand,

You'll find upon the instant
A supply for your demand.

CHORUS

No! wait for the wagons,
The new army wagons,
The fat contract wagons,
Till the fifteenth of July.

No swindling fat contractors
    Shall block the people's way,
Nor rebel compromisers—
    'Tis treason's reckoning day.
Then shout again our war-cry,
    To Richmond onward move!
We now can crush the traitors,
    And that we mean to prove!

CHORUS

No! wait for the wagons,
The fat contract wagons;
If red-tape so wills it,
Wait till the Judgment day.

My Maryland

BY JAMES RYDER RANDALL

This author remained an unreconstructed rebel until his death. This was his plea for Maryland to join the Confederacy.

The despot's heel is on thy shore,
    Maryland!
His torch is at thy temple door,
    Maryland!
Avenge the patriotic gore

That flecked the streets of Baltimore,
And be the battle-queen of yore,
   Maryland, my Maryland!

Hark to an exiled son's appeal,
   Maryland!
My Mother State, to thee I kneel,
   Maryland!
For life and death, for woe and weal,
Thy peerless chivalry reveal,
And gird thy beauteous limbs with steel,
   Maryland, my Maryland!

Thou wilt not cower in the dust,
   Maryland!
Thy beaming sword shall never rust,
   Maryland!
Remember Carroll's sacred trust,
Remember Howard's warlike thrust,
And all thy slumberers with the just,
   Maryland, my Maryland!

Come! 'tis the red dawn of the day,
   Maryland!
Come with thy panoplied array,
   Maryland!
With Ringgold's spirit for the fray,
With Watson's blood at Monterey,
With fearless Lowe and dashing May,
   Maryland, my Maryland!

Dear Mother, burst the tyrant's chain,
   Maryland!
Virginia should not call in vain,
   Maryland!
She meets her sisters on the plain,—
"*Sic semper!*" 'tis the proud refrain
That baffles minions back amain,
   Maryland!

Arise in majesty again,
  Maryland, my Maryland!

Come! for thy shield is bright and strong,
  Maryland!
Come! for thy dalliance does thee wrong,
  Maryland!
Come to thine own heroic throng
Stalking with Liberty along,
And chant thy dauntless slogan-song,
  Maryland, my Maryland!

I see the blush upon thy cheek,
  Maryland!
For thou wast ever bravely meek,
  Maryland!
But lo! there surges forth a shriek,
From hill to hill, from creek to creek,
Potomac calls to Chesapeake,
  Maryland, my Maryland!

Thou wilt not yield the Vandal toll,
  Maryland!
Thou wilt not crook to his control,
  Maryland!
Better the fire upon thee roll,
Better the shot, the blade, the bowl,
Than crucifixion of the soul,
  Maryland, my Maryland!

I hear the distant thunder hum,
  Maryland!
The Old Line's bugle, fife and drum,
  Maryland!
She is not dead, nor deaf, nor dumb;
Huzza! she spurns the Northern scum!
She breathes! She burns! She'll come! She'll come!
  Maryland, my Maryland!

Confederate Song

BY E. LLOYD WALES

This is Louisiana's contribution to Civil War balladry. It was written by a young captain in the Confederate army in 1861.

Rally 'round our country's flag!
Rally, boys, nor do not lag;
Come from every vale and crag,
Sons of Liberty!

Northern vandals tread our soil,
Forth they come for blood and spoil,
To the homes we've gained with toil,
Shouting, "Slavery!"

Traitorous Lincoln's bloody band
Now invades this freeman's land,
Armed with sword and firebrand,
'Gainst the brave and free.

Arm ye then, for fray and fight,
March ye forth both day and night,
Stop not till the foe's in sight,
Sons of chivalry.

Eulogy to General Sherman

BY ALFRED W. ARRINGTON

Curiously enough, this eulogic ballad is by an eminent North Carolina jurist, a member of a distinguished family.

Have ye read in truthful story,
Or on fiction's legends hoary,
Aught that rings with real glory
Louder than our Sherman's name?
Through campaigns of conquest, vaster

Than before were trod by master
Of the sword, without disaster,
He hath marched to deathless fame!
Less a man than weird magician,
He hath stormed each strong position,
Pushed the foe to swift perdition,
But with arms his reason wrought;
Spurning battle's frantic thunder,
As a crude and cruel blunder,
He hath crushed rebellion under
Blasting bolts of quicker thought!
Mercy, mild, he proved God's daughter,
Dearest pearl from Eden's water;
Still disdaining useless slaughter,
Wise, he flanked the Red sea's flood.
Loyal in his country's quarrel,
True unto the highest moral,
He condemned the greenest laurel,
If bedewed with needless blood.
Vengeance vain he left to others;
Rebel sons he knew were brothers
And he felt they might have mothers
Tender as his own true wife.
He would only doom assailing
Hosts of death, while trumpets wailing,
Mourned the hearts in battle failing:
He but warred with weaponed life.
Those who cried for quarter round him,
Pity's kindly angel found him;
Widows lone, and orphans crowned him
With the love of grateful tears.
War's wild mandates he did season
With the eloquence of reason,
Seeking still to woo back treason
To its faith of former years.
Since he passed the purple border

Of which civil strife is warder,
Never did a ruthless order
Shame our Sherman's gentle hand.
Small in words but great in action,
Ne'er a demon of distraction
Dared to class him with a fraction
Narrower than his native land.
Glory's record shows the traces
Of the mighty ones, whose faces
Triumphed over alien races,
Conquerors of the weak alone.
But our hero's stern persistence,—
Vanquished warriors in resistance,
Brave as ever has existence,
Kindred bravery to his own.
Pray for Sherman's preservation,
Ye who seek the land's salvation;
Hopes, the highest of the nation,
Cling for life unto his name.
Praise him for his posts forsaken,
Laud him for Savannah taken,
Cheer him till the world awaken
With the echoes of his fame.

The Sword of Robert E. Lee

BY ABRAM J. RYAN

*Father Ryan was known as "the poet-priest of the Confederacy." He
reached the height when he penned this tribute to a noble American.*

Forth from its scabbard, pure and bright,
　　Flashed the sword of Lee!
Far in the front of the deadly fight,
High o'er the brave in the cause of Right
Its stainless sheen, like a beacon light,
　　Led us to Victory!

Out of its scabbard, where, full long,
  It slumbered peacefully,
Roused from its rest by the battle's song,
Shielding the feeble, smiting the strong,
Guarding the right, avenging the wrong,
  Gleamed the sword of Lee!

Forth from its scabbard, high in air
  Beneath Virginia's sky—
And they who saw it gleaming there,
And knew who bore it, knelt to swear
That where that sword led they would dare
  To follow and to die!

Out of its scabbard! Never hand
  Waved sword from stain as free,
Nor purer sword led braver band,
Nor braver bled for a brighter land,
Nor brighter land had a cause so grand,
  Nor cause a chief like Lee!

Forth from its scabbard! How we prayed
  That sword might victor be;
And when our triumph was delayed,
And many a heart grew sore afraid,
We still hoped on while gleamed the blade
  Of noble Robert Lee!

Forth from its scabbard all in vain
  Bright flashed the sword of Lee;
'Tis shrouded now in its sheath again,
It sleeps the sleep of our noble slain,
Defeated, yet without a stain,
  Proudly and peacefully!

✦ ✦ ✦

Company K

By Ethel Lynn Beers

This touching Civil War ballad was written by the author of "All Quiet Along the Potomac."

There's a cap in the closet,
Old, tattered, and blue,
That would be of little value,
It may be, to you;
But a crown jewel-studded
Could not buy it today,
With the letters of honor,
Brave "Company K."

The head that it sheltered
Needs shelter no more;
Dead heroes make holy
The trifles they wore;
So a wreath better winning
Than laurel and bay
Seems the cap of the soldier,
Marked "Company K."

For eyes have looked steady
Its visor beneath
O'er the work of the reaper,
Whose harvest is Death.
Let the muster-roll meagre
So mournfully say
How foremost in danger
Went "Company K"—

Whose footsteps unbroken
Came up to the town,
Where rampart and bastion
Looked fearfully down—

Who, closing up breaches,
Yet kept on their way,
Till guns downward pointing
Faced "Company K."

Like cameras fearful
Stood cannon aloof,
Till the signal was given
To strike off a proof
Of the soul of a soldier,
To send up to Him.
(Pray God that He knew them,
Though bloody and dim!)

Who faltered or shivered?
Who shunned battle-smoke?
Whose fire was uncertain?
Whose battle-line broke?
Go ask it of History
Years from Today
And the record shall tell you,
Not "Company K."

Tho' my darling is sleeping
Today with the dead,
And the daisies and clover
Bloom over his head,
I smile, tho' I'm crying
As I lay it away,
That battle-worn cap
Lettered "Company K."

General Jackson Crosses Jordan

By Martha Keller

General Jackson was accidentally wounded by his own troops at Chancellorsville on May 2, 1863 and died on May 10th.

❧ 150 ❧

The air of heaven was black with smoke,
Black with battle, loud with lead,
When Thomas Jonathan Jackson spoke,
And these were the words that Jackson said,

As the blood of his arm ran over his breast
And he lay and bled with his hand in Lee's:
"Let us pass over the river and rest—
Rest in the shade of the trees."

By the roads and ridges, creeks and crags,
  Where men would follow, he led them on,
Led the rebels in bloody rags
  From dawn to dark and dark to dawn.
With bandages for their battle flags—
  They followed Jackson to hell and gone.

The arm he lost was a mortal loss.
(He lost his left, but Lee his right.)
The one more river he had to cross
Was wicked water and black as night.

But over Jordan, deep and wide,
As wide a water as kingdom come,
A flock of angels on either side—
Waited for to carry him home.

He was a deacon, good and grim.
  He, alone, was a mighty host,
A rebel yell and a battle hymn.
  His were the men that marched the most.
Stonewall wasn't the word or him—
  He was a phantom, he was a ghost.

The angels waiting on either bank
Blew for him till their trumpets burst.
But he slipped so fast around the flank
That he got to heaven first.

In clouds as white as a cloud of tents,
There in a sunshine bright as braid,
He called the roll of his regiments—
And rested in the shade.

His were the men no men could beat.
(He won his battles by breaking rules.)
With empty bellies and bloody feet,
(Regulations were made for fools,)
He led them up to the judgment seat—
(Fast as horses, tough as mules.)

Soon We'll Have the Union Back

By Charles Graham Halpine

During the Lincoln-McClellan Presidential campaign in 1864 this was General McClellan's marching song.

Good people all, both great and small,
I sing a tale of pity,
My hand I fling across the string,
To waken up the ditty;
A ruined land that once was grand
Is not a joking matter,
Though Abe, we know, the more our woe,
The more his jokes he'll clatter.
    Oh, M'Clellan,
    Georgie B. M'Clellan,
    Shall we have the Union back?
    Tell us "Mac"—M'Clellan.

All evils sure we could endure,
Thrice all the ills we suffer,
Could we but glance on any chance
Our Union to recover;

There gleams one way a flash of day.
But one bright bow of promise—
Good Lord, alack! just give us "Mac";
And take Abe Lincoln from us!
    Oh, M'Clellan,
    Georgie B. M'Clellan,
    The one to bring our Union back
    Is only "Mac"—M'Clellan.

Then not a rag of our old flag
Should ever part asunder;
"Fair terms of peace if you will cease—
If not we'll give you thunder!"
A million swords to back our words
Beneath M'Clellan gleaming,
And soon you know, Jeff D. and Co.,
For France they will be steaming.
    Oh, M'Clellan,
    Georgie B. M'Clellan,
    Soon we'll have our prisoners back
    Under "Mac"—M'Clellan.

The people all, both great and small,
Except the sons of "shoddy,"
Are on the track for Little Mac—
They're with him soul and body;
For well they know the nation's woe
Can never be abated,
Till in command of all the land
Our chief we have instated.
    Oh, M'Clellan,
    Georgie B. M'Clellan,
    The Union will come leaping back
    Under "Mac"—M'Clellan.

Shoo, Fly, Don't Bother Me

By T. Brigham Bishop

This author was a song writer in the Civil War days and is supposed to have written this after listening to some colored soldiers complaining about the flies.

I think I hear the angels sing,
I think I hear the angels sing,
I think I hear the angels sing;
The angels now are on the wing.
I feel, I feel, I feel that's what my mother said,
The angels pouring 'lasses down
Upon this darkey's head.

CHORUS

Shoo, fly, don't bother me,
Shoo, fly, don't bother me,
Shoo, fly, don't bother me,
I belong to Company G.
I feel, I feel, I feel, I feel like a morning star.
I feel, I feel, I feel, I feel like a morning star.

If I sleep in the sun this darkey knows,
If I sleep in the sun this darkey knows,
If I sleep in the sun this darkey knows,
A fly comes sting him on the nose.
I feel, I feel, I feel, that's what my mother said,
Whenever this darkey goes to sleep
He must cover up his head.

To General Butler

By "Bay State"

Despite history's adverse opinion of Ben Butler's character and generalship, someone thought he was good at the time.

Ben Butler, my boy,
It gives me much joy,
Of your brave words and acts to hear.
So prompt and so quick,
Your are truly a "Brick",
Knowing not the meaning of fear.
As a lawyer bold
We know you of old,
In many a "hard knotty case."
But now on the field,
Convinced you'll not yield;
You are just the man for the place.
Be true to your trust,
And bring to the dust
The rebels where'er they are found.
Inform them, dear Ben,
They've mistaken the men
If they think the North is not sound.
We know you are right,
Wherever you fight,
In upholding the Stripes and the Stars.
We know they are wrong,

Where'er they belong,
Who follow the stripes and the bars.
See to it our flag
Displaces that rag,
Symbolic of despot and slave;
From Georgia to Maine
It must wave again
"O'er the land of the free and the brave."
We will anxiously wait
To hear of your fate,
Entreating God's blessing on you;
For one thing we know,
"Come weal or come woe,"
To the Union you'll ever be true.

He'll Be Back By-And-By

ANONYMOUS

It took a brave mother to sing this while her husband was fighting in the Civil War for $13 a month, and flour cost $24 a barrel.

The wife of a soldier was starving with hunger,
    And close by her side was a poor little lad;
I've seen many children, but never one younger,
    Who seemed so depressed at the loss of his dad.
'Oh, where is my father?' the boy kept on asking,
    'I wish he would come, for I do feel so cold!'
And then, in reply to the little one's asking,
    Why, this was the tale that the poor woman told:

CHORUS

He'll be back by-and-by, it is true all I've told you,
    So cheer up, my darling, and don't sob and cry;
Your father, my lad, is a brave Union soldier,
    Tho' torn from us now, he'll be back by-and-by.

Oh, father, dear father, pray, why did you leave us?
    And why from your boy to the war did you go?
I've prayed to the One up above to receive us,
    And as he said this the boy fell in the snow.
The mother then clutched him more tightly and firmer
    Than e'er she had done! How the poor soul did weep!
For in the still night you could hear the faint murmur.
    And these were the words as she hushed him to sleep:
— *Chorus*

The boy then awoke, and "dear father" was crying,
    The mother, poor soul, how she burst into tears;
She knew very well that her poor boy was dying,
    It had come now to this was the worst of her fears,
"Oh, father, come quickly," his faint voice was call-
    ing,
    As he laid back his head in her arms, and he died
On that cold winter's night, as the snow fast was fall-
    ing.
    I heard a faint sound as the poor mother cried:
— *Chorus*

When Johnny Comes Marching Home

By Patrick S. Gilmore

The author of this gay and cheering ballad was bandmaster to General Benjamin Butler when the latter was in command of New Orleans. Although written some time during the Civil War, this song did not achieve its greatest popularity until the time of the Spanish-American War, of which it became almost a trade mark.

When Johnny comes marching home again, hurrah,
    hurrah!
We'll give him a hearty welcome then, hurrah, hurrah!
The men will cheer, the boys will shout,
The ladies they will all turn out.

CHORUS

And we'll all feel gay when Johnny comes marching home.
And we'll all feel gay when Johnny comes marching home.

The old church bell will peal with joy, hurrah, hurrah!
To welcome home our darling boy, hurrah, hurrah!
The village lads and lassies say
With roses they will strew the way. — *Chorus*

Get ready for the Jubilee, hurrah, hurrah!
We'll give the hero three times three, hurrah, hurrah!
The laurel wreath is ready now
To place upon his loyal brow. — *Chorus*

Let love and friendship on that day, hurrah, hurrah!
Their choicest treasures then display, hurrah, hurrah!
And let each one perform some part,
To fill with joy the warrior's heart. — *Chorus*

We Are the Boys of Potomac's Ranks

ANONYMOUS

*Although most of the Civil War songs were in turn lachrymose, sen-
timental, and lugubrious, occasional writers acquired the humorous
perspective which allowed them to laugh. Sung to the tune of "When
Johnny Comes Marching Home", this ballad makes fun of the endless
defeats which the Union seemed to suffer before Grant took command.
These verses seem as spontaneous and of as diverse authorship as the
later ones of "Mademoiselle from Armentières."*

We are the boys of Potomac's ranks,
Hurrah! Hurrah!
We are the boys of Potomac's ranks,
We ran with McDowell, retreated with Banks,

And we'll all drink stone blind—
Johnny, fill up the bowl.

We fought with McClellan, the Rebs, shakes, and fever,
    Hurrah! Hurrah!
We fought with McClellan, the Rebs, shakes, and fever,
But Mac joined the navy on reaching James River,
And we'll all drink stone blind—
Johnny, fill up the bowl.

They gave us John Pope, our patience to tax,
    Hurrah! Hurrah!
They gave us John Pope, our patience to tax,
Who said that out West he'd seen naught but gray
        backs,
And we'll all drink stone blind—
Johnny, fill up the bowl.

He said his headquarters were in the saddle,
    Hurrah! Hurrah!
He said his headquarters were in the saddle,
But Stonewall Jackson made him skedaddle,
And we'll all drink stone blind—
Johnny, fill up the bowl.

Then Mac was recalled, but after Antietam,
    Hurrah! Hurrah!
Then Mac was recalled, but after Antietam,
Abe gave him a rest, he was too slow to beat 'em,
And we'll all drink stone blind—
Johnny, fill up the bowl.

Oh, Burnside, then he tried his luck,
    Hurrah! Hurrah!
Oh, Burnside, then he tried his luck,
But in the mud so fast got stuck,
And we'll all drink stone blind—
Johnny, fill up the bowl.

Then Hooker was taken to fill the bill,
  Hurrah! Hurrah!
Then Hooker was taken to fill the bill,
But he got a black eye at Chancellorsville,
And we'll all drink stone blind—
Johnny, fill up the bowl.

Next came General Meade, a slow old plug,
  Hurrah! Hurrah!
Next came General Meade, a slow old plug,
For he let them get away at Gettysburg,
And we'll all drink stone blind—
Johnny, fill up the bowl.

Marching Through Georgia

By Henry Clay Work

The writer of this enduringly popular ballad, as well as others such as "Sleeping for the Flag", was also a devoted temperance worker who finds a second claim to fame as author of the classic "Father, Dear Father, Come Home with Me Now." Work was a strong Unionist whose father was imprisoned for his activities as a member of the Illinois underground railway.

Bring the good old bugle, boys, we'll sing another
    song—
Sing it with a spirit that will start the world along—
Sing it as we used to sing it, fifty thousand strong,
While we were marching through Georgia.

CHORUS

"Hurrah! Hurrah! We bring the jubilee!
  Hurrah! Hurrah! the flag that makes you
    free!"
So we sang the chorus from Atlanta to the sea,
While we were marching through Georgia.

How the darkeys shouted when they heard the joyful
    sound!
How the turkeys gobbled which our commissary found!
How the sweet potatoes even started from the ground,
While we were marching through Georgia. — *Chorus*

Yes, and there were Union men who wept with joyful
    tears
When they saw the honored flag they had not seen for
    years;
Hardly could they be restrained from breaking forth
    in cheers,
While we were marching through Georgia. — *Chorus*

"Sherman's dashing Yankee boys will never reach the
    coast!"
So the saucy rebels said, and 'twas a handsome boast.
Had they not forgot, alas! to reckon with the host,
While we were marching through Georgia. — *Chorus*

So we made a thoroughfare for Freedom and her train,
Sixty miles in latitude — three hundred to the main;
Treason fled before us, for resistance was in vain,
While we were marching through Georgia. — *Chorus*

The Faded Coat of Blue

By J. H. McNaughton

*Some Civil War songs, such as Charles C. Sawyer's "Weeping, Sad,
and Lonely" were so lachrymose that their recitation was forbidden in
some army units for fear that they might completely destroy morale.
Here is another tear-jerker through which one can read the dread story
of heavy casualty lists.*

My brave lad he sleeps in his faded coat of blue;
In a lonely grave unknown lies the heart that beat so
    true;

He sank faint and hungry among the famished brave,
And they laid him sad and lonely within his nameless
grave.

No more the bugle calls the weary one,
Rest, noble spirit, in thy grave unknown!
I'll find you and know you, among the good and true,
When a robe of white is giv'n for the faded coat of
blue.

He cried, "Give me water and just a little crumb,
And my mother she will bless you through all the
years to come;
Oh! tell my sweet sister, so gentle, good and true,
That I'll meet her up in heaven, in my faded coat of
blue." — *Chorus*

Tramp, Tramp, Tramp

BY GEORGE F. ROOT

*George F. Root, professor at the Boston Academy of Music, was one
of the most productive Northern writers of Civil War songs, many of
which achieved considerable success. In addition to the two printed
here, he wrote "The Battle Cry of Freedom", "The Vacant Chair",
and other ballads. "Tramp, Tramp, Tramp" has retained its popularity
through the years.*

In the prison cell I sit,
  Thinking, mother dear, of you,
And our bright and happy home so far away,
  And the tears they fill my eyes,
Spite of all that I can do,
  Tho' I try to cheer my comrades and be gay.

Tramp, tramp, tramp, the boys are marching,
  Oh, cheer up, comrades, they will come,
And beneath the starry flag we shall breathe the air
    again,
Of freedom in our own beloved home.

In the battle front we stood
  When the fiercest charge they made,
And they swept us off a hundred men or more,
  But before we reached their lines
They were beaten back dismayed
  And we heard the cry of vict'ry o'er and o'er. —
Chorus

So within the prison cell
  We are waiting for the day
That shall come to open wide the iron door,
  And the hollow eye grows bright,
And the poor heart almost gay,
  As we think of seeing friends and home once more.
— *Chorus*

Tenting Tonight

By Walter Kittredge

Although defeatist in tone, this song so well descibed the tragedy of fratricide that it achieved great popularity in both Civil War camps. It achieved currency on a mouth-to-mouth basis, for its author was unable to find a publisher, although he had issued a collection of Northern songs several years before.

We're tenting tonight on the old camp ground,
Give us a song to cheer our weary hearts,
A song of home and the friends we love so dear.

Many are the hearts that are weary tonight,
Waiting for the war to cease;
Many are the hearts looking for the right
To see the dawn of peace.
Tenting tonight, tenting tonight,
Tenting on the old camp ground.

We've been tenting tonight on the old camp ground,
Thinking of the days gone by, of the loved ones at
    home
That gave us the hand, and the tear that said "good-
    bye!" — *Chorus*

We are tired of war on the old camp ground,
Many are dead and gone, of the brave and true,
Who've left their homes, others been wounded long.
    — *Chorus*

We've been fighting today on the old camp ground,
Many are lying near, some are dead,
And some are dying, many are in tears.

Many are the hearts that are weary tonight,
Wishing for the war to cease;
Many are the hearts looking for the right,
To see the dawn of peace.
Dying tonight, dying tonight,
Dying on the old camp ground.

✦ ✦ ✦

Just Before the Battle, Mother

BY GEORGE F. ROOT

Perhaps due to the youth of many of the contestants, the Civil War produced a surprising number of mawkish ballads. Their sentimental excesses often inspired parody. One unauthorized version of this song ran as follows:

> Just before the battle, mother,
> I was drinking mountain dew.
> When I saw the Rebels marching,
> To the rear I quickly flew.

As with so many of these compositions, although written in the North, this was equally popular in the South.

Just before the battle, mother,
I am thinking most of you;
While upon the field we're watching,
With the enemy in view.
Comrades brave are 'round me lying,
Filled with thoughts of home and God;
For well they know upon the morrow
Some will sleep beneath the sod.

CHORUS

Farewell, mother, you may never
Press me to your heart again;
But, oh, you'll not forget me, mother,
If I'm numbered with the slain.

Oh! I long to see you, mother,
And the loving ones at home;
But I'll never leave our banner
'Till in honor I can come.
Tell the enemy around you
That their cruel words, we know,
In every battle kill our soldiers
By the help they give the foe. — *Chorus*

We Are Coming, Father Abraham

By James Sloan Gibbons

As the losses of the Civil War mounted, Lincoln in 1862 asked the various states to supply "three hundred thousand more" men. When the required number of men was not forthcoming, further demands for manpower provoked the draft riots of 1863. It is interesting to note that the music for this song was composed by Stephen Foster, then living in obscure poverty in New York City.

We are coming, Father Abraham, three hundred thousand more,
From Mississippi's winding stream and from New England's shore;
We leave our ploughs and workshops, our wives and children dear,
With hearts too full for utterance, with but a silent tear;
We dare not look behind us, but steadfastly before:
We are coming, Father Abraham, three hundred thousand more!

If you look across the hilltops that meet the northern sky,
Long moving lines of rising dust your vision may descry;
And now the wind, an instant, tears the cloudy veil aside,
And floats aloft our spangled flag in glory and in pride,
And bayonets in the sunlight gleam, and bands brave music pour,
We are coming, Father Abraham, three hundred thousand more!

If you look all up our valleys where the growing har-
vests shine,
You may see our sturdy farmer boys fast forming into
line;
And children from their mothers' knees are pulling
at the weeds,
And learning how to reap and sow against their country's needs;
And a farewell group stands weeping at every cottage
door:
We are coming, Father Abraham, three hundred thousand more!

You have called us, and we're coming, by Richmond's
bloody tide
To lay us down, for Freedom's sake, our brothers'
bones beside,
Or from foul treason's savage grasp to wrench the
murderous blade,
And in the face of foreign foes its fragments to parade.
Six hundred thousand loyal men and true have gone
before:
We are coming, Father Abraham, three hundred thousand more!

The Battle Hymn of
the Republic

By Julia Ward Howe

The wife of the famous Massachusetts reformer wrote this greatest song to come out of the Civil War at dawn one morning after witness-ing on the previous afternoon a review of Union troops and a minor military engagement. The poem was published in The Atlantic Monthly *for February, 1862. While it attracted some attention, the general pre-occupation with the war obscured most literary efforts. It achieved its immediate great popularity with the troops in the field.*

Mine eyes have seen the glory of the coming of the
  Lord:
He is trampling out the vintage where the grapes of
  wrath are stored;
He hath loosed the lightning of his terrible swift
  sword:
  His truth is marching on.

I have seen Him in the watch fires of a hundred cir-
  cling camps;
They have builded Him an altar in the evening dews
  and damps;
I can read His righteous sentence by the dim and flar-
  ing lamps.
  His day is marching on.

I have read a fiery gospel writ in burnished rows of
  steel:
"As ye deal with my contemners, so with you my
  grace shall deal;
Let the Hero, born of woman, crush the serpent with
  his heel,
  Since God is marching on."

He has sounded forth the trumpet that shall never call
  retreat;
He is sifting out the hearts of men before his judgment seat:
Oh! be swift, my soul, to answer Him! be jubilant, my
  feet!
  Our God is marching on.

In the beauty of the lilies Christ was born across the
  sea,
With a glory in His bosom that transfigures you and
  me;
As He died to make men holy, let us die to make men
  free,
  While God is marching on.

Ye Cavaliers of Dixie

By Benjamin F. Porter

This was another great Confederate song, sung to the traditional tune of "Ye Mariners of England".

Ye Cavaliers of Dixie!
Who guard the Southern shores,
Whose standards brave the battle storm
Which o'er our border roars.
Your glorious sabers draw once more,
And charge the Northern foe;
And reap their columns deep,
And reap their columns deep,
And reap their columns deep.

CHORUS

Where the raging tempests blow,
Where the raging tempests blow,
And the iron hail in floods descends,
And the bloody torrents flow.

Ye cavaliers of Dixie!
Though dark the tempest lower,
What arms will wear the tyrant's chains,
What dastard heart will cower?
Bright o'er the night a sign shall rise
To lead to victory!
And your swords reap their hordes,
Where the battle tempests blow;
Where the iron hail in floods descends,
And the bloody torrents flow. — *Chorus*

The South! she needs no ramparts,
No lofty towers to shield;
Your bosoms are her bulwarks strong,
Breastworks that never yield!
The thunder of your battle blades
Shall sweep the servile foe;

While their gore stains the shore,
Where the battle tempests blow;
Where the iron hail in floods descends,
And the bloody torrents flow. — *Chorus*

The battle flag of Dixie
With crimson field shall flame;
Her azure cross and silver stars
Shall light her sons to fame!
When peace with olive branch returns,
That flag's white folds shall grow
Still bright on every height,
When storm has ceased to blow,
And the battle tempests roar no more;
Nor the bloody torrents flow. — *Chorus*

The Bonnie Blue Flag

BY HARRY McCARTHY

One of the most popular of Southern marching songs, this was composed for a vaudeville presentation at a New Orleans theater. Its popularity so infuriated "Beast" Butler when he was in command of the city that he arrested its publisher and threatened to fine anyone caught singing it.

We are a band of brothers, and native to the soil,
Fighting for the property we gained by honest toil;
And when our rights were threatened, the cry rose
    near and far:
Hurrah for the bonnie Blue Flag that bears a single
    star!
  Hurrah! hurrah! for the bonnie Blue Flag
  That bears a single star.

So long as the Union was faithful to her trust,
Like friends and like brothers, kind were we and just;
But now when Northern treachery attempts our rights
    to mar,
We hoist on high the bonnie Blue Flag that bears a
    single star.

First, gallant South Carolina nobly made the stand;
Then came Alabama, who took her by the hand;
Next, quickly Mississippi, Georgia, and Florida—
All raised the flag, the bonnie Blue Flag that bears a
    single star.

Ye men of valor, gather round the banner of the right;
Texas and fair Louisiana join us in the fight.
Davis, our loved President, and Stephens, statesmen
    are;
Now rally round the bonnie Blue Flag that bears a
    single star.

And here's to brave Virginia! the Old Dominion State
With the young Confederacy at length has linked her
    fate.
Impelled by her example, now other States prepare
To hoist on high the bonnie Blue Flag that bears a
    single star.

Then here's to our Confederacy; strong we are and
    brave,
Like patriots of old we'll fight, our heritage to save;
And rather than submit to shame, to die we would
    prefer;
So cheer for the bonnie Blue Flag that bears a single
    star.

Then cheer, boys, cheer, raise the joyous shout,
For Arkansas and North Carolina now have both gone
    out;
And let another rousing cheer for Tennessee be given,
The single star of the bonnie Blue Flag has grown to
    be eleven!
    Hurrah! hurrah! for the bonnie Blue Flag
    That bears a single star.

John Brown's Body

BY THOMAS B. BISHOP

This is a true folk song in the sense that it was widely sung in the North and that both its origin and its author are shrouded in obscurity. The words have been attributed to Thomas B. Bishop and they were sung to a Negro folk melody popular in the Carolinas.

John Brown's body lies a-mould'ring in the grave,
John Brown's body lies a-mould'ring in the grave,
John Brown's body lies a-mould'ring in the grave,
His soul is marching on.

CHORUS

Glory! Glory Hallelujah!
Glory! Glory Hallelujah!
Glory! Glory Hallelujah!
His soul is marching on.

He's gone to be a soldier in the army of the Lord'.
His soul is marching on. — *Chorus*

John Brown's knapsack is strapped upon his back.
His soul is marching on. — *Chorus*

His pet lambs will meet him on the way,
And they'll go marching on. — *Chorus*

They'll hang Jeff Davis on a sour apple tree,
As they go marching on. — *Chorus*

Now for the Union let's give three rousing cheers,
As we go marching on.
Hip. Hip, hip, hip, Hurrah! — *Chorus*

What the Engines Said

Opening of the Pacific Railroad, May 12, 1869

By Bret Harte

Bret Harte, who wrote the classic "Outcasts of Poker Flat," caught the spirit of the great railroad era in this fine ballad. That was the era when the states were at last banded together by the great ribbons of steel.

What was it the Engines said,
Pilots touching,—head to head
Facing on the single track,
Half a world behind each back?
This is what the Engines said,
Unreported and unread.

With a prefatory screech,
In a florid Western speech,
Said the Engine from the West:
"I am from Sierra's crest;
And if altitude's a test,
Why, I reckon, it's confessed
That I've done my level best."

❦ 173 ❦

Said the Engine from the EAST:
"They who work best talk the least.
S'pose you whistle down your brakes;
What you've done is no great shakes,—
Pretty fair,—but let our meeting
Be a different kind of greeting.
Let these folks with champagne stuffing,
Not their Engines, do the *puffing*.

"Listen! Where Atlantic beats
Shores of snow and summer heats;
Where the Indian autumn skies
Paint the woods with wampum dyes,—
I have chased the flying sun,
Seeing all he looked upon,
Blessing all that he has blessed,
Nursing in my iron breast
All his vivifying heat,
All his clouds about my crest;
And before my flying feet
Every shadow must retreat."

Said the Western Engine, "Phew!"
And a long, low whistle blew.
"Come, now, really that's the oddest
Talk for one so very modest.
You brag of your East! *You* do?
Why, *I* bring the East to *you*!
All the Orient, all Cathay,
Find through me the shortest way;
And the sun you follow here
Rises in my hemisphere.
Really,—if one must be rude,—
Length, my friend, ain't longtitude."

Said the Union: "Don't reflect, or
I'll run over some Director."
Said the Central: "I'm Pacific;

But, when riled, I'm quite terrific.
Yet to-day we shall not quarrel,
Just to show these folks this moral,
How two Engines—in their vision—
Once have met without collision."

This is what the Engines said,
Unreported and unread;
Spoken slightly through the nose,
With a whistle at the close.

Heaven Bell A-Ring

ANONYMOUS

*Even the poor slaves were not denied their channel of articulation,
as this fervent ballad will testify.*

My Lord, my Lord, what shall I do?
And a Heav'n bell a-ring and praise God.
What shall I do for a hidin' place?
And a Heav'n bell a-ring and praise God.
I run to de sea, but de sea run dry!
I run to de gate, but de gate shut fast!
No hidin' place for a sinner dere.
Say when you get to Heav'n say you 'member me:
Remember me, poor fallen soul.
Say when you get to Heav'n say your work shall
    prove:
Your righteous Lord shall prove 'em well;
Your righteous Lord shall find you out.
He cast out none that come by faith!
You look to de Lord with a tender heart.
I wonder where poor Monday dere;
For I am gone and sent to hell.
We must harkee what de wordly say.
Say Christmas come but once a year;
Say Sunday come but once a week.

Johnny Appleseed

By WILLIAM HENRY VENABLE

A Ballad of the Old Northwest

At the very birth of the nineteenth century, if you were one of the pioneers scattered through the Ohio territory you might have been greeted by a young man appearing out of nowhere. He would be leading a horse, bearing bags of apple seeds on its back. That was Jonathan Chapman, known in every log cabin in the territory as Johnny Appleseed. There are apple orchards bearing today that were planted by Johnny.

A midnight cry appalls the gloom,
    The puncheon door is shaken:
"Awake! arouse! and flee the doom!
    Man, woman, child, awaken!

"Your sky shall glow with fiery beams
    Before the morn breaks ruddy!
The scalpknife in the moonlight gleams,
    Athirst for vengeance bloody!"

Alarumed by the dreadful word
    Some warning tongue thus utters,
The settler's wife, like mother bird,
    About her young ones flutters.

Her first-born, rustling from a soft
    Leaf-couch, the roof close under,
Glides down the ladder from the loft,
    With eyes of dreamy wonder.

Reprinted by courtesy of Dodd, Mead & Co.

The pioneer flings open wide
  The cabin door naught fearing;
The grim woods drowse on every side,
  Around the lonely clearing.

"Come in! come in! not like an owl
  Thus hoot your doleful humors;
What fiend possesses you to howl
  Such crazy, coward rumors!"

The herald strode into the room;
  That moment, through the ashes,
The back-log struggled into bloom
  Of gold and crimson flashes.

The glimmer lighted up a face,
  And o'er a figure darted,
So eerie, of so solemn grace,
  The bluff backwoodsman started.

The brow was gathered to a frown,
  The eyes were strangely glowing,
And, like a snow-fall drifting down,
  The stormy beard went flowing.

The tattered cloak that round him clung
  Had warred with foulest weather;
Across his shoulders broad were flung
  Brown saddlebags of leather.

One pouch with hoarded seed was packed,
  From Penn-land cider presses;
The other garnered book and tract
  Within its creased recesses.

A glance disdainful and austere,
  Contemptuous of danger,
Cast he upon the pioneer,
  Then spake the uncouth stranger:

"Heed what the Lord's anointed saith;
  Hear one who would deliver
Your bodies and your souls from death;
  List ye to John the Giver.

"Thou trustful boy, in spirit wise
  Beyond thy father's measure,
Because of thy believing eyes
  I share with thee my treasure.

"Of precious seed this handful take;
  Take next this Bible Holy:
In good soil sow both gifts, for sake
  Of Him, the meek and lowly.

"Farewell! I go!—the forest calls
  My life to ceaseless labors;
Wherever danger's shadow falls
  I fly to save my neighbors.

"I save; I neither curse nor slay;
  I am a voice that crieth
In night and wilderness. Away!
  Whoever doubteth, dieth!"

The prophet vanished in the night,
  Like some fleet ghost belated:
Then, awe-struck, fled with panic fright
  The household, evil-fated.

They hurried on with stumbling feet,
  Foreboding ambuscado;
Bewildered hope told of retreat
  In frontier palisado.

But ere a mile of tangled maze
  Their bleeding hands had broken,
Their home-roof set the dark ablaze,
  Fulfilling doom forespoken.

The savage death-whoop rent the air!
　A howl of rage infernal!
The fugitives were in Thy care,
　Almighty Power eternal!

Unscathed by tomahawk or knife,
　In bosky dingle nested,
The hunted pioneer, with wife
　And babes, hid unmolested.

The lad, when age his locks of gold
　Had changed to silver glory,
Told grandchildren, as I have told,
　This western wildwood story.

Told how the fertile seeds had grown
　To famous trees, and thriven;
And oft the Sacred Book was shown,
　By that weird Pilgrim given.

Remember Johnny Appleseed,
　All ye who love the apple,
He served his kind by Word and Deed,
　In God's grand greenwood chapel.

❖ ❖ ❖

Jim Bludso

By John Hay

Gone are the great days of the Mississippi sidewheelers and their hardy pilots, who raced their enormous craft till their boilers were ready to burst. Lincoln's young secretary John Hay, later to become Secretary of State under President William McKinley, authored this undying drama of one of the classic races along the Father of Waters.

Wal, no! I can't tell whar he lives,
    Because he don't live, you see;
Leastways, he's got out of the habit
    Of livin' like you and me.
Where have you been for the last three years
    That you haven't heard folks tell
How Jemmy Bludso passed in his checks,
    The night of the Prairie Belle?

He weren't no saint—them engineers
    Is all pretty much alike—
One wife in Natchez-under-the-Hill,
    And another one here in Pike.
A keerless man in his talk was Jim,
    And an awkward man in a row —
But he never funked, and he never lied;
    I reckon he never knowed how.

And this was all the religion he had—
    To treat his engines well;
Never be passed on the river;
    To mind the pilot's bell;
And if ever the Prarie Belle took fire,
    A thousand times he swore,
He'd hold her nozzle agin the bank
    Till the last soul got ashore.

All boats have their day on the Mississip,
 And her day come at last.
The Movastar was a better boat,
 But the Belle she wouldn't be passed;
And so come tearin' along that night—
 The oldest craft on the line,
With a nigger squat on her safety valve,
 And her furnace crammed, rosin and pine.

The fire burst out as she cleared the bar,
 And burnt a hole in the night,
And quick as a flash she turned, and made
 To that willer-bank on the right.
There was runnin' and cursin', but Jim yelled out
 Over the infernal roar,
"I'll hold her nozzle agin the bank
 Till the last galoot's ashore."

Through the hot black breath of the burnin' boat
 Jim Bludso's voice was heard,
And they all had trust in his cussedness,
 And knowed he would keep his word.
And, sure's you're born, they all got off
 Afore the smokestacks fell—
And Bludso's ghost went up alone
 In the smoke of the Prairie Belle.

He weren't no saint—but at jedgment
 I'd run my chance with Jim,
'Longside of some pious gentlemen
 That wouldn't shook hands with him.
He'd seen his duty, a dead-sure thing—
 And went for it thar and then:
And Christ ain't agoing to be too hard
 On a man that dies for men.

✦ ✦ ✦

A Husband's Revenge

ANONYMOUS

*Warning! Not to be read immediately after a tiff with the Missus.
You might get an idea.*

A man whose name was Johnny Sands,
That married Betty Hague,
Although she brought him gold and lands,
She proved a terrible plague;
She proved a terrible plague.

Says he, "Then I will drown myself;
The river runs below."
"I pray you do, you silly elf;
I wished it long ago;
I wished it long ago."

"For fear that I should courage lack
And try to save my life,
Pray tie my hands behind my back."
"I will," replied his wife;
"I will," replied his wife.

She tied them fast as you might think,
And when securely done,
"Now stand here upon the brink
While I prepare to run;
While I prepare to run."

And down the hill his loving bride
Now ran with all her force
To push him in. He stepped aside,
And she fell in, of course:
And she fell in, of course.

From Neely's *Tales and Songs of Southern Illinois*

Oh, splashing, splashing like a fish,
"Oh, save me, Johnny Sands!"
"I can't, my dear, though much I wish,
For you have tied my hands;
For you have tied my hands."

The Swapping Song

Anonymous

Apparently the old Kentucky mountaineers liked to exchange what they had for something they had not, in this case with questionable results.

When I was a little boy I lived by myself,
And all the bread and cheese I had kept upon the shelf.

REFRAIN

To my wing wong waddle ding,
A jack-straw straddle ding,
A John fair faddle ding,
A long way's home.

The rats and the mice did give me such a life,
I had to go to London to get me a wife.

The creeks were wide and the streets were narrow,
And I had to bring her home in an old wheelbarrow.

Oh, my foot slipped and I got a fall,
And away went the wheelbarrow, wife and all.

I swapped my wheelbarrow and got me a mare,
And then I rode from tare to tare.

I swapped my mare and got me a mule,
And then I rode like a gol-darn fool.

I swapped my mule and I got me a cow,
And in that trade I just learned how.

I swapped my cow and got me a calf,
And in that trade I just lost half.

I swapped my calf and got me a sheep,
And then I rode till I fell asleep.

I swapped my sheep and got me a hen,
And la! What a pretty thing I had then.

I swapped my hen and got me a rat,
And I sat it on a hayrack for two little cats.

I swapped my rat and got me a mole,
And the dog-gone thing went straight to its hole.

The Preacher
and the Bear

ANONYMOUS

*Wasn't a certain ballad collector's
face red at a party where a lovely
English lady sang this? He had
never heard it before!*

A colored preacher went a-hunting,
It was on a Sunday morn.
Of course, it was against his religion,
But he took his gun along.

He shot himself some very fine quail,
A 'possum, a buck and a hare,
And, on the way returning to his home,
He met a great, big grizzly bear.

The bear marched out into the middle of the road,
The better his victim to see,
And the parson got so excited
That he climbed a persimmon tree.

That bear reared up and he shook that tree,
But the parson held on with vim,
And he rolled his eyes toward the Ruler of the skies,
And these words prayed to Him:

CHORUS

"Oh, Lawd, you deliv'rd li'l Dan'el frum de lion's
    den;
Li'l Jonah frum de belly ob de whale, an' den,
De Hebrew chillun frum de fi'y fu'nace,
De good book do declah.
Now, Lawd, ef'n you kain' help me,
Fo' goodness sake doan help dat beah."

Preacher. "Now Mist Beah, le's you an' me reason dis
      out, hunh?"
Bear.   "G-r-r-r-r!"
Preacher. "Nice ol' bear."
Bear.   "G-r-r-r-r!"
Preacher. "Good ol' bear."
Bear.   "G-r-r-r-r."
Preacher. "Ef'n Ah come down an' let y'll tek jes' one
      li'l bite, den would yeh gwan 'way an'
      leab me lone?"
Bear.   "G-r-r-r-r-e-e-ah!"
Preacher. "Oh, yeh would, hey? H-e-e-e-ha! Well, Ah's
      gwine teh stay right up whah Ah is."

The preacher sat up there thinking:
"What will my congregation say,
Ef'n they should heah dat Wuthy Parson Brown
Went huntin' on de Sabbaf Day?"

He climbed higher up into the tree,
In hopes some help to call,
But the limb broke loose from under his feet
And the parson began to fall.

The bear looked up and he frothed at the mouth,
As the parson came tumbling down,
But the parson got out his razor
Before he hit the ground.

The bear began to growl and the parson to shout,
Till they made an awful din,
And he cast his eyes to the Ruler of the skies
And once more prayed to Him.

CHORUS

"Oh, Lawd, you deliv'ed li'l Dan'el frum de Lion's
        den:
Li'l Jonah frum de belly ob de whale, an' den,
De Hebrew chillun frum de fi'y furnace,
De Scripters do recite.
Now, Lawd, ef'n you doan he'p dat beah
Youse gwine teh see a pow'ful fight."

There Was an Old Soldier

ANONYMOUS

*When Father once took me to a Kickapoo Indian medicine show, this
tickled my childish risibilities no end.*

O there was an old soldier and he had a wooden leg,
He had no tobaccy, no tobaccy could he beg.
Another old soldier was as sly as a fox,
He always had tobaccy in the old tobaccy box.

Said the one old soldier, "Won't you give me a
    chew?"
Said the other old soldier, "I'll be damned if I do.
Save up your money and put away your rocks,
And you'll always have tobaccy in the old tobaccy
    box."

Well, the same old soldier was feelin' very bad.
He says, "I'll get even, I will, begad!"
He goes to a corner, takes a rifle from a peg,
And stabs the other soldier with a splinter from his
    leg.

There was an old hen and she had a wooden foot,
And she made her nest by a gooseberry root,
And she laid more eggs than any on the farm;
And another wooden foot wouldn't do her any harm.

Lasca

By Frank Desprez

*"Lasca" will persist through the years as one of America's finest and most
dramatic ballads. Love, hatred, and courage are vividly set down here
for our enjoyment.*

I want free life, and I want fresh air;
And I sigh for the canter after the cattle,
The crack of the whips like shots in battle,
The medley of hoofs and horns and heads
That wars and wrangles and scatters and spreads;
The green beneath and the blue above,
And dash and danger, and life and love—
And Lasca!
              Lasca used to ride
On a mouse-grey mustang close by my side,
With blue serape and bright-belled spur;
I laughed with joy as I looked at her!

Reprinted from *Songs of the Cattle Trail and Cow Camp,* published by
Duell, Sloan, and Pearce, Inc.

Little knew she of books or creeds;
An Ave Maria sufficed her needs;
Little she cared save to be at my side,
To ride with me, and ever to ride,
From San Saba's shore to Lavaca's tide.
She was as bold as the billows that beat,
She was as wild as the breezes that blow:
From her little head to her little feet,
She was swayed in her suppleness to and fro
By each gust of passion; a sapling pine
That grows on the edge of a Kansas bluff
And wars with the wind when the weather is rough,
Is like this Lasca, this love of mine.

She would hunger that I might eat,
Would take the bitter and leave me the sweet;
But once, when I made her jealous for fun
At something I whispered or looked or done,
One Sunday, in San Antonio,
To a glorious girl in the Alamo,
She drew from her garter a little dagger,
And—sting of a wasp—it made me stagger!
And inch to the left, or an inch to the right,
And I shouldn't be maundering here tonight;
But she sobbed, and sobbing, so quickly bound
Her torn reboso about the wound
That I swiftly forgave her. Scratches don't count
          In Texas, down by the Rio Grande.

Her eye was brown—a deep, deep brown;
Her hair was darker than her eye;
And something in her smile and frown,
Curled crimson lip and instep high,
Showed that there ran in each blue vein,
Mixed with the milder Aztec strain,
The vigorous vintage of Old Spain.

She was alive in every limb
With feeling, to the finger tips;
And when the sun is like a fire,
And sky one shining, soft sapphire
One does not drink in little sips.

The air was heavy, the night was hot,
I sat by her side and forgot, forgot;
Forgot the herd that were taking their rest,
Forgot that the air was close oppressed,
That the Texas norther comes sudden and soon,
In the dead of the night or the blaze of the noon;
That, once let the herd at its breath take fright,
Nothing on earth can stop their flight;
And woe to the rider, and woe to the steed,
That falls in front of their mad stampede!

Was that thunder? I grasped the cord
Of my swift mustang without a word.
I sprang to the saddle, and she clung behind.
Away! on a hot chase down the wind!
But never was fox-hunt half so hard,
And never was steed so little spared.
For we rode for our lives. You shall hear how we fared
    In Texas, down by the Rio Grande.

The mustang flew, and we urged him on;
There was one chance left, and you have but one—
Halt, jump to the ground, and shoot your horse;
Crouch under his carcass, and take your chance;
And if the steers in their frantic course
Don't batter you both to pieces at once,
You may thank your star; if not, goodbye
To the quickening kiss and the long-drawn sigh,
And the open air and the open sky,
        In Texas, down by the Rio Grande.

The cattle gained on us, and just as I felt
For my old six-shooter behind in my belt,

Down came the mustang, and down came we,
Clinging together—and, what was the rest?
A body that spread itself on my breast,
Two arms that shielded my dizzy head,
Two lips that hard to my lips were prest;
Then came thunder in my ears,
As over us surged the sea of steers,
Blows that beat blood into my eyes,
And when I could rise—
Lasca was dead!

I gouged out a grave a few feet deep,
And there in the Earth's arms I laid her to sleep;
And there she is lying, and no one knows;
And the summer shines, and the winter snows;
For many a day the flowers have spread
A pall of petals over her head;
And the little grey hawk hangs aloft in the air,
And the sly coyote trots here and there,
And the black snake glides and glitters and slides
Into the rift of a cottonwood tree;
And the buzzard sails on,
And comes and is gone,
Stately and still, like a ship at sea.
And I wonder why I do not care
For the things that are, like the things that were.
Does half my heart lie buried there
          In Texas, down by the Rio Grande?

Billy Boy

ANONYMOUS

Oh, where have you been, Billy boy, Billy boy,
Oh, where have you been, charming Billy?
I have been to seek a wife, she's the joy of my young
     life,
She's a young thing and cannot leave her mother.

Did she ask you to come in, Billy boy, Billy boy,
Did she ask you to come in, charming Billy?
She did ask me to come in, with a dimple in her chin,
She's a young thing and cannot leave her mother.

Did she ask you to sit down, Billy boy, Billy boy,
Did she ask you to sit down, charming Billy?
She did ask me to sit down, with a curtsey to the
    ground,
She's a young thing and cannot leave her mother.

Did she set for you a chair, Billy boy, Billy boy,
Did she set for you a chair, charming Billy?
Yes, she set for me a chair, she's got ringlets in her
    hair,
She's a young thing and cannot leave her mother.

How old is she, Billy boy, Billy boy,
How old is she, charming Billy?
She's three times six, four times seven, twenty-eight
    and eleven,
She's a young thing and cannot leave her mother.

How tall is she, Billy boy, Billy boy,
How tall is she, charming Billy?
She's as tall as any pine and as straight's a pumpkin
    vine,
She's a young thing and cannot leave her mother.

Can she make a cherry pie, Billy boy, Billy boy,
Can she make a cherry pie, charming Billy?
She can make a cherry pie, quick's a cat can wink her
    eye,
She's a young thing and cannot leave her mother.

Does she often go to church, Billy boy, Billy boy,
Does she often go to church, charming Billy?
Yes, she often goes to church, with her bonnet white
    as birch,
She's a young thing and cannot leave her mother.

Can she make a pudding well, Billy boy, Billy boy,
Can she make a pudding well, charming Billy?
She can make a pudding well, I can tell it by the smell,
She's a young thing and cannot leave her mother.

Can she make a feather-bed, Billy boy, Billy boy,
Can she make a feather-bed, charming Billy?
She can make a feather-bed, place the pillows at the
    head,
She's a young thing and cannot leave her mother.

Can she card and can she spin, Billy boy, Billy boy,
Can she card and can she spin, charming Billy?
She can card and she can spin, she can do most any-
    thing,
She's a young thing and cannot leave her mother.

Finnigan's Wake

Anonymous

Irish-American Vaudeville Tune, c. 1870

*When I was a boy there was a man in our town called "Muggy Day"
John Doyle. After a "dhrop o' the craythur" John's rendition of "Finnigan's Wake" was excellent; a few more, and it was magnificent.*

Tim Finnigan lived in Walker Street,
An Irish gentleman mighty odd;
He'd a beautiful brogue so rich and sweet,
And to rise in the world he carried the hod.
But you see, he'd a sort of tippling way,
For the love of the liquor poor Tim was born;
And to help him on his work each day,
He'd a drop of the craythur every morn.

> *With my philalloo, hubbaboo, whack hurroo, boys,*
> *Didn't we sing till our jaws did ache,*
> *And shout and laugh and drink and sing,*
> *Oh, it's lots of fun at Finnigan's wake.*

One morning Tim was rather full,
His head felt heavy, which made him shake,
He fell from the ladder and broke his skull,
So they carried him home, himself to wake.
They tied him up in a nice clean sheet,
And laid him out upon the bed,
Wid a gallon of whiskey at his feet,
And a barrel of praties at his head.

> With my philalloo, hubbaboo, whack hurroo, boys,
> Didn't we sing till our jaws did ache,
> And shout and laugh and drink and sing,
> Oh, it's lots of fun at Finnigan's wake.

His friends assembled at the wake,
Miss Finnigan call'd out for the lunch,
First they brought in tay and cake,
Then pipes, tobacco, and whiskey punch;
Biddy O'Brien began to cry,
Such a pretty corpse she never did see,
Arrah, Tim Mavourneen, why did you die?
"Ah! hould your gab," said Paddy McGree.

> With my philalloo, hubbaboo, whack hurroo, boys,
> Didn't we sing till our jaws did ache,
> And shout and laugh and drink and sing,
> Oh, it's lots of fun at Finnigan's wake.

Then Peggy O'Connor tuck up the job,
"Biddy," says she, "you're wrong, I'm sure,"
But Biddy gave her a pelt in the gob,
And we left her sprawling on the flure;
Oh, then the war did soon enrage!
'Twas woman to woman, and man to man,
Shillelagh law did soon engage!
And a row and a ruction soon began.

> With my philalloo, hubbaboo, whack hurroo, boys,
> Didn't we sing till our jaws did ache,

And shout and laugh and drink and sing,
Oh, it's lots of fun at Finnigan's wake.

Then Mickey Mollaney raised his head,
When a gallon of whiskey flew at him,
It missed, an' falling on the bed,
The liquor scatter'd over Tim;
Be-dad he revives, see how he rises,
And Timothy, rising from the bed,
Saying, "Whirl your liquor round like blazes!
Arrah! Gudaguddug, do you think I'm dead?"

With my philalloo, hubbaboo, whack hurroo, boys,
Didn't we sing till our jaws did ache,
And shout and laugh and drink and sing,
Oh, it's lots of fun at Finnigan's wake.

Jim Fisk

By WILLIAM J. SCANLAN

In 1872 New York was stunned at the killing of Jim Fisk by Ed
Stokes on the stairway of the Broadway Central Hotel. Beautiful Josie
Mansfield was the cause of it all. Stokes served a short time in jail,
the principal eyewitness having skipped to China where, it is said, he
lived well at Stokes' expense.

If you'll listen a while I'll sing you a song
Of this glorious land of the free;
And the difference I'll show 'twixt the rich and the
    poor,
In a trial by jury, you'll see.
If you've plenty of stamps you can hold up your head
And walk from your own prison door,
But they'll hang you up high if you've no friends and
    no gold,
Let the rich go, but hang up the poor.

I'll sing of man who's now dead in his grave,
A good man as ever was born;
Jim Fisk he was called and his money he gave
To the outcast, the poor and forlorn.
We all know he loved both women and wine,
But his heart it was right, I am sure;
Though he lived like a prince in a palace so fine,
Yet he never went back on the poor.

Jim Fisk was a man wore his heart on his sleeve,
No matter what people might say;
And he did all his deeds, both the good and the bad,
In the broad open light of the day.
With his grand six-in-hand, on the beach at Long
    Branch,
He cut a big dash to be sure;
But Chicago's great fire showed the world that Jim
    Fisk
With his wealth still remembered the poor.

Now what do you think of the trial of Stokes,
Who murdered this friend of the poor?
When such men get free is there anyone safe
To step outside their own door?
Is there one law for the poor and one for the rich?
It seems so, at least so I say;
If they hang up the poor, why surely the rich
Ought to swing up the very same way.

Charles Guiteau

ANONYMOUS

*On July 2, 1881, while talking to Secretary of State James G. Blaine
in a Washington railroad station, President James Abram Garfield was
assassinated by Charles Jules Guiteau, a demented office-seeker. As per
the prevailing custom, such an event called for a ballad.*

My name is Charles Guiteau,
My name I'll never deny
To leave my aged parents
In sorrow for to die.
Little did they think I
While in my youthful bloom
I'd be taken to the scaffold
To meet my fatal doom.

My sister came to see me
To bid her last farewell;
She threw her arms around my neck
And the tears so bitterly fell.
Said she, "My darling brother,
This day you sure will die
For the murder of James A. Garfield
Upon the scaffold high."

'Twas down at the depot
I tried to make my escape,
The crowd it gathered around me—
I found it was too late.
The jury found me guilty,
The clerk he wrote it down;
On the thirtieth day of April
I was sentenced to be hung.

My name is Charles Guiteau,
My name I'll never deny
To leave my aged parents
In sorrow for to die.
Little did they think I
While in my youthful bloom
I'd be taken to the scaffold
To meet my fatal doom.

✦ ✦ ✦

Down with the Rag, and Up with the Flag

By Monroe H. Rosenfeld

In 1888 they were singing this, extolling the virtues of Harrison and Morton over Cleveland and Thurman, and we've been hearing similar sentiments in every campaign since.

March on beneath the starry flag,
To victory again,
We'll down the red bandanna rag
With flag that bears no stain;
The war-cry rings thro'out the land,
It sounds from sea to sea,
Protection's right shall win the fight,
Triumphant it shall be.

CHORUS

Down with the rag, up with the flag,
As we march 'neath the banner true!
On to fight, strike for the right,
For the Red, the White and the Blue.
Tip, tip, Tippecanoe, true blue
Tip, tip, Tippecanoe, true blue.
Down with the rag, up with the flag,
For the Red, the White, and the Blue.

Their sham reforms we'll sweep away,
As billows sweep the shore,
Tho' Grover, boys, would like to stay,
He'll guide the ship no more;
Its doom is written on the sky,
The snuffy rag must go;
We'll march along to freedom's song
And lay their banner low.

We'll give the nation's glorious trust
To Indiana's son,
We'll trail their banner in the dust,
Its course shall soon be run;
So let them float their snuffy rag,
And wave it to the sky.
Beneath the true and starry flag,
We'll conquer till we die!

Riding on the Elevated Road

By T. B. KELLEY

*In the midst of an uproar of protest, the L started operating. Sparks,
cinders, and smoke from the engines blew in the windows; horses ran
away in terror; the rumble kept people awake. Finally all this blended
into the symphony of New York. How we old timers miss these annoyances!*

Upon the elevated train
I often take a ride:
Along the second storey rooms,
The blinds are open wide;
Of course when I am looking out,
Some curious things I see;
And now I'll try to tell of those
That interested me.

CHORUS

Riding on the elevated railroad train,
In a cosy little seat beside the window pane,
Many things I see to interest me,
While riding on the elevated train.

Now there's a little dwelling place,
The folks are going to dine;
I see the table thickly spread,
With everything that's fine.
And here's a man with eyes intent
Upon the morning news;
And here's a fellow that lies in bed
As if he had the blues.

Now here's a woman washing clothes
With all her might and main;
And there's a pretty sewing girl
Who glances at the train.
Oh! there's a grand piano,
And a lady seems to play;
While near her hands a little bird
To sing its merry lay.

Oh! There's a woman holding up
A baby very small;
And yonder sits a tailor
With his back against the wall;
While just beside, two idle men
Are seated playing cards;
And people here are drinking beer
With "mutual regards."

I see a picture of distress,
A barely furnished room,
Three little ragged children
With faces full of gloom.
So many and so varied
Are the sights that come to view,
I'm sure I'd try your patience
If I told them all to you.

The Little Brown Jug

ANONYMOUS

*Perhaps the most famous of all drinking ballads—the uninhibited love
of a drunkard for his bottle. It has the charm of great honesty.*

My wife and I live all alone,
In a little hut we call our own,
She loves gin and I love rum,
Tell you what it is, don't we have fun?

CHORUS

Ha, ha, ha! 'Tis you and me,
Little brown jug, don't I love thee?
Ha, ha, ha! 'Tis you and me,
Little brown jug, don't I love thee?

If I had a cow that gave such beer,
I'd dress her in the finest sheer,
Feed her on the choicest hay,
And milk her twenty times a day.

'Tis gin that makes my friends my foes,
'Tis gin that makes me wear old clothes,
But seeing you are so near my nose,
Tip her up and down she goes.

When I go toiling on my farm,
Take little brown jug under my arm,
Set it under some shady tree,
Little brown jug, don't I love thee?

Then came the landlord tripping in,
Round top hat and a peaked chin,
In his hand he carried a cup,
Says I, "Old fellow, give us a sup."

If all the folks in Adam's race
Were put together in one place,
Then I'd prepare to drop a tear
Before I'd part with you, my dear.

The Man on the
Flying Trapeze

ANONYMOUS

*A short while ago this enduring ballad had a country-wide revival. I
remember its being sung in a circus when I was very young. How long
ago was that? I have nothing to say.*

Once I was happy, but now I'm forlorn,
Like an old coat, all tattered and torn,
Left in this wide world to fret and to mourn,
Betrayed by a maid in her teens.
Oh, the girl that I loved she was handsome,
I tried all I knew her to please,
But I could not please one quarter as well
As the man on the flying trapeze.

He would fly through the air
With the greatest of ease,
This daring young man
On the flying trapeze;
His movements were graceful,
All girls he could please,
And my love he purloined away.

Her father and mother were both on my side,
And very hard tried to make her my bride.
Her father he sighed, and her mother she cried
To see her throw herself away.
'Twas all no avail, she'd go there every night
And throw him bouquets on the stage,
Which caused him to meet her; how he ran me down
To tell you would take a whole page.

One night I as usual called at her dear home,
Found there her father and mother alone.
I asked for my love, and soon they made known
To my horror that she'd run away.
She packed up her goods and eloped in the night
With him with the greatest of ease;
From three stories high he had lowered her down
To the ground on his flying trapeze.

Some months after this, I chanced in a hall,
Was greatly surprised to see on the wall
A bill in red letters that did my heart gall,
That she was appearing with him.
He taught her gymnastics and dressed her in tights
To help him to live at his ease,
And made her assume a masculine name,
And now she goes on the trapeze.

CHORUS

She floats through the air
With the greatest of ease,
You'd think her a man
On the flying trapeze.
She does all the work
While he takes his ease,
And that's what became of my love.

The Dying Hobo

By Bob Hughes

All in an empty box car one cold and dreary day
Beside a railroad water tank, a dying hobo lay,
His chum he sat beside him with low and bended head,
And listened to the last sad words the dying hobo said.

"I'm headed now for far away where prospects are all
    bright,
Where cops don't hound a hobo, or pinch a man on
    sight,
Tell Brooklyn Jack and Murph and Jo just what I tell
    to you,
I've caught a fast train on the fly and now I'm going
    through.

"I'm going to a better land where brakies ain't so
    mean,
Where wieners grow on bushes and where dogs is never
    seen,
Where no one knows of rockpiles and when you wants
    a ride,
The Boss Con says asmilin', "Pardner, won't you get
    inside?"

"Oh, pard, I hear the whistle, I must catch her on the
fly,
It's my last ride—gimme a drink of whiskey 'fore I
die."
The hobo smiled. His head fell back, he'd sung his last
refrain,
His pardner swiped his shirt and coat and hopped the
eastbound train.

The Bootblack's Christmas

By Barney Mullelly

*Our forefathers, without the complications of modern life, were not
afraid of the frankly sentimental. Tragedy in the old days was simple
and understandable. A broken heart was just that, and tears were not
idle tears. Here is one of the heartbreakers.*

A bootblack slept in a dry-goods box, it was on a
Christmas eve,
Tho' all alone in his scanty home in Santa Claus he
did believe;
He slept on rags and straw, then placed his little shoes
outside,
Just as he hung his stockings up before his mother
died.
The night rolled on and no Santa came, but a thief
crept soft and low,
As he stole away those little shoes that were left stand-
ing in the snow.

CHORUS

Sad, sad, indeed, to see the lad standing in the storm
alone,
Beside the empty dry-goods box that served him as a
home;
And the look of disappointment—Santa Claus did him
refuse,

But saddest of all was to hear him call: "Santa Claus, bring back my shoes."
But a moment's time had scarcely passed till I was beside the lad.
What makes you weep, my dear boy? I said have you indeed not got a dad?
Oh, no, kind sir, he said, with a beseeching look to me.
My poor mother died a year ago, papa was lost at sea.
I started back when I heard this tale, for I was returning home.
Then I scanned his face, what did I trace? It was the outline of my own.
I grasped the box, as I held my child in a father's fond embrace.
I could feel that my brain was whirling and the hot tears rolled down my face.
On a whaleship I sailed for a six months' voyage to sea.
I was wrecked and cast on a foreign shore, where none could hear from me.
The truth was clear, my wife so dear, from earth had passed away.
I'd play'd the part with broken heart of Santa Claus that Christmas day.

CHORUS

Thank God, indeed, to find my boy, although in the storm alone,
Beside the empty dry-goods box that served him as a home.
I dispelled his disappointment. Santa Claus will not refuse.
For your father has come, my own dear son. I will buy for you new shoes!

✦ ✦ ✦

The Ballad of the Oysterman

By Oliver Wendell Holmes

Dr. Oliver Wendell Holmes managed to be not only one of the greatest physicians of his time, but a humorist who has stood the test of the years.

It was a tall young oysterman lived by the riverside,
His shop was just upon the bank, his boat was on the
   tide;
The daughter of a fisherman, that was so straight and
   slim,
Lived over on the other bank, right opposite to him.

It was the pensive oysterman that saw a lovely maid,
Upon a moonlight evening, a sitting in the shade;
He saw her wave her handkerchief, as much as if to
   say,
"I'm wide awake, young oysterman, and all the folks
   away."

Then up arose the oysterman, and to himself said he,
"I guess I'll leave the skiff at home, for fear that
   folks should see;
I read it in the story-book, that, for to kiss his dear,
Leander swam the Hellespont,—and I will swim this
   here."

And he has leaped into the waves, and crossed the
   shining stream,
And he has clambered up the bank, all in the moonlight gleam;
O there were kisses sweet as dew, and words as soft
   as rain,—
But they have heard her father's step, and in he leaps
   again!

Out spoke the ancient fisherman,—"O what was that,
  my daughter?"
" 'Twas nothing but a pebble, sir, I threw into the
  water."
"And what is that, pray tell me, love, that paddles off
  so fast?"
"It's nothing but a porpoise, sir, that's been a swimming past."

Out spoke the ancient fisherman,—"Now bring me
  my harpoon!
I'll get into my fishing-boat, and fix the fellow soon."
Down fell that pretty innocent, as falls a snow-white
  lamb,
Her hair drooped round her pallid cheeks, like sea-
  weed on a clam.

Alas for those two loving ones! she waked not from
  her swound,
And he was taken with the cramp, and in the waves
  was drowned;
But Fate has metamorphosed them, in pity of their
  woe,
And now they keep an oyster-shop for mermaids down
  below.

The Letter Edged in Black

ANONYMOUS

Oh, he rang the bell and whistled while he waited,
And then he said, "Good morning to you, Jack."
But he little knew the sorrow that he brought me
When he handed me a letter edged in black.

CHORUS

As I heard the postman whistling yester morning,
Coming down the pathway with his pack,
Oh, he little knew the sorrow that he brought me
When he handed me that letter edged in black.

With trembling hand I took the letter from him,
I broke the seal and this is what it said:
"Come home, my boy, your dear old father wants you!
Come home, my boy, your dear old mother's dead!"
    —*Chorus*

"The last words that your mother ever uttered—
'Tell my boy I want him to come back,'
My eyes are blurred, my poor old heart is breaking,
For I'm writing you this letter edged in black."
    —*Chorus*

I bow my head in sorrow and in silence,
The sunshine of my life it all has fled,
Since the postman brought that letter yester morning
Saying, "Come home, my boy, your poor old mother's
    dead!" —*Chorus*

"Those angry words, I wish I'd never spoken,
You know I never meant them, don't you, Jack?
May the Angels bear me witness, I am asking
Your forgiveness in this letter edged in black."
    —*Chorus*

Where is Your Boy Tonight?

ANONYMOUS

Life is teeming with evil snares,
The gates of sin are wide,
The rosy fingers of pleasure wave,
And beckon the young inside.

❧ 209 ❧

Man of the world with open purse,
Seeking your own delight,
Pause ere reason is wholly gone—
Where is your boy tonight?

Sirens are singing on every hand,
Luring the ear of youth,
Gilded falsehood with silver notes
Drowneth the voice of truth.
Dainty ladies in costly robes,
Your parlours gleam with light,
Fate and beauty your senses steep—
Where is your boy tonight?

Tempting whispers of royal spoil
Flatter the youthful soul
Eagerly entering into life,
Restive of all control.
Needs are many, and duties stern
Crowd on the weary sight;
Father, buried in business cares,
Where is your boy tonight?

Pitfalls lurk in the flowery way,
Vice has a golden gate:
Who shall guide the unwary feet
Into the highway straight?
Patient worker with willing hand,
Keep the home hearth bright,
Tired mother, with tender eyes—
Where is your boy tonight?

Turn his feet from the evil paths
Ere they have entered in:
Keep him unspotted while yet he may,
Earth is so stained with sin;
Ere he has learned to follow wrong,
Teach him to love the right;
Watch ere watching is wholly vain—
Where is your boy tonight?

Abdullah
Bulbul
Amir

ANONYMOUS

The sons of the Prophet are valiant and bold,
  And quite unaccustomed to fear;
And the bravest of all was a man, so I'm told,
  Called Abdullah Bulbul Amir.

When they wanted a man to encourage the van,
  Or harass the foe from the rear,
Storm fort or redoubt, they were sure to call out
  For Abdullah Bulbul Amir.

There are heroes in plenty, and well known to fame,
  In the legions that fight for the Czar;
But none of such fame as the man by the name
  Of Ivan Petrofsky Skovar.

He could imitate Irving, tell fortunes by cards,
  And play on the Spanish guitar;
In fact, quite the cream of the Muscovite guards
  Was Ivan Petrofsky Skovar.

One day this bold Muscovite shouldered his gun,
   Put on his most cynical sneer,
And was walking downtown when he happened to run
   Into Abdullah Bulbul Amir.

"Young man," said Bulbul, "is existence so dull
   That you're anxious to end your career?
Then, infidel, know you have trod on the toe
   Of Abdullah Bulbul Amir.

"So take your last look at the sea, sky and brook,
   Make your latest report on the war;
For I mean to imply you are going to die,
   O Ivan Petrofsky Skovar."

So this fierce man he took his trusty chibouk,
   And murmuring, "Allah Akbar!"
With murder intent he most savagely went
   For Ivan Petrofsky Skovar.

The Sultan rose up, the disturbance to quell,
   Likewise, give the victor a cheer.
He arrived just in time to bid hasty farewell
   To Abdullah Bulbul Amir.

A loud-sounding splash from the Danube was heard
   Resounding o'er meadows afar;
It came from the sack fitting close to the back
   Of Ivan Petrofsky Skovar.

There lieth a stone where the Danube doth roll,
   And on it in characters queer
Are "Stranger, when passing by, pray for the soul
   Of Abdullah Bulbul Amir."

A Muscovite maiden her vigil doth keep
   By the light of the pale northern star,
And the name she repeats every night in her sleep
   Is Ivan Petrofsky Skovar.

The Lane County Bachelor

ANONYMOUS

After reading this no man will raise hell about a lone mosquito keeping him awake all night unless he is a sissy.

My name is Frank Bolar, 'n ole bachelor I am,
I'm keepin' ole bach on an elegant plan,
You'll find me out West in the county of Lane,
Starvin' to death on a government claim;
My house it is built of the national soil,
The walls are erected accordin' to Hoyle,
The roof has no pitch, but is level and plain,
And I always get wet when it happens to rain.

CHORUS

But hurrah for Lane county, the land of the free,
The home of the grasshopper, bedbug and flea:
I'll sing loud her praises and boast of her fame
While starving to death on my government claim.

My clothes they are ragged, my language is rough,
My head is casehardened, both solid and tough;
The dough it is scattered all over the room
And the floor would get scared at the sight of a broom;
My dishes are dirty and some in the bed
Covered with sorghum and government bread;
But I have a good time, and live at my ease
On common sop-sorghum, old bacon and grease.

CHORUS

But hurrah for Lane county, the land of the West,
Where the farmers and laborers are always at rest,
Where you've nothing to do but sweetly remain
And starve like a man on your government claim.

How happy am I when I crawl into bed,
And a rattlesnake rattles his tail at my head,
And a gay little centipede, void of all fear,
Crawls over my pillow and into my ear,
And the nice little bedbug, so cheerful and bright,
Keeps me a-scratching full half of the night,
And the gay little flea, with toes sharp as a tack,
Plays "Why don't you catch me?" all over my back.

CHORUS

But hurrah for Lane county, where blizzards arise,
Where the winds never cease and the flea never dies,
Where the sun is so hot if in it you remain
'Twill burn you quite black on your government claim.

How happy I am on my government claim,
Where I've nothing to lose and nothing to gain,
Nothing to eat and nothing to wear,
Nothing from nothing is honest and square.
But here I am stuck, and here I must stay,
My money's all gone and I can't get away;
There's nothing will make a man hard and profane
Like starving to death on a government claim.

CHORUS

Then come to Lane county, there's room for you all,
Where the winds never cease and the rains never fall;
Come join in the chorus and boast of her fame
While starving to death on your government claim.

Now, don't get discouraged, ye poor hungry men,
We're all here as free as a pig in a pen;
Just stick to your homestead and battle your fleas,
And pray to your Maker to send you a breeze.
Now a word to claim-holders who are bound for to
    stay;
You may chew your hardtack till you're toothless and
    gray,
But as for me, I'll no longer remain
And starve like a dog on my government claim.

Farewell to Lane county, farewell to the West;
I'll travel back East to the girl I love best;
I'll stop in Missouri and get me a wife,
And live on corn dodgers the rest of my life.

The Jam on Gerry's Rock

ANONYMOUS

This one apparently originated in Scotland but through the years has become part of the lore of the state of Maine.

Come all ye jolly Shanty Boys, wherever you may be,
I would have you pay attention and listen unto me, .
While I tell you of some Shanty Boys, so noble, true
 and brave,
Who broke the jam on Garyon's Rock, and met with a
 watery grave.

It being Sunday morning, as you will quickly hear,
The logs were rolling mountain high, and they could
 not keep them clear;
Our foreman says, "Prepare, my boys, your hearts
 devoid all fear,
To break the jam on Garyon's Rock, with their riggin,
 so they will go clear."

It being Sunday morning, they thought it hardly
 right,
While some of them were idling, others they did hang
 back;
Six young Canadian Shanty Boys they volunteered to
 go,
To break the jam on Garyon's Rock, with their leader,
 young Munroe.

They had not rolled off many of the logs, when the
  foreman he did say,
"I would have you be on your guard, for the jam will
  soon give way."
He had no more than spoke the word, when the jam
  did break and go,
And it carried away those six brave boys, and their
  leader, young Munroe.

When the comrades of the camp that night this sad-
  ness came to hear,
To search for their dead bodies to the river they did
  prepare;
Unto their sad misfortune, sorrow, grief and woe,
All bruised and mangled on the shore lay the head of
  young Munroe.

We picked it up most carefully, smoothed down his
  beautiful hair;
There was one fair form amongst the rest, whose cries
  did ring in the air;
There was one fair form amongst the rest, a maid
  from Saginaw town;
Her moans and cries did rise to the skies, for her true
  love lay there drowned.

We buried him quite decently, all on the fifteenth of
  May;
Come all you jolly Shanty Boys and for your comrade
  pray;
Engraved upon a hemlock tree, there on the bank it
  grew,
Is the name and the date and the drowning of that
  hero, young Munroe.

His mother was a widow, she lived down by the river
  side;
Miss Clark, she was a noble girl, and his intended
  bride;

The wages of her own true love, the boss to her did
    pay;
And quite a sum of money she received from the
    Shanty Boys next day.

When she received the money, she thanked them every
    one;
But it was not her lot for to enjoy it long;
Scarcely three weeks had passed away when she was
    called to go—
Her last request was, "Let me rest by the side of
    young Munroe."

The Death of
Jesse James

ANONYMOUS

*The spelling of the elder James boy's first name on the old copy I
unearthed was "Jessie," which I accepted as authentic; this might
have brought the wrath of the whole state of Missouri on my unsus-
pecting head. But a distinguished Missouri author and, incidentally,
an old friend of the James family corrected me. "Jesse" it is.*

It was on a Wednesday night, the moon was shining
    bright,

They robbed the Glendale train.
And the people they did say, for many miles away,
'Twas the outlaws Frank and Jesse James.

Jesse had a wife to mourn all her life,
The children they were brave.
'Twas a dirty little coward shot Mister Howard,
And laid Jesse James in his grave.

It was Robert Ford, the dirty little coward,
I wonder how he does feel,
For he ate of Jesse's bread and he slept in Jesse's bed,
Then he laid Jesse James in his grave.

It was his brother Frank that robbed the Gallatin
bank,
And carried the money from the town.
It was in this very place that they had a little race,
For they shot Captain Sheets to the ground.

They went to the crossing not very far from there,
And there they did the same;
And the agent on his knees he delivered up the keys
To the outlaws Frank and Jesse James.

It was on a Saturday night, Jesse was at home
Talking to his family brave,
When the thief and the coward, little Robert Ford,
Laid Jesse James in his grave.

How people held their breath when they heard of
Jesse's death,
And wondered how he ever came to die.
'Twas one of the gang, dirty Robert Ford,
That shot Jesse James on the sly.

Jesse went to his rest with his hand on his breast.
The devil will be upon his knee.
He was born one day in the county of Clay,
And came from a solitary race.

The Old Oaken Bucket

By Samuel Woodworth

Paradoxically enough, this piece extolling the virtues of water as a beverage originated in a barroom. Mr. Samuel Woodworth, a New York printer, finished his brandy at Mr. Mallory's bar and commended it over all other drinks. Mr. Mallory replied, "No, you're mistaken. There's a drink surpassing all others—fresh water from the old oaken bucket that hung in the well." After a wistful pause, tears came to Mr. Woodworth's eyes as he softly murmured, "Very true." He had another brandy to think about it.

How dear to this heart are the scenes of my childhood,
When fond recollections present them to view!—
The orchard, the meadow, the deep-tangled wildwood,
And every loved spot which my infancy knew!

The wide-spreading pond, and the mill that stood by
    it;
The bridge, and the rock where the cataract fell;
The cot of my father, the dairy-house nigh it;
And e'en the rude bucket that hung in the well,—
The old oaken bucket, the iron-bound bucket,
The moss-covered bucket which hung in the well.

That moss-covered vessel I hailed as a treasure;
For often at noon, when returned from the field,
I found it the source of an exquisite pleasure,—
The purest and sweetest that nature can yield.
How ardent I seized it, with hands that were glowing,
And quick to the white-pebbled bottom it fell!
Then soon, with the emblem of truth over-flowing,
And dripping with coolness, it rose from the well,—
The old oaken bucket, the iron-bound bucket,
The moss-covered bucket arose from the well.

How sweet from the green, mossy brim to receive it,
As, poised on the curb, it inclined to my lips!
Not a full, blushing goblet could tempt me to leave it,

The brightest that beauty or revelry sips.
And now, far removed from the loved habitation,
The tear of regret will intrusively swell,
As fancy reverts to my father's plantation,
And sighs for the bucket that hangs in the well,—
The old oaken bucket, the iron-bound bucket,
The moss-covered bucket that hangs in the well.

Captain Jinks

ANONYMOUS

I am Captain Jinks of the Horse Marines,
I often live beyond my means,
I sport young ladies in their 'teens,
 To cut a swell in the army.
I teach the ladies how to dance,
How to dance, how to dance,
I teach the ladies how to dance,
 For I'm their pet in the army.
Spoken: Ha! Ha! Ah!

CHORUS

I'm Captain Jinks of the Horse Marines,
I give my horse good corn and beans;
Of course it's quite beyond my means,
 Though a captain in the army.

I joined the corps when twenty-one,
Of course I thought it capital fun,
When the enemy came then off I run,
 I wasn't cut out for the army.

When I left home mamma she cried,
Mamma she cried, mamma she cried,
  "He ain't cut out for the army."
Spoken: No, she thought I was too young, but then,
  I said, "Ah! Mamma."—*Chorus*

The first day I went out to drill,
The bugle-sound made me quite ill,
At the balance step my hat it fell,
  And that wouldn't do for the army.
The officers they all did shout,
They all cried out, they all did shout,
The officers they all did shout,
  "Oh, that's the curse of the army."
Spoken: Of course my hat *did* fall off, but, ah!
  Nevertheless,—*Chorus*

My tailor's bill came in so fast,
Forced me one day to leave at last,
And ladies, too, no more did cast
  Sheep's eyes at me in the army.
My creditors at me did shout,
At me did shout, at me did shout,
My creditors at me did shout,
  "Why, kick him out of the army."
Spoken: I said, "Ah, gentlemen, ah! Kick *me* out of the
  army? Perhaps you are not aware that . . . *Chorus*

✦   ✦   ✦

Casey at the Bat

By Ernest Lawrence Thayer

When Ernest Lawrence Thayer wrote this ballad there was much speculation as to which ball player he was alluding to. We Boston boys were resentful, thinking he meant Mike "King" Kelley, the $10,000 Beauty of the Bostons, the highest-priced player up to that time. The famous actor De Wolf Hopper delighted his era with his superb rendition of this masterpiece.

It looked extremely rocky for the Mudville nine that
    day,
The score stood four to six with but an inning left to
    play.
And so, when Cooney died at first, and Burrows did
    the same,
A pallor wreathed the features of the patrons of the
    game.
A straggling few got up to go, leaving there the rest,
With that hope which springs eternal within the hu-
    man breast.

For they thought if only Casey could get a whack at
    that,
They'd put up even money with Casey at the bat.
But Flynn preceded Casey, and likewise so did Blake,

And the former was a pudding and the latter was a
    fake;
So on that stricken multitude a death-like silence sat,
For there seemed but little chance of Casey's getting
    to the bat.
But Flynn let drive a single to the wonderment of all,
And the much despised Blakey tore the cover off the
    ball,
And when the dust had lifted and they saw what had
    occurred,
There was Blakey safe on second, and Flynn a-hug-
    ging third.
Then from the gladdened multitude went up a joyous
    yell,
It bounded from the mountain top and rattled in the
    dell,
It struck upon the hillside, and rebounded on the flat,
For Casey, mighty Casey, was advancing to the bat.
There was ease in Casey's manner as he stepped into
    his place,
There was pride in Casey's bearing and a smile on
    Casey's face,
And when responding to the cheers he lightly doffed
    his hat,
No stranger in the crowd could doubt, 'twas Casey at
    the bat.
Ten thousand eyes were on him as he rubbed his
    hands with dirt,
Five thousand tongues applauded as he wiped them
    on his shirt;
And while the writhing pitcher ground the ball into
    his hip—
Defiance gleamed from Casey's eyes — and a sneer
    curled Casey's lip.
And now the leather-covered sphere came hurtling
    through the air,

And Casey stood a-watching it in haughty grandeur
    there;
Close by the sturdy batsman the ball unheeded sped—
"That hain't my style," said Casey—"Strike one,"
    the Umpire said.
From the bleachers black with people there rose a
    sullen roar,
Like the beating of the storm waves on a stern and
    distant shore,
"Kill him! kill the Umpire!" shouted some one from
    the stand—
And it's likely they'd have done it had not Casey
    raised his hand.
With a smile of Christian charity great Casey's visage
    shone,
He stilled the rising tumult and he bade the game go
    on;
He signalled to the pitcher and again the spheroid
    flew,
But Casey still ignored it and the Umpire said,
    "Strike two."
"Fraud!" yelled the maddened thousands, and the
    echo answered "Fraud."
But one scornful look from Casey and the audience
    was awed;
They saw his face grow stern and cold; they saw his
    muscles strain,
And they knew that Casey would not let that ball go
    by again.

The sneer is gone from Casey's lip; his teeth are
    clenched with hate,
He pounds with cruel violence his bat upon the plate;
And now the pitcher holds the ball, and now he lets
    it go,
And now the air is shattered by the force of Casey's
    blow.

Oh! somewhere in this favored land the sun is shining
  bright,
The band is playing somewhere, and somewhere hearts
  are light.
And somewhere men are laughing, and somewhere
  children shout;
But there is no joy in Mudville—mighty Casey has
  "Struck Out."

Casey's Revenge

By Ernest Lawrence Thayer

This sequel was written in 1888, about a month after the same author gave us his immortal "Casey At The Bat." It was published in The San Francisco Examiner.

There were saddened hearts in Mudville, for a week
  or even more,
There were muttered oaths and curses—every fan in
  town was sore.
"Just think," said one, "how soft it looked with
  Casey at the bat!
And then to think he'd go and spring a bush league
  trick like that."

All his past fame was forgotten; he was now a hopeless "Shine,"
They called him "Strike-Out Casey" from the Mayor
  down the line,
And as he came to bat each day his bosom heaved a
  sigh,
While a look of hopeless fury shone in mighty Casey's
  eye.

The lane is long, someone has said, that never turns
  again,

And Fate, though fickle, often gives another chance to
 men.
And Casey smiled—his rugged face no longer wore a
 frown;
The pitcher who had started all the trouble came to
 town.

All Mudville had assembled; ten thousand fans had
 come
To see the twirler who had put big Casey on the bum;
And when he stepped into the box the multitude went
 wild.
He doffed his cap in proud disdain—but Casey only
 smiled.
"Play Ball!" the umpire's voice rang out, and then
 the game began;
But in that throng of thousands there was not a single
 fan
Who thought that Mudville had a chance; and with
 the setting sun
Their hopes sank low—the rival team was leading
 four to one.

The last half of the ninth came round, with no change
 in the score;
But when the first man up hit safe the crowd began to
 roar.
The din increased, the echo of ten thousand shouts
 was heard
When the pitcher hit the second and gave four balls
 to the third.

Three men on base—nobody out—three runs to tie the
 game!
A triple meant the highest niche in Mudville's hall of
 fame!

But here the rally ended and the gloom was deep as
  night
When the fourth one fouled to catcher and the fifth
  flew out to right.

A dismal groan in chorus came—a scowl was on each
  face—
When Casey walked up, bat in hand, and slowly took
  his place;
His bloodshot eyes in fury gleamed; his teeth were
  clinched in hate,
He gave his cap a vicious hook and pounded on the
  plate.

But fame is fleeting as the wind, and glory fades away.
There were no wild and woolly cheers, no glad acclaim
  this day.
They hissed and groaned and hooted as they clamored,
  "Strike him out",
But Casey gave no outward sign that he had heard
  this shout.

The pitcher smiled and cut one loose; across the
  plate it sped;
Another hiss, another groan—"Strike one!" the umpire said.
Zip! Like a shot, the second curve broke just below
  his knee—
"Strike two!" the umpire roared aloud; but Casey
  made no plea.

No roasting for the umpire now—his was an easy lot,
But here the pitcher whirled again—was that a rifle
  shot?
A whack! A crack! And out through space the leather
  pellet flew—
A blot against the distant sky, a speck against the
  blue!

Above the fence in center field, in rapid whirling flight
The sphere sailed on; the blot grew dim and then was
   lost from sight.
Ten thousand hats were thrown in air, ten thousand
   threw a fit;
But no one ever found the ball that mighty Casey hit!

Oh, somewhere in this favored land dark clouds may
   hide the sun,
And somewhere bands no longer play and children
   have no fun;
And somewhere over blighted lives there hangs a
   heavy pall;
But Mudville hearts are happy now, for Casey hit the
   ball!

Slide,

Kelly,

Slide

BY JOHN W. KELLY

*Back in 1889 this great monologist wrote this ballad joshing his friend
"King" Kelly, the great ball player who was the slowest runner in the
game and the greatest base-stealer.*

I played a game of baseball. I belong to Casey's nine!
The crowd was feeling jolly and the weather it was
   fine;

A nobler lot of players I think were never found,
When the omnibusses landed that day upon the
ground.
The game was quickly started, they sent me to the bat;
I made two strikes. Says Casey, ''What are you strik-
ing at?''
I made the third, the catcher muffed, and to the
ground it fell;
I run like a divil to first base, where the gang began
to yell:

CHORUS

Slide, Kelly, slide! Your running's a disgrace!
Slide, Kelly, slide! Stay there, hold your base!
If someone doesn't steal you, and your batting doesn't
fail you,
They'll take you to Australia! Slide, Kelly, slide!

'Twas in the second inning they called on me, I think,
To take the catcher's place while he went to get a
drink:
But something was the matter, sure I couldn't see the
ball:
And the second one came in, broke my muzzle, nose
and all.
The crowd up in the grandstand they yelled with all
their might.
I ran toward the club house, I thought there was a
fight.
'Twas the most unpleasant feeling I ever felt before:
I knew they had me rattled, when the gang began to
roar: — *Chorus*

They sent me out to centre field, I didn't want to go.
The way my nose was swelling up, I must have been
a show;
They said on me depended victory or defeat;

If a blind man was to look at us he'd know that we
   were beat.
Sixty-four to nothing! was the score when we got
   done,
And everybody there but me said they had lots of fun.
The news got home ahead of me, they heard I was
   knocked out.
The neighbors carried me in the house, and then began to shout: — *Chorus*

The Cumberland

BY HERMAN MELVILLE

It was a surprise to discover this by the author of Moby Dick, Typee,
etc.

Some names there are of telling sound,
   Whose vowelled syllables free
Are pledge that they shall ever live renowned;
   Such seems to be
A Frigate's name (by present glory spanned)—
   The Cumberland.
      Sounding name as e'er was sung,
      Flowing, rolling on the tongue—
      Cumberland! Cumberland!

She warred and sunk. There's no denying
   That she was ended—quelled;
And yet her flag above her fate is flying,
   As when it swelled
Unswallowed by the swallowing sea: so grand—
   The Cumberland.
      Goodly name as e'er was sung,
      Roundly rolling on the tongue—
      Cumberland! Cumberland!

What need to tell how she was fought—
  The sinking flaming gun—
The gunner leaping out the port—
  Washed back, undone!
Her dead unconquerably manned
  The Cumberland.
      Noble name as e'er was sung,
      Slowly roll it on the tongue—
      Cumberland! Cumberland!

Long as hearts shall share the flame
  Which burned in that brave crew,
Her fame shall live—outlive the victor's name;
  For this is due.
Your flag and flag-staff shall in story stand—
  Cumberland!
      Sounding name as e'er was sung,
      Long they'll roll it on the tongue—
      Cumberland! Cumberland!

The Johnstown Flood

BY JOE FLYNN

*On May 31, 1889 the dam burst and the flood rolled down on Johnstown,
Pennsylvania. 2200 lives were lost.*

On a balmy day in May, when nature held full sway,
  And the birds sang sweetly in the sky above;
A lovely city lay serene in a valley deep in green,
  Where thousands dwelt in happiness and love.
But soon the scene was changed, for just like a thing
    deranged,
  A storm came crashing through the quiet town;
The wind raved and shrieked, thunder rolled, light-
    ning streaked,
  And the rain it poured in awful torrents down.

Then the cry of distress rings from East to West,
  And our whole dear country now is plunged in woe;
For the thousands burned and drowned in the city of
    Johnstown,
  All were lost in that great overflow.

Like the Paul Revere of old, comes a rider, brave and
    bold,
  On a big bay horse he's flying like a deer;
And he is shouting warnings shrill: Quickly fly off to
    the hills!
  But the people smile and show no signs of fear.
Ah, but ere they turned away, the brave rider and his
    bay,
  And the many thousand souls he tried to save;
For they had no time to spare or to offer up a prayer,
  They were hurled at once into a watery grave. —
    Chorus

'Twas a scene no tongue can tell, homes strewn about
    pell-mell,
  Infants torn away from loving mothers' arms;
Strong men battling for their lives, husbands for their
    wives,
  And no one left protecting them from harm.
Fathers, mothers, children, all, both young, old, great,
    and small,
  Were thrown about like chaff before the wind;
When the fearful raging flood, rushing where the city
    stood,
  Leaving thousands dead and dying there behind. —
    Chorus

Soon the houses piled on high, reaching far up to the
    sky,
  And containing dead and living human freight;

Loud shrieks soon rent the air from the wounded lying
  there,
  With no chance to help avert their dreadful fate.
But a fearful cry arose, like the screams of battling
  foes,
  For that dreadful sick'ning pile was now on fire;
While pouring prayers to heaven, they were burned
  as in an oven.
  And that burning heap had formed their funeral
  pyre. —*Chorus*

Poverty's Tears Ebb and Flow

BY EDWARD HARRIGAN

*Harrigan was a famous actor, dramatist, and ballad writer during the
'80s and '90s.*

Oh, nature she gives us the snow and the rain,
The piercing cold wind and the dew;
Misfortune she gives us both sorrow and pain,
To the many and not to the few.
The years come and go, old time moves along,
Still bearing his burden of woe;
Forever and ever 'twill be the old song,
While poverty's tears ebb and flow.

CHORUS

Forever and ever 'twill be the same song,
While poverty's tears ebb and flow;
Forever and ever 'twill be the same song,
While poverty's tears ebb and flow.

Ye fathers and mothers, ye sisters and sons,
Remember that God made us all;
Ye rich, help the poor and the weak little ones,
Go and answer sweet charity's call.
For life's but a span on time's endless road,

Good deeds inculcated will grow;
Go help the afflicted and lighten their load,
Where poverty's tears ebb and flow. — *Chorus*

Oh, pause in your pleasures, ye wealthy and grand,
Remember that hunger's abroad;
Oh, turn to the needy and stretch forth a hand,
Oh, now listen to sympathy's chord.
Its sweet holy strain encircles the soul
Of the ragged, the fallen, and low;
So pause in your pleasures, seek charity's goal,
When poverty's tears ebb and flow. — *Chorus*

The wine cup it's laden with sin and deceit.
Be careful, my friends, how you quaff;
While merry and jolly its bitter is sweet,
There's a deep, hidden sting in its laugh.
Oh, man is a fool when drink rides the mind,
Not knowing a friend from a foe;
Believing and trusting, he falls on behind,
When poverty's tears ebb and flow. — *Chorus*

The Bowery

By CHARLES H. HOYT

*This is Hoyt's most famous
song and was sung in his
play, "A Trip to China-
town."*

Oh! the night that I struck New York,
I went out for a quiet walk;
Folks who are "on to" the city say,
Better by far that I took Broadway;
But I was out to enjoy the sights,
There was the Bowery ablaze with lights;
I had one of the devil's own nights!
I'll never go there any more!

The Bow'ry, the Bow'ry!
They say such things and they do strange things
On the Bow'ry! The Bow'ry!
I'll never go there any more!

I had walked up but a block or two,
When up came a fellow and me he knew;
Then a policeman came walking by,
Chased him away, and I asked him, "Why?"
"Wasn't he pulling your leg?" said he;
Said I, "He never laid hands on me!"
"Get off the Bow'ry, you yap!" said he;
I'll never go there any more. — *Chorus*

I went into an auction store,
I never saw any thieves before;
First he sold me a pair of socks,
Then, said he, "How much for the box?"
Someone said, "Two dollars!" I said, "Three!"
He emptied the box and he gave it to me;
"I sold you the box, not the socks," said he.
I'll never go there any more! — *Chorus*

I went into a concert hall,
I didn't have a good time at all;
Just the minute that I sat down
Girls began singing, "New Coon in Town."
I got up and I spoke out free,

"Somebody put that man out!" said she.
A man called a bouncer attended to me.
I'll never go there any more! — *Chorus*

I went into a barber shop,
He talked till I thought he would never stop;
I said, "Cut it short." He misunderstood,
Clipped down my hair as close as he could;
He shaved with a razor that scratched like a pin,
He took off my whiskers and most of my chin;
That was the worst scrape I ever got in.
I'll never go there any more! — *Chorus*

I struck a place that they called a "dive,"
I was in luck to get out alive;
When the policeman heard my woes,
Saw my black eyes and my battered nose,
"You've been held up!" said the "copper" fly!
"No, sir! But I've been knocked down!" said I.
Then he laughed, but I couldn't see why!
I'll never go there any more. — *Chorus*

The Prodigal Son

BY BILL NYE

This ballad was a great favorite, written by Bill Nye for his theatrical offering, "The Cadi."

There was an old man and he had two sons,
He did, he did.
He lived on a ranch, so the story runs,
He did, he did.
'Twas built on a grand old Queen Ann plan,
Right next to the new Jerusalem,
The vicinity, it does not matter a d - - n,
Sing tra la la la la la la,
Sing tra la la la la la la.

The elder son was a goodly man,
He was, he was.
And built on the Moody and Sankey plan,
He was, he was.
With calm and sanctimonious face,
He talked about love and undying grace,
And hoped for a seat in the Heavenly place,
Sing tra la la la la la la,
Sing tra la la la la la la.

The younger son was a son of a gun,
He was, he was.
He shuffled the cards and played for mon,
He did, he did.
He wore a red necktie and a high standing collar,
Would go with the boys and get full and then holler.
O, he was a regular Jim Dandy loller,
Sing tra la la la la la la,
Sing tra la la la la la la.

The old fellow's purse was long and fat,
It was, it was.
The Prodigal he was quite on to that,
He was, he was.
And he of the sweet sanctimonious smile,
Just kept his weather eye on the pile,
And hoped he would get there after a while,
Sing tra la la la la la la,
Sing tra la la la la la la.

To divide on the square, he did it his best,
He did, he did.
The Prod took his share and went out West,
He did, he did.
Fell in with some cowboys and had a great time,
Woke up in the morning with nary a dime,
Stranded way out in a foreign clime,
Sing tra la la la la la la,
Sing tra la la la la la la.

A telegraph man in his office sat,
Out West, out West,
When in rushed a tramp without a hat,
Or coat, or vest.
"Come send this message right over the track,
The Prod is a wreck and is coming back,
Have plenty of veal for one on the rack,"
Sing tra la la la la la la,
Sing tra la la la la la la.

The answer he got was short and direct,
It was, it was.
It read, "Yours received go to blazes. Collect"
It did, it did.
The Prod he was used to this knock down of Fate,
So pawned his suspenders and put on a skate,
And started for home on a limited freight,
Sing tra la la la la la la,
Sing tra la la la la la la.

To a lawyer's office he went next day,
He did, he did.
And sued the old folks for pay while away,
He did, he did.
Got out an injunction and put them out,
O, he was a la-la, you hear me shout.
That's the sort of a Prod I'm singing about,
Sing tra la la la la la la,
Sing tra la la la la la la.

That's all the yarn "Yours truly" knows,
It is, it is.
I've gone as far as the parable goes,
I have, I have.
I've never heard what became of Pa,
The religious brother is tending bar
And the Prod, I believe, is driving a car,
Sing tra la la la la la la,
Sing tra la la la la la la.

Down Went McGinty

By Joseph Flynn

"Did you see him?" "Who?" "McGinty." Some of us remember when that was a great joke to pull on the unwary. Joe Flynn used to sing his ballad at the Old Howard theater in Boston and I went in to see him; but I didn't dare tell my mother. The Old Howard is not Carnegie Hall.

Sunday morning just at nine,
Dan McGinty dressed so fine,
Stood looking up at every high stone wall;
When his friend young Pat McCann
Says, "I'll bet five dollars, Dan,
I could carry you to the top without a fall";
So on his shoulders he took Dan;
To climb the ladder he began,
And he soon commenced to reach up near the top;
When McGinty, cute old rogue,
To win the five he did let go,
Never thinking just how far he'd have to drop.

Down went McGinty to the bottom of the wall,
And though he won the five, he was more dead than
alive,
Sure his ribs and nose and back were broke from get-
ting such a fall,
Dress'd in his best suit of clothes.

From the hospital Mac went home,
When they fix'd his broken bone,
To find he was the father of a child;
So to celebrate it right,
His friend he went to invite,
And he soon was drinking whiskey fast and wild;
The he waddled down the street
In his Sunday suit so neat
Holding up his head as proud as John the Great;
But in the sidewalk was a hole,
To receive a ton of coal,
That McGinty never saw till just too late.

Down went McGinty to the bottom of the hole,
Then the driver of the cart give the load of coal a
start,
And it took us half an hour to dig McGinty from the
coal,
Dress'd in his best suit of clothes.

Now McGinty raved and swore,
About his clothes he felt so sore,
And an oath he took he'd kill the man or die;
So he tightly grabbed his stick
And hit the driver a lick,
Then he raised a little shanty on his eye;
But two policemen saw the muss
And they soon join'd in the fuss,

Then they ran McGinty in for being drunk;
And the Judge says with a smile,
"We will keep you for a while
In a cell to sleep upon a prison bunk."

CHORUS

Down went McGinty to the bottom of the jail,
Where his board would cost him nix, and he stay'd
    exactly six,
They were big long months he stopped, for no one
    went his bail,
Dress'd in his best suit of clothes.

Now the Ginty thin and pale,
One fine day got out of jail,
And with joy to see his boy was nearly wild;
To his home he quickly ran
To meet his wife Bedaley Ann,
But she'd skipped away and took along the child;
Then he gave up in despair,
And he madly pull'd his hair,
As he stood one day upon the river shore,
Knowing well he couldn't swim,
He did foolishly jump in,
Although water he had never took before.

CHORUS

Down went McGinty to the bottom of the bay,
And he must be very wet for they haven't found him
    yet,
But they say his ghost comes round the docks before
    the break of day,
Dress'd in his best suit of clothes.

✦ ✦ ✦

The Irish Jubilee

By James Thornton

Many have attempted, but few have ever finished this old vaudeville favorite of the '90s. The breath gives out.

Oh, a short time ago, boys, an Irishman named
    Doherty,
Was elected to the senate by a very large majority,
He felt so elated that he went to Dennis Cassidy,
Who owned a barroom of very large capacity,
He said to Cassidy, "Go over to the brewer,
For a thousand kegs of lager beer and give it to the
    poor,
Then go over to the butcher shop and order up a ton of
    meat,
Be sure and see the boys and girls have all they want
    to drink and eat;
Send out invitations in twenty different languages,
And don't forget to tell them to bring their own sand-
    wiches;
They've made me their senator, and to show my grati-
    tude,
They'll have the finest supper ever eaten in this lati-
    tude.
Tell them that the music will be furnished by O'Raf-
    ferty,
Assisted on the bagpipes by Felix McCafferty,
Whatever the expenses are remember I'll put up in the
    tin,
And anyone who doesn't come, be sure and do not let
    them in."

Cassidy at once sent out the invitations
And every one that came was a credit to their nations,
Some came on bycycles because they had no fare to
    pay,

And those who didn't come at all made up their minds
    to stay away,
Two by two they marched in the dining hall
Young men and old men, and girls that were not men
    at all,
Blind men and deaf men, and men who had their teeth
    in pawn,
Single men and double men, and men that had their
    glasses on,
Before many minutes nearly ev'ry chair was taken,
Till the front rooms and mushrooms were packed to
    suffocation;
When everyone was seated, they started to lay out the
    feast,
Cassidy said, "Rise up and give up each a cake of
    yeast,"
He then said, as manager he would try to fill the chair,
We then sat down and we looked at the bill of fare;
There was pigs head and gold fish, mocking birds and
    ostriches,
Ice cream and cold cream, vaseline and sandwiches.

Blue fish, green fish, fishooks and partridges,
Fish balls, snow balls, cannon balls and cartridges,
Then we ate oatmeal till we could hardly stir about,
Ketchup and hurry up, sweet kraut and sour kraut,
Dressed beef and naked beef, and beef with all its
    dresses on,
Soda crackers, firecrackers, limburg cheese with
    tresses on,
Roast ribs and spare ribs, and ribs that we couldn't
    spare,
Reindeer and snow dear, dear me and antelope,
And women ate so mushmellon, the men said they
    cantelope;
Red herrings, smoked herrings, Herrins from Old
    Erin's Isle,

Bologna and fruit cake, and sausages a half a mile;
There was hot corn and cold corn, corn salve and
honeycomb,
Reed birds, read books, sea bass and sea foam;
Fried liver, baked liver, Carter's little liver pills,
And everyone was wondering who was going to pay
the bills.

For dessert we had toothpicks, ice picks and skipping
rope,
And washed them all down with a big piece of shaving
soap,
We ate ev'ry thing that was down on the bill of fare,
Then looked on the back to see if any more was there,
Then the band played hornpipes, gas pipes and Irish
reels,
And we danced to the music of "The Wind that
Shakes the Barley Fields,"
The piper played old tunes and spittoons, so very fine,
That in came Peiper Heidsick and handed him a glass
of wine:
They welted the floor till they could be heard for miles
around,
When Gallagher was in the air his feet were never on
the ground,
A finer lot of dancers you never set your eyes upon,
And those who couldn't dance at all were dancing
with their slippers on,
Some danced jig steps, door steps and Highland flings
And Murphy took his knife out and tried to cut a
pigeon's wing.
When the dance was over Cassidy then told us
To join hands together and sing this good old chorus:
Should old acquaintance be forgot
Wherever they may be—
Think of the good old times we had
At the Irish Jubilee.

Where the Chicken Got the Axe

By William P. Glenroy

*Oh! for the days of the amateur minstrel show when the local comic
would bring down the house with this ballad.*

In the country once a farmer killed
A rooster with an axe
Just by striking him a single little blow,
But I noticed he took extra care
To land upon his neck,
And the poor young rooster gave his final crow.
Then a man who stood beside me
Said the farmer was a brute,
And they had some words that caused them both to
    fight.
When the farmer threw his axe aside
I saw that he was mad,
And he struck the man a blow with all his might.

CHORUS

And he got it where the chicken got the axe,
Just because he made too many sassy cracks.
But the blow he failed to check,
It landed square upon his neck,
Just exactly where the chicken got the axe.

In a poker game a sharper sat,
And thought he had a cinch
With a countryman who lives at Pumpkinsville.
When the jay drew one the sharper said:
"He's drawing for a flush,"
And he saw his chance in case his hand he'd fill.
Then from underneath the table
He took out four lovely jacks
Where he had them laid away to make a haul.
Then they both bet all their money,

Put their watches up as well,
And the sharper with a smile said, I will call.

CHORUS

And he got it where the chicken got the axe,
For of course you know that aces they beat jacks.
And the jay contented sat,
For he had four aces pat,
To give it where the chicken got the axe.

Here Lies an Actor

BY PAUL DRESSER

This author also wrote "The Banks of The Wabash". He was a brother of Theodore Dreiser.

One evening I was strolling thro' the city of the dead,
Where folks have slept for many years, while birds
    sang overhead,
The little mound of baby, of father and mother dear,
To see them there united filled mine eye with many a
    tear;
I saw the grassy spot where my dear old grandpa lay,
And brothers, sisters scattered 'round, a mass of silent
    clay;
But that which mostly touched me was an open spot
    of ground,
These words upon a tombstone I saw above the
    mound:

CHORUS

"Here lies an actor, in life played many parts,
He had his joys and sorrows, was oftimes sad at heart;
May his sleep here be peaceful, beneath the bright
    blue skies,
While passing drop a flower where an actor lies."

Many people passed the grave that day, I knew not
　　whence they came,
The old, the young, the deaf, some gray, decrepit,
　　blind and lame;
A silent throng of faces they moved with gentle tread,
Each searching for a loved one in the city of the dead.
The one spot seemed forsaken, no one it seemed drew
　　nigh,
No tears were shed unless perchance they came down
　　from the sky;
But being naught but stranger, with nothing else to
　　do,
Those words impressed me vividly, again I read them
　　through: — *Chorus*

While pondering there, a little child with innocence
　　and grace,
It seemed to me celestial, a babe with angel face,
Came up and scattered o'er that spot some flowers
　　rich and rare,
Then kneeling by the actor's grave bow'd down her
　　head in prayer:
"Oh, God! protect my papa, throughout the night and
　　day,
I beg you treat him kindly, he's 'mong strangers far
　　away,
For, oh, we loved him dearly," she said in accents
　　mild;
Please hear the prayer, oh, Father, of an actor's only
　　child.

✦　✦　✦

The Fatal Wedding

By W. H. Windom

The wedding bells were ringing on a moonlight winter's night,
And the church was decorated, all within was gay and
bright.
A mother with her baby came and saw the lights
aglow,
She thought how these same bells chimed out for her
three years ago;
"I'd like to be admitted, sir," she told the sexton old,
"Just for the sake of baby to protect him from the
cold."
He told her that the wedding there was for the rich
and grand,
And with the eager watching crowd outside she'd
have to stand.

CHORUS

While the wedding bells were ringing, while the bride
and groom were there
Marching up the aisle together, while the organ pealed
an air;

Telling tales of fond affection, vowing never more to part—
Just another fatal wedding, just another broken heart.

She begged the sexton once again to let her pass inside.
"For baby's sake you may step in," the gray haired man replied.
"If anyone knows reason why this couple should not wed,
Speak now, or hold your peace forever," soon the preacher said.
"I must object," the woman cried in voice so meek and mild,
"That bridegroom is my husband, sir, and this our little child."
"What proof have you?" the preacher asked. "My infant," she replied.
She raised the babe, then knelt to pray—the little one had died.

The parents of the bride then took the outcast by the arm,
"We'll care for you through life," they said, "you saved our child from harm."
The parents, bride and outcast wife then quickly drove away;
The bridegroom died by his own hand before the break of day.
No wedding feast was spread that night; two graves were dug next day,
One for the darling baby, and in one the father lay.
The story, it has oft been told by firesides warm and bright,
Of parents, bride and outcast wife, and a fatal wedding night.

My Mother Was a Lady

By Edward B. Marks

A Denver newspaperman and myself were watching a performance of an old melodrama at the American Music Hall there and enjoying it thoroughly. Between the acts the girls who served drinks sang this ballad of long ago. While we did not actually cry in our beer, we both felt an upsurge of chivalry in our hearts.

Two drummers sat at dinner, in a grand hotel one day,
While dining they were chatting in a jolly sort of way,
And when a pretty waitress brought them a tray of
 food,
They spoke to her familiarly in a manner rather rude;
At first she did not notice them or make the least re-
 ply,
But one remark was passed that brought the tear
 drops to her eye,
And facing her tormentor, with cheeks now burning
 red,
She looked a perfect picture as appealingly she said:

Reprinted by arrangement with Edward B. Marks Music Corp.

"My mother was a lady—like yours you will allow,
And you may have a sister, who needs protection now,
I've come to this great city to find a brother dear,
And you wouldn't dare insult me, Sir, if Jack were
    only here."

It's true one touch of nature, it makes the whole world
    kin,
And ev'ry word she uttered seemed to touch their
    hearts within,
They sat there stunned and silent, until one cried in
    shame,
"Forgive me, Miss! I meant no harm, pray tell me
    what's your name?"
She told him and he cried again, "I know your
    brother, too,
Why, we've been friends for many years and he often
    speaks of you,
He'll be glad to see you, and if you'll only wed,
I'll take you to him as my wife, for I love you since
    you said:— *Chorus*

The House by the Side of the Road

By SAM WALTER FOSS

There are hermit souls that live withdrawn
In the place of their self-content;
There are souls like stars, that dwell apart,
In a fellowless firmament;
There are pioneer souls that blaze their paths
Where highways never ran—

From Dreams in Homespun, *published by Lothrop, Lee, and Shepard Co.*

But let me live by the side of the road
And be a friend to man.

Let me live in a house by the side of the road,
Where the race of men go by—
The men who are good and the men who are bad,
As good and as bad as I.
I would not sit in the scorner's seat,
Or hurl the cynic's ban—
Let me live in a house by the side of the road
And be a friend to man.

I see from my house by the side of the road,
By the side of the highway of life,
The men who press with the ardor of hope,
The men who are faint with the strife.
But I turn not away from their smiles nor their tears,
Both parts of an infinite plan—
Let me live in a house by the side of the road
And be a friend to man.

I know there are brook-gladdened meadows ahead,
And mountains of wearisome height;
That the road passes on through the long afternoon
And stretches away to the night.
But still I rejoice when the travelers rejoice,
And weep with the strangers that moan,
Nor live in my house by the side of the road
Like a man who dwells alone.

Let me live in my house by the side of the road,
It's here the race of men go by—
They are good, they are bad, they are weak, they are
    strong,
Wise, foolish—so am I;
Then why should I sit in the scorner's seat,
Or hurl the cynic's ban?
Let me live in my house by the side of the road
And be a friend to man.

After the Ball

By CHARLES K. HARRIS

One night at a party at The Lambs Club in New York, I heard Charlie Harris sing his famous ballad in public for the last time. Some of the younger members had never heard it before, but they have never forgotten it.

A little maiden climbed an old man's knee,
Begged for a story, "Do, Uncle, please;
Why are you single, why live alone?
Have you no babies, have you no home?"
"I had a sweetheart, years, years ago,
Where she is now, pet, you will soon know.
List to the story, I'll tell it all,
I believed her faithless, after the ball.

CHORUS

"After the ball is over, after the break of morn,
After the dancers' leaving, after the stars are gone;
Many a heart is aching, if you could read them all;
Many's the hopes that have vanished, after the ball.

"Bright lights were flashing in the grand ballroom,
Softly the music, playing sweet tunes,
There came my sweetheart, my love, my own,
'I wish some water; leave me alone!'
When I returned, dear, there stood a man,
Kissing my sweetheart as lover can.
Down fell the glass, pet, broken, that's all,
Just as my heart was, after the ball. — *Chorus*

"Long years have passed, child, I've never wed,
True to my lost love, though she is dead,
She tried to tell me, tried to explain,
I would not listen, pleadings were vain;
One day a letter came, from that man,
He was her brother, the letter ran.
That's why I'm lonely, no home at all,
I broke her heart, pet, after the ball." — *Chorus*

The Company Store

BY ISAAC HANNA

We were just emerging from the panic of 1893 when this rough-hewn ballad appeared, expressing the indignation of the coal miners over an intolerable condition.

The lot of the miner
At best is quite hard.
We work for good money,
Get paid with a card;
We scarcely can live,
And not a cent more,
Since we're paid off in checks
On the company store.

Those great coal monopolies
Are growing apace,
They are making their millions
By grinding our face;
Unto their high prices
The people pay toll,
While they pay fifty cents
For mining their coal.

They keep cutting our wages
Time after time,
Where we once had a dollar
We now have a dime;
While our souls are near famished,
Our bodies are sore;
We are paid off in checks
On the company store.

Though hard we may labor,
But little we have;
We are robbed of our rights,
Though we fought for the slave.

Published by the University of Pennsylvania Press.

Monop'ly keeps grasping
For more and still more;
They will soon earn the earth
Through the company store.

We sign them a contract
As agreed between men,
Though it holds us like slaves,
It never holds them;
And when they've exhausted
The old contract score,
They capped the climax
With the company store.

The old pirates and brigands
Who fought hand to hand,
Who would scuttle a ship
Or pillage the land,
Have formed a collusion
And all come on shore,
And now ply their trade
Through the company store.

But when those old worthies
Are called to their doom,
I think honest business
Will enjoy a great boom;
And when they are finally
Called from our shore,
I hope they'll take with them
The company store.

The Coxey Army

BY WILLIE WILDWAVE

During the panic of 1893 an army of the unemployed, headed by Jacob S. Coxey, marched on Washington to demand relief. No harm was done and Coxey's army was soon disbanded.

Bring the good old bugle, boys, we want to tell in song
The Coxey army's marching from the town of Massillon,
Soon they'll meet old Grover, a good four million strong,
     Marching in the Coxey Army!

CHORUS

Hurrah! hurrah! we want the jubilee!
Hurrah! hurrah! hard workingmen are we!
We only want a chance to live in this land of the free,
     Marching in the Coxey Army!

Coxey is our leader, from the State of Ohio,
When we get to Washington, he'll let legislators know
That we are all workingmen, and not tramps ''on the go,''
     Marching in the Coxey Army! — *Chorus*

Yes, we have Union men—men who fought in sixty-one,
Who faced ev'ry danger 'neath the broiling Southern sun,
Out of work, they're marching on to Washington—
     Marching in the Coxey Army! — *Chorus*

Bring the good old bugle, boys, let all join in the song,
We'll let the politicians know, they've tried our patience long,
We cry for honest labor, four million people strong,
     Marching in the Coxey Army! — *Chorus*

Ballad of Robert Ross

By Obadiah Cyrus Auriner

On March 6, 1894, Robert Ross was murdered in Troy, New York while fighting to preserve the purity of the ballot.

Martyr blood has stained our streets,
People, bow your heads.
Murder bred in foul retreats
Triumphs; bow your heads.
Civic pride and honor groan,
Stricken. tottering from their throne,
Quenched their pride, their glory flown,
People, bow your heads.

Shame's base blood doth stain our cheeks,
People, bow your heads,
In each patriot's face it speaks,
Bidding bow our heads.
All our manhood's chivalry
Withers like a blighted tree,
Stung by fierce conspiracy,—
People, bow your heads.

'Twas a hero's blood that flowed,
People, lift your heads,
Manhood's spirit in him glowed
Kinglike, lift your heads.
Look, once more here was a man
After God's primeval plan,
Noble blood as ever ran,—
People, lift your heads.

Though he's dead and in his grave,
People, lift your heads.
Clods cannot keep down the brave,
Therefore, lift your heads!
Lo! how swiftly from that seed
Springs the harvest for our need,
Kindred souls with strength to feed,—
People, lift your heads.

Blow the trumpet in the street,
People, rear your heads!
Thunder with your thronging feet,

Marching, rear your heads!
Swift, resistless, troops of fate,
Sweep away the foeman's gate,
Trample down the walls of hate,—
People, rear your heads!

Praise no martyr's ghost can ease,
People, rear your heads!
Deeds must Ross's soul appease,
Straightway rear your heads.
His fair city's name restore,
Build her walls of truth once more,
And his soul goes on before,—
People, rear your heads!

The Face on the Barroom Floor

By H. Antoine D'Arcy

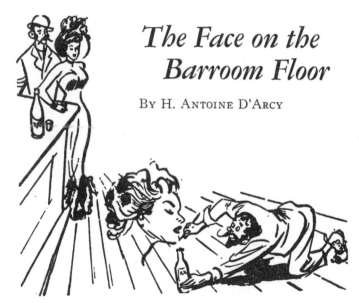

Hughie D'Arcy always insisted to me that the title of his celebrated work was not "The Face on the Barroom Floor" but "The Face upon the Floor." I reluctantly bow to popular usage and include "Barroom" in the title. Maurice Barrymore, brilliant father of Ethel, John, and

*Lionel, spread the ballad's fame by his recitation. Years after, when I
was playing with the two boys in "The Jest," Hughie sent them an
autographed copy. Seated in his dressing room, Jack read it to Lionel and
me with the pathos which only Jack could command.*

'Twas a balmy summer evening, and a goodly crowd
was there,
Which well-nigh filled Joe's barroom on the corner of
the square,
And as songs and witty stories came through the door
A vagabond crept slowly in and posed upon the floor.

"Where did it come from?" someone said: "The wind
has blown it in."
"What does it want?" another cried. "Some whisky,
rum or gin?"
"Here, Toby, seek him, if your stomach's equal to the
work—
I wouldn't touch him with a fork, he's filthy as a
Turk."

This badinage the poor wretch took with stoical good
grace;
In fact, he smiled as though he thought he'd struck
the proper place.
"Come, boys, I know there's kindly hearts among so
good a crowd—
To be in such good company would make a deacon
proud.

"Give me a drink—that's what I want—I'm out of
funds, you know;
When I had cash to treat the gang, this hand was
never slow.
What? You laugh as though you thought this pocket
never held a sou;
I once was fixed as well, my boys, as any one of you.

"There, thanks; that's braced me nicely; God bless
you one and all;

Next time I pass this good saloon, I'll make another
call.
Give you a song? No, I can't do that, my singing days
are past;
My voice is cracked, my throat's worn out, and my
lungs are going fast.

"Say! Give me another whisky, and I'll tell you what
I'll do—
I'll tell you a funny story, and a fact, I promise, too.
That I was ever a decent man not one of you would
think;
But I was, some four or five years back. Say, give me
another drink.

"Fill her up, Joe, I want to put some life into my
frame—
Such little drinks, to a bum like me, are miserably
tame;
Five fingers—there, that's the scheme—and corking
whisky, too.
Well, here's luck, boys; and, landlord, my best regards
to you.

"You've treated me pretty kindly, and I'd like to tell
you how
I came to be the dirty sot you see before you now.
As I told you, once I was a man, with muscle, frame
and health,
And, but for a blunder, ought to have made considerable wealth.

"I was a painter—not one that daubed on bricks and
wood
But an artist, and, for my age, was rated pretty good.
I worked hard at my canvas and was bidding fair to
rise,
For gradually I saw the star of fame before my eyes.

"I made a picture, perhaps you've seen, 'tis called the
　　'Chase of Fame,'
It brought me fifteen hundred pounds and added to
　　my name.
And then I met a woman—now comes the funny part—
With eyes that petrified my brain, and sunk into my
　　heart.

"Why don't you laugh? 'Tis funny that the vagabond
　　you see
Could ever love a woman and expect her love for me;
But 'twas so, and for a month or two her smiles were
　　freely given,
And when her loving lips touched mine it carried me
　　to heaven.

"Did you ever see a woman for whom your soul you'd
　　give,
With a form like the Milo Venus, too beautiful to live;
With eyes that would beat the Koh-i-noor, and a
　　wealth of chestnut hair?
If so, 'twas she, for there never was another half so
　　fair.

"I was working on a portrait, one afternoon in May,
Of a fair-haired boy, a friend of mine, who lived across
　　the way,
And Madeline admired it, and, much to my surprise,
Said that she'd like to know the man that had such
　　dreamy eyes.

"It didn't take long to know him, and before the
　　month had flown
My friend had stolen my darling, and I was left alone;
And, ere a year of misery had passed above my head,
The jewel I had treasured so had tarnished, and was
　　dead.

"That's why I took to drink, boys. Why, I never saw
  you smile,
I thought you'd be amused, and laughing all the while.
Why, what's the matter, friend? There's a teardrop
  in your eye,
Come, laugh, like me; 'tis only babes and women that
  should cry.

"Say, boys, if you give me just another whisky, I'll
  be glad,
And I'll draw right here a picture of the face that
  drove me mad.
Give me that piece of chalk with which you mark the
  baseball score—
You shall see the lovely Madeline upon the barroom
  floor."

Another drink, and with chalk in hand the vagabond
  began
To sketch a face that well might buy the soul of any
  man.
Then, as he placed another lock upon the shapely head,
With a fearful shriek, he leaped and fell across the
  picture—dead.

Dot Leedle Loweeza

BY CHARLES FOLLEN ADAMS

*There was a time when no amateur concert or Sunday evening in the
parlor was complete without one German dialect recitation. Adams wrote
under the name "Yawcob Strauss," and this particular piece used to have
us in stitches.*

How dear to dis heart vas mine grandchild, Loweeza!
Dot shveet leedle taughter of Yawcob, mine son!
I nefer was tired to hug und to shqveeze her
Vhen home I get back, und der day's vork vas done.
Vhen I vas avay, oh, I know dot she miss me,

For vhen I come homevards, she rushes, bell-mell,
Und poots out dot shveet leedle mout' for to kiss me
Her "darling oldt gampa," dot she loves so vell.

Katrina, mine frau, she could not do mitoudt her,
She vas sooch a gomfort to her day py day;
Dot shild she make efry von habby aboudt her,
Like sunshine she drife all dheir troubles avay;
She hold der vool yarn vhile Katrina she vind it,
She prings her dot camfire bottle to shmell;
She fetch me mine pipe, too, vhen I don'd can find it,
Dot plue-eyed Loweeza dot lofe me so vell.

How shveet, vhen der toils off der veek vas all ofer,
Und Sunday vas come, mit its quiet und rest,
To valk mit dot shild 'mong der daisies und clofer,
Und look off der leedle birds building dheir nest!
Her pright leedle eyes how dhey shparkle mit pleas-
    ure,
Her laugh it rings oudt shust so clear like a bell;
I dink dhere was nopody haf sooch a treasure
As dot shmall Loweeza dot lofe me so vell.

Vhen vinter vas come, mit its coldt, shtormy veddher,
Katrina und I ve musd sit in der house
Und dalk off der bast, by der fireside togeddher,
Or blay mit dot taughter off our Yawcob Strauss.
Oldt age, mit its wrinkles, pegins to remind us
Ve gannot shtay long mid our shildren to dvell;
But soon ve shall meet mit der poys left pehind us,
Und dot shveet Loweeza dot lofe us so vell.

✦ ✦ ✦

The Kid's Last Fight

ANONYMOUS

The roaring crowds at the ringside always know that every fight might be a kid's last. Death or glory, or a career cutting out paper dolls, awaits them all.

Us two was pals, the Kid and me;
'Twould cut no ice if some gayzee,
As tough as hell, jumped either one,
We'd both light in and hand him some.

Both of a size, the Kid and me,
We tipped the scales at thirty-three;
And when we'd spar 'twas give and take,
I wouldn't slug for any stake.

One day we worked out at the gym,
Some swell guy hangin' round called "Slim"
Watched us and got stuck on the Kid,
Then signed him up, that's what he did.

This guy called "Slim" he owned a string
Of lightweights, welters, everything;
He took the Kid out on the road,
And where they went none of us knowed.

I guessed the Kid had changed his name,
And fightin' the best ones in the game.

I used to dream of him at night,
No letters came—he couldn't write.

In just about two months or three
I signed up with Bucktooth McGee.
He got me matched with Denver Brown,
I finished him in half a round.

Next month I fought with Brooklyn Mike,
As tough a boy who hit the pike;
Then Frisco Jim and Battlin' Ben,
And knocked them all inside of ten.

I took 'em all and won each bout,
None of them birds could put me out;
The sportin' writers watched me slug,
Then all the papers run my mug.

"He'd rather fight than eat," they said,
"He's got the punch, he'll knock 'em dead."
There's only one I hadn't met,
That guy they called "The Yorkshire Pet."

He'd cleaned 'em all around in France,
No one in England stood a chance;
And I was champ in U.S.A.,
And knocked 'em cuckoo every day.

Now all McGee and me could think
Was how we'd like to cross the drink,
And knock this bucko for a row,
And grab a wagon load of dough.

At last Mac got me matched all right,
Five thousand smackers for the fight;
Then me and him packed up our grip,
And went to grab that championship.

I done some trainin' and the night
Set for the battle sure was right;

The crowd was wild, for this here bout
Was set to last till one was out.

The mob went crazy when the Pet
Came in, I'd never seen him yet;
And then I climbed up through the ropes,
All full of fight and full of hopes.

The crowd gave me an awful yell,
('Twas even money at the bell)
They stamped their feet and shook the place;
The Pet turned 'round, I saw his face!

My guts went sick, that's what they did,
For Holy Gee, it was the Kid!
We just had time for one good shake,
We meant it, too, it wasn't fake.

Whang! went the bell, the fight was on,
I clinched until the round was gone,
A-beggin', that he'd let me take
The fall for him—he wouldn't fake.

Hell, no, the Kid was on the square,
And said we had to fight it fair,
The crowd had bet their dough on us—
We had to fight (the honest cuss).

The referee was yellin', "Break,"
The crowd was sore and howlin', "Fake."
They'd paid their dough to see a scrap,
And so far we'd not hit a tap.

The second round we both begin.
I caught a fast one on my chin;
And stood like I was in a doze,
Until I got one on the nose.

I started landin' body blows,
He hooked another on my nose,

That riled my fightin' blood like hell,
And we was sluggin' at the bell.

The next round started, from the go
The millin' we did wasn't slow,
I landed hard on him, and then,
He took the count right up to ten.

He took the limit on one knee,
A chance to get his wind and see;
At ten he jumped up like a flash
And on my jaw he hung a smash.

I'm fightin', too, there, toe to toe,
And hittin' harder, blow for blow,
I damn soon knowed he couldn't stay,
He rolled his eyes—you know the way.

The way he staggered made me sick,
I stalled, McGee yelled, "Cop him quick!"
The crowd was wise and yellin', "Fake,"
They'd seen the chance I wouldn't take.

The mob kept tellin' me to land,
And callin' things I couldn't stand;
I stepped in close and smashed his chin,
The kid fell hard; he was all in.

I carried him into his chair,
And tried to bring him to for fair,
I rubbed his wrists, done everything,
A doctor climbed into the ring.

And I was scared as I could be,
The Kid was starin' and couldn't see;
The doctor turned and shook his head;
I looked again—the Kid was dead!

Bury Me Not on the Lone Prairie

ANONYMOUS

"O bury me not on the lone prairie!"
These words came low and mournfully
From the pallid lips of a youth who lay
On his dying bed at the close of day.

"O bury me not on the lone prairie,
Where the wild coyotes will howl o'er me,
Where the buzzards beat and the wind goes free;
O bury me not on the lone prairie!

"O bury me not on the lone prairie,
In a narrow grave six foot by three,
Where the buffalo paws o'er a prairie sea;
O bury me not on the lone prairie!

"O bury me not on the lone prairie,
Where the wild coyotes will howl o'er me,
Where the rattlesnakes hiss and the crow flies free;
O bury me not on the lone prairie!

"O bury me not," and his voice faltered there,
But we took no heed of his dying prayer;
In a narrow grave just six by three
We buried him there on the lone prairie.

The Hell-Bound Train

ANONYMOUS

A Texas cowboy on a barroom floor
Had drunk so much he could hold no more;
So he fell aslep with a troubled brain
To dream that he rode on the hell-bound train.

The engine with human blood was damp,
And the headlight was a brimstone lamp;
An imp for fuel was shoveling bones,
And the furnace roared with a thousand groans.

The tank was filled with lager beer,
The devil himself was engineer;
The passengers were a mixed-up crew—
Churchman, atheist, Baptist, Jew;

The rich in broadcloth, poor in rags,
Handsome girls and wrinkled hags;
Black men, yellow, red and white,
Chained together—fearful sight.

The train rushed on at an awful pace
And sulphur fumes burned hands and face;
Wilder and wilder the country grew,
Fast and faster the engine flew.

Loud and terrible thunder crashed.
Whiter, brighter lightning flashed;
Hotter still the air became
Till clothes were burned from each shrinking frame.

Then came a fearful ear-splitting yell,
Yelled Satan, "Gents, the next stop's hell!"
'Twas then the passengers shrieked with pain
And begged the devil to stop the train.

He shrieked and roared and grinned with glee,
And mocked and laughed at their misery,
"My friends, you've bought your seats on this road
I've got to go through with the complete load.

"You've bullied the weak, you've cheated the poor,
The starving tramp you've turned from the door,
You've laid up gold till your purses bust,
You've given play to your beastly lust.

"You've mocked at God in your hell-born pride.
You've killed and you've cheated; you've plundered
and lied,
You've double-crossed men and you've swore and
you've stole,
Not a one but has perjured his body and soul.

"So you've paid full fare and I'll carry you through;
If there's one don't belong, I'd like to know who,
And here's the time when I ain't no liar,
I'll land you all safe in the land of fire.

"There your flesh will scorch in the flames that roar,
You'll sizzle and scorch from rind to core."
Then the cowboy awoke with a thrilling cry,
His clothes were wet and his hair stood high.

And he prayed as he never until that hour
To be saved from hell and the devil's power.
His prayers and his vows were not in vain
And he paid no fare on the hell-bound train.

Rock Me to Sleep

By Elizabeth Akers Allen

Backward, turn backward, O time, in your flight;
Make me a child again, just for tonight!
Mother, come back from that echoless shore;
Take me again in your heart as of yore—
Kiss from my forehead the furrows of care,
Smooth the few silver threads out of my hair,
Over my slumbers your loving watch keep—
Rock me to sleep, mother—rock me to sleep!

Backward, turn backward, O tide of the years!
I am so weary of toil and of tears—
Toil without recompense, tears all in vain—

Take them and give me my childhood again!
I have grown weary of dust and decay—
Weary of flinging my soul-wealth away—
Weary of sowing for others to reap—
Rock me to sleep, mother—rock me to sleep!

Tired of the hollow, the base, the untrue,
Mother, O mother, my heart calls for you!
Many a summer the grass has grown green,
Blossomed and faded—our faces between—
Yet with strong yearning and passionate pain,
Long I tonight for your presence again;
Come from the silence so long and so deep—
Rock me to sleep, mother—rock me to sleep!

Come, let your brown hair, just lighted with gold,
Fall on your shoulders again as of old—
Let it drop over my forehead tonight,
Shading my faint eyes away from the light!
For, with its sunny-edged shadows once more,
Haply will throng all the visions of yore;
Lovingly, softly, its bright billows sweep—
Rock me to sleep, mother—rock me to sleep!

Mother, dear mother! the years have been long
Since last I listened to your lullaby song;
Sing, then, and unto my soul it shall seem
Womanhood's years have been only a dream;
Clasped to your heart in a loving embrace,
With your light lashes just sweeping my face,
Never hereafter to wake or to weep—
Rock me to sleep, mother—rock me to sleep!

The Flat River Girl

ANONYMOUS

Come all you fine young fellows with hearts so fond
    and true,

Never believe in women for you are lost if you do;
But if you ever see one with a long, brown chestnut
  curl,
Just think of Jack Haggerty and his Flat River girl.

Her form was like the dove, so slender and so neat,
Her long, brown chestnut curl hung to her tiny feet,
Her voice it was like music or the murmur of the breeze
As she whispered that she loved me as we strolled
  among the trees.

She was the blacksmith's daughter from the Flat
  River side,
And I always had intended for to make her my bride;
But one day on the river a letter I received;
She said that from her promise she craved to be re-
  lieved.

To her mother, Jane Tucker, I lay all the blame,
She caused her to leave me and to blacken my name;
I counted her my darling, what a lady for a wife!
When I think of her treachery it nearly takes my life.

Come all you fine young fellows with hearts so warm
  and true,
Never believe in a woman; you are lost if you do;
But if you ever see one with a long, brown chestnut
  curl,
Just think of Jack Haggerty and his Flat River girl!

Sam Bass and How His Career Was Short

Anonymous

Sam Bass was born in Indiana, it was his native home,
And at the age of seventeen young Sam began to roam.

❧ 272 ❧

Sam first came out to Texas a cowboy for to be—
A kinder-hearted fellow you seldom ever see.

Sam used to deal in race stock, one called the Denton
    mare,
He matched her in scrub races, and took her to the
    Fair.
Sam used to coin the money and spent it just as free,
He always drank good whisky wherever he might be.

Sam left the Collins' ranch in the merry month of May
With a herd of Texas cattle the Black Hills for to see,
Sold out in Custer City and then got on a spree—
A harder set of cowboys you seldom ever see.

On their way back to Texas they robbed the U.P. train,
And then split up in couples and started out again.
Joe Collins and his partner were overtaken soon,
With all their hard-earned money they had to meet
    their doom.

Sam made it back to Texas all right side up with care;
Rode into the town of Denton with all his friends to
    share.
Sam's life was short in Texas; three robberies did he
    do,
He robbed all the passengers, mail, and express cars
    too.

Sam had four companions—four bold and daring
    lads—
They were Richardson, Jackson, Joe Collins, and Old
    Dad;
Four more bold and daring cowboys the rangers never
    knew,
They whipped the Texas Rangers and ran the boys in
    blue.

Sam had another companion, called Arkansas for
    short,

Was shot by a Texas ranger by the name of Thomas
  Floyd;
Oh, Tom is a big six-footer, and thinks he's mighty fly,
But I can tell you his racket—he's a deadbeat on the
  sly.

Jim Murphy was arrested, and then released on bail;
He jumped his bond at Tyler and then took the train
  for Terrell;
But Mayor Jones had posted Jim and that was all a
  stall,
'Twas only a plan to capture Sam before the coming
  fall.

Sam met his fate at Round Rock, July the twenty-first,
They pierced poor Sam with rifle balls and emptied out
  his purse.
Poor Sam he is a corpse and six foot under clay,
And Jackson's in the bushes, trying to get away.

Jim had borrowed Sam's good gold and didn't want
  to pay,
The only shot he saw was to give poor Sam away.
He sold out Sam and Barnes and left their friends to
  mourn—
Oh, what a scorching Jim will get when Gabriel blows
  his horn.

Perhaps he's got to heaven, there's none of us can say,
But if I'm right in my surmise he's gone the other way.

✦ ✦ ✦

Father, Dear Father,
Come Home With Me Now

By Henry Clay Work

How many sorely tempted footsteps did these tragic lines lead safely past the saloon door and on to the happy home? Ah, but if they paused, sniffing the aromatic odors from the swinging doors, then the Lord pity the poor hungry children.

Father, dear Father, come home with me now,
  The clock in the steeple strikes one;
You said you were coming right home from the shop,
  As soon as your day's work was done;
Our fire has gone out, our house is all dark,
  And Mother's been watching since tea,
With poor brother Benny so sick in her arms,
  And no one home to help her but me.
Come home! Come home! Come home!
  Please, Father, *dear* Father, come home.

CHORUS

Hear the sweet voice of the child,
Which the night winds repeat as they roam;

❦ 275 ❦

Oh, who could resist this most plaintive of prayers,
"Please, Father, dear Father, come home."

Father, dear Father, come home with me now,
   The clock in the steeple strikes two;
The night has grown colder, and Benny is worse,
   But he has been calling for you;
Indeed he is worse, Ma says he will die,
   Perhaps before morning shall dawn;
And this is the message she sent me to bring:
   "Come quickly, or he will be gone." — *Chorus*

Father, dear Father, come home with me now,
   The clock in the steeple strikes three;
The house is so lonely, the hours are so long,
   For poor weeping Mother and me;
Yes, we are alone; poor Benny is dead,
   And gone with the angels of light;
And these were the very last words that he said:
   "I want to kiss Papa good night." — *Chorus*

The New Colossus

By EMMA LAZARUS

The deep feeling of this poem comes from the heart, for Emma Lazarus was herself a child of the oppressed. When France presented us with the Statue of Liberty our officials could not decide what to do with it. For several years it was left to rust in a vacant lot. Popular subscription, spurred by Miss Lazarus, paid for its erection at the mouth of New York Harbor. There it stands, giving hope to immigrants from over the sea, and on its base is a part of this ballad.

Not like the brazen giant of Greek fame,
With conquering limbs astride from land to land,
Here at our sea-washed, sunset gates shall stand
A mighty woman with a torch, whose flame
Is the imprisoned lightning, and her name

Mother of Exiles. From her beacon-hand
Glows world-wide welcome; her mild eyes command
The air-bridged harbor that twin cities frame.
"Keep, ancient lands, your storied pomp!" cries she
With silent lips. "Give me your tired, your poor,
Your huddled masses yearning to breathe free,
The wretched refuse of your teeming shore.
Send these, the homeless, tempest tossed to me,
I lift my lamp beside the golden door!"

There Is a Tavern in the Town

ANONYMOUS

Change the word "tavern" to "night club" and the sentiment is the same as when this classic was written. One thing I'll say for liquor: It has inspired lots of good songs.

There is a tavern in the town,
And there my dear love sits him down, sits him down,
And drinks his wine mid laughter free,
And never, never thinks of me.

Fare thee well for I must leave thee,
Do not let this parting grieve thee,

And remember that the best of friends must part.
   must part.

Adieu, adieu, kind friends, adieu,
I can no longer stay with you, stay with you,
I'll hang my harp on the weeping willow tree
And may the world go well with thee.

He left me for a damsel dark, damsel dark,
Each Friday night they used to spark, used to spark,
And now my love once true to me
Takes that dark damsel on his knee.

O dig my grave both wide and deep, wide and deep,
Put tombstones at my head and feet, head and feet,
And on my breast carve a turtle dove
To signify I died of love.

The Eagle's Song

BY RICHARD MANSFIELD

Like many other great actors, Richard Mansfield had other talents. He wrote the novel "Blown Away" and many excellent verses. "The Eagle's Song" will appeal to intelligent patriots, for whom this book is intended.

The lioness whelped, and the sturdy cub
Was seized by an eagle and carried up,
And homed for a while in an eagle's nest,
And slept for a while on an eagle's breast;
And the eagle taught it the eagle's song:
"To be stanch, and valiant, and free, and strong!"

The lion whelp sprang from the eyrie nest,
From the lofty crag where the queen birds rest;
He fought the King on the spreading plain,
And drove him back o'er the foaming main.
He held the land as a thrifty chief,

And reared his cattle, and reaped his sheaf,
Nor sought the help of a foreign hand,
Yet welcomed all to his own free land!

Two were the sons that the country bore
To the Northern lakes and the Southern shore;
And Chivalry dwelt with the Southern son,
And Industry lived with the Northern one.
Tears for the time when they broke and fought!
Tears was the price of the union wrought!
And the land was red in a sea of blood,
Where brother for brother had swelled the flood!

And now that the two are one again,
Behold on their shield the word "Refrain!"
And the lion cubs twain sing the eagle's song:
"To be stanch, and valiant, and free, and strong!"
For the eagle's beak, and the lion's paw,
And the lion's fangs, and the eagle's claw,
And the eagle's swoop, and the lion's might,
And the lion's leap, and the eagle's sight,
Shall guard the flag with the word "Refrain!"
Now that the two are one again!

The Orphan Girl, or
No Bread for the Poor

ANONYMOUS

"No home, no home," cried an orphan girl
　　At the door of a princely hall,
As she trembling stood on the polished steps
　　And leaned on the marble wall.

Her clothes were torn and her head was bare
　　And she tried to cover her feet

With her dress that was tattered and covered with
    snow,
    Yes, covered with snow and sleet.

Her dress was thin and her feet were bare
    And the snow had covered her head.
"Oh, give me a home," she feebly cried,
    "A home and a piece of bread."

"My father, alas, I never knew."
    Tears dimmed the eyes so bright.
"My mother sleeps in a new-made grave,
    'Tis an orphan that begs tonight.

"I must freeze," she cried as she sank on the steps
    And strove to cover her feet
With her ragged garments covered with snow,
    Yes, covered with snow and sleet.

The rich man lay on his velvet couch
    And dreamed of his silver and gold
While the orphan girl in her bed of snow
    Was murmuring, "So cold, so cold."

The night was dark and the snow fell fast
    As the rich man closed his door.
And his proud lips curled with scorn as he said,
    "No bread, no room for the poor."

The morning dawned but the orphan girl
    Still lay at the rich man's door
And her soul had fled to that home above
    Where there's bread and room for the poor.

Willie the Weeper

Anonymous

Listen to the story of Willie the Weeper.
Willie the Weeper was a chimney sweeper.

He had the hop habit and he had it bad;
Listen and I'll tell you of a dream he had.

He went to a hop joint the other night,
Where he knew the lights were always shining bright,
And, calling for a chink to bring some hop,
He started in smoking like he wasn't gonna stop.

After he'd smoked about a dozen pills,
He said, "This ought to cure all my aches and ills."
And turning on his side he fell asleep,
And dreamt he was a sailor on the ocean deep.

He played draw poker as they left the land,
And won a million dollars on the very first hand.
He played and he played till the crew went broke.
Then he turned around and took another smoke.

He came to the island of Siam,
Rubbed his eyes and said, "I wonder where I am,"
Played craps with the king and won a million more,
But had to leave the island 'cause the king got sore.

He went to Monte Carlo where he played roulette,
And couldn't lose a penny but won every bet—
Played and he played till the bank went broke.
Then he turned around and took another smoke.

Then he thought he'd better be sailing for home,
And chartered a ship and sailed away alone.
Ship hit a rock. He hit the floor.
Money was gone and the dream was o'er.

Now this is the story of Willie the Weeper;
Willie the Weeper was a chimney sweeper.
Someday a pill too many he'll take,
And dreaming he's dead, he'll forget to awake.

Natchez Nan and Her Gambling Man

BY C. H. WHEELER

Derringer Dan was a gambling man
 Who plied his trade on the Nellie Bly,
Whose paddles dipped in the Mississipp
 As the swampy banks slid by.
The backs he glimmed as the cards he skimmed
 With never a crooked move;
Early and late he shuffled them straight,
 For his heart held naught but love.

The guiding force who mapped his course
 Was his sweetheart, Natchez Nan;
The captain's daughter who loved the water,
 And worshipped Derringer Dan,
As with smiling lips he stacked his chips
 In towers blue, white, and red.
She lived in dreams of New Orleans
 And the day when they would wed.

The whistle blew for Belle Bayou
  With its landing piled with bales;
The lusty shouts of the roustabouts
  Answered the planter's hails.
Then up the plank with swagger and swank
  Came a gent with a long mustache,
Clerical frock, and a pearl in his stock,
  Who looked like ready cash.

Handsome Hank strolled up the plank—
  A pearler, rake, and scamp;
A "nigger robber" and "poker dauber,"
  From an up-state mussel camp.
He bartered pearls with crib-line girls
  At "Natchez Under the Hill,"
And would oft' flim-flam a digger of clams;
  In fact, he'd been known to kill.

Natchez Nan watched Derringer Dan
  When Hank horned into the game.
She heard Dan say in his quiet way,
  "My friend, I have heard your fame
As a wizard at cards in the mussel yards,
  So forgive me if I must chide.
Retain your gloves, but your coat remove—
  Those sleeves are much too wide!"

Nan saw the flash, the crimson splash,
  As Dan sank to the floor;
With a panther's glide she stood beside
  Her love who lived no more.
He faced his God, but his two-barreled rod
  Was safe in the hand of Nan,
Who slammed a ball in the cabin wall
  Through the heart of the pearler man.

"Your game was rank," she sneered at Hank,
  " 'Twas a rotten card you played.

You yellow scum, you lousy bum,
  Your last draw is a spade.
You did away with my fiance,
  Now we'll follow him on his trip."
And the captain's daughter who loved the water
  Hopped into the Mississipp.

Prismatic

Boston

By

ARTHUR MACY

When the new Boston Library was opened in 1895 a Common Councilman was horrified to discover the figures of two nude boys in the St. Gaudens sculpture over the portals. The city was in an uproar, but nothing was done about it.

Fair city by the famed Batrachian Pool,
Wise in the teachings of the Concord School;
Home of the Eurus, paradise of cranks,
Stronghold of thrift, proud in your hundred banks;
Land of the mind-cure and the abstruse book,

The Monday lecture and the shrinking Cook;
Where twin-lensed maidens, careless of their shoes,
In phrase Johnsonian oft express their views;
Where realistic pens invite the throng
To mention "spades," lest "shovels" should be wrong;
Where gaping strangers read the thrilling ode
To Pilgrim Trousers on the West-End road;
Where strange sartorial questions as to pants
Offend our "sisters, cousins, and our aunts;"
Where men expect by simple faith and prayer
To lift a lid and find a dollar there;
Where labyrinthine lanes that sinuous creep
Make Theseus sigh and Ariadne weep;
Where clubs gregarious take commercial risks
'Mid fluctuations of alluring disks;
Where Beacon Hill is ever proud to show
Her reeking veins of liquid indigo;
To thee, fair land, I dedicate my song,
And tell how simple, artless minds go wrong.
A Common Councilman, with lordly air,
One day went strolling down through Copley Square.
Within his breast there beat a spotless heart;
His taste was pure, his soul was steeped in art.
For he had worshipped oft at Cass's shrine,
Had daily knelt at Cogswell's fount divine,
And chaste surroundings of the City Hall
Had taught him much, and so he knew it all.
Proud, in a sack coat and a high silk hat,
Content in knowing just "where he was at,"
He wandered on, till gazing toward the skies,
A nameless horror met his modest eyes;
For where the artist's chisel had engrossed
An emblem fit on Boston's proudest boast,
There stood aloft, with graceful equipoise,
Two very small, unexpurgated boys.

Filled with solicitude for city youth,
Whose morals suffer when they're told the truth,

Whose ethic standards high and higher rise,
When taught that God and nature are but lies,
In haste he to the council chamber hied,
His started fellow-member called aside,
His fearful secret whispering disclosed,
Till all their separate joints were ankylosed.
Appalling was the silence at his tale;
Democrats turned red, Republicans turned pale.
What mugwumps turned 't is difficult to think,
But probably they compromised on pink.
When these stern moralist had their breaths regained,
And told how deeply they were shocked and pained,
They then resolved how wrong our children are,
Said, "Boys should be contented with a scar,"
Rebuked Dame Nature for her deadly sins,
And damned trustees who foster "Heavenly Twins."

O Councilmen, if it were left for you
To say what art is false and what is true,
What strange anomalies would the world behold!
Dolls would be angels, dross would count for gold;
Vice would be virtue, virtues would be taints;
Gods would be devils, Councilmen be saints;
And this sage law by your wise minds be built:
"No boy shall live if born without a kilt."
Then you'd resolve, to soothe all moral aches,
"We're always right, but God has made mistakes."

✦ ✦ ✦

There Are Moments When One Wants to Be Alone

By Gus C. Weinberg

Gus's many old friends in the theatre will enjoy reading this as much as I do re-introducing it.

Now every boy remembers when he smoked his first
    cigar—
  When he lit it, how it filled him with delight.
I was happy when I started, but I hadn't smoked it far,
  When the things about me didn't seem so bright.
I saw my friends a-grinning, things about me started
    spinning—
  I hastened to the woodshed, oh, I thought my heart
    would break.
    There are moments when one wants to be alone—
That is one of them, that is one of them;

I like my friends devotedly, I'm awful fond of company,
But there are moments when one wants to be alone.

The colored man is fond of promenading late at night,
And when the coast is clear he makes a swoop;
He'll watch his chance, and when the silvery moon is out of sight,
He crawls into his neighbor's chicken-coop;
The neighbors think it's awful queer the way those pullets disappear;
Our colored man trots homeward with a chicklet in each arm.
There are moments when one wants to be alone—
That is one of them, that is one of them;
But then this colored man ain't proud, you'll often see him in a crowd,
But there are moments when he wants to be alone.

'Twas late the other evening, I was coming from the club,
And I had a jag that was simply out of sight;
I'd upset the ash-barrels, and I'd yell to keep my spirits up—
I'm a regular Pine Ridge Indian when I'm tight.
I sang so loud and long and deep I aroused a policeman from his sleep;
He grabbed me and he told me that I had to go with him.
There are moments when one wants to be alone—
That is one of them, that is one of them;
Next day in court I was a sight, the Judge said that my song was right,
And for fifteen long, long days I sat alone.

Have you ever been to parties where a girl gets up to sing
With a voice that you could use for boiling eggs.

She has studied Italian opera and all that sort of
thing,
And then she will not stop until one begs;
Oh, how you'd like to get away, but, of course, you
know you have to stay.
Just listen and I'll show just exactly how she sings:
There are moments when one wants to be alone—
That is one of them, that is one of them;
Of course, she's got a lovely voice, and it would make
our hearts rejoice.
But those are moments that she ought to be alone.

An Alderman was going to attend a fancy ball,
And he had to rent a suit to wear that night,
And he had to wear the darned thing, but it didn't fit
at all—
Why, he could scarcely breathe, it was so tight.
And when they danced the Boston Dip, then something
gave an awful rip;
He hastened from the ballroom while he sang this
little tune:
There are moments when one wants to be alone—
That is one of them, that is one of them;
Oh, he could dance the whole night long, and mingle
in the giddy throng,
But there are moments when he wants to be alone.

The boys all like to play a little poker now and then.
And wrestle with the jack-pots half the night;
Yes, it's nice to rake in jack-pots and to raise it five or
ten;
And each one thinks his game is out of sight.
And oft they play till early dawn, and oft a fellow's
money's gone;
This happens very frequently—I'll show you how it's
done.
There are moments when one wants to be alone—

That is one of them, that is one of them;
Of course, he'd like to play all night—to play the game
    is his delight,
  But there are moments when one wants to be alone.

All Bound Round With
A Woolen String

ANONYMOUS

Remember Senator Frank Bell singing this in "Way Down East"? He used to knock us off our seats and lay us in the aisles where we nearly died in convulsions of laughter.

I once knew a man and he wasn't very rich
And when he died he didn't leave much;
But a great big hat, with a big broad brim
And it was all bound round round with a woolen string.
The first time that my wife I saw
She was sucking cider through a straw.
Says I to her: "Show me, Miss Shaw,
How you suck cider through that straw."

CHORUS

All bound round with a woolen string,
All bound round with a woolen string,
All bound round with a woolen string,
All bound round with a wool - - e - - n string.

Then, cheek by cheek and jaw by jaw,
We sucked that cider through that straw;
And when that little straw did slip
By Gosh, I sipped some cider from her lips.
And now I've got a mother-in-law
From sucking cider through that straw;
With a great big hat with a great big brim,
All bound round with a woolen string. — *Chorus*

The last time that I used a straw
The cider through the bung to draw
I tried to show my sister-in-law
How two could drink with but one straw.
This little trick my wife she saw,
She let me have it on the jaw,
And then she said to my sister-in-law,
"You go right home and live with Maw." — *Chorus*

I came near being a widower,
For sucking cider through a straw
With a great big hat, with big broad brim
All bound round with a woolen string. — *Chorus*

Break the News to Mother

By CHARLES K. HARRIS

*Written in 1897, this was a highly popular ballad during the Spanish-
American War.*

While shot and shell were screaming upon the battle-
field;
The boys in blue were fighting their noble flag to
shield;
Came a cry from their brave captain, "Look, boys!
our flag is down;
Who'll volunteer to save it from disgrace?"
"I will," a young voice shouted, "I'll bring it back or
die;"
Then sprang into the thickest of the fray;
Saved the flag and gave his young life, all for his
country's sake.
They brought him back and softly heard him say:

CHORUS

"Just break the news to Mother. She knows how dear
I love her,

And tell her not to weep for me, For I'm not coming
home.
Just say there is no other can take the place of Mother;
Then kiss her dear, sweet lips for me, and break the
news to her.''

From afar a noted general had witnessed this brave
deed.
''Who saved our flag? speak up, lads; twas noble,
brave, indeed!''
''There he lies sir'', said the captain, ''he's sinking
very fast;''
Then slowly turned away to hide a tear.
The general in a moment, knelt down beside the boy,
Then gave a cry that touched all hearts that day.
''It's my son, my brave, young hero; I thought you
safe at home.''
''Forgive me, Father, for I ran away.'' — *Chorus*

The Battleship Maine

BY WILLIE WILDWAVE

On February 12, 1898 the battleship Maine *was blown up in Havana
Harbor, arousing the fury of the people until we were plunged into an
unnecessary and inglorious war with Spain. The cause of the disaster
has never been determined.*

Oh, shipmates, come gather and list to my story,
  It's a terrible accident that happened of late;
Over two hundred brave tars died in their glory,
  When the battleship *Maine* met her sad fate.
February the fifteenth—a date we will treasure—
  Its memory is freighted with sorrow and pain;
'Tis a pity that God up above us should measure
  Such a sad end to the battleship *Maine*.

On that ill-fated day, about ten in the evening,
  Havana's fair city was peaceful and still:

But little we thought how bitter the grieving
    Ere morning's light would our sad hearts fill.
A flash from starboard caused our brave ship to quiver,
    Then a sound like a thunderbolt over the main,
Which made every heart in Havana to quiver,
    God help our brave tars on the battleship *Maine.*

The dead and the dying they littered the waters,
    In a moment the work of destruction was o'er;
Bang, bang! went the shells; bang, bang! went the
    mortars,
    While madly the waves about our ship tore.
Down in the deep soon our brave ship was sinking,
    Officers and men were almost insane;
But not one brave tar his duty was shrinking,
    God bless every man on the battleship *Maine.*

Was it an accident? Let time tell the story,
    And don't blame the bard if he casts a doubt;
The black Spanish dogs—their red hands are gory,
    Brave Cuba for years has given them bout.
Let our Consul—brave Lee—make a thorough inspec-
    tion.
    We're sure that he'll make the mongrels explain;
Too long have we tarried at poor Cuba's subjection,
    But can we forget our battleship *Maine?*

Let Washington tremble at their base inaction,
    Too long have we stood Spain's gibes and Spain's
    sneers;
They'll find out, ere long, they're but a small faction
    And soon they will heed American tears.
God bless our brave tars who in Cuba are sleeping,
    Let sweet holy music play its soft strain;
America grieves and sadly is weeping
    For her gallant sons on the battleship *Maine.*

A Hot Time in the Old Town

BY JOE HAYDEN & JAMES DILLON

I can still hear the boys singing this as they marched off to the Spanish-American War in 1898.

Come along, get you ready, wear your bran', bran'
    new gown,
For dere's gwine to be a meeting in that good, good
    old town,
Where you knowded ev'rybody and dey all knowded
    you;
And you've got a rabbit's foot to keep away de hoodoo.
When you hear that the preaching does begin,
Bend down low for to drive away your sin.
And when you gets religion you want to shout and
    sing,
There'll be a hot time in the old town to-night, my
    baby.

CHORUS

When you hear dem a bells go ding, ling, ling.
All join 'round and sweetly you must sing;
And when the verse am through in the chorus all join
    in,
There'll be a hot time in the old town to-night.

There'll be girls for ev'rybody in that good, good old
    town,
For dere's Miss Consola Davis an' dere's Miss Gon-
    dolia Brown,
And dere's Miss Johanna Beasly, she am all dressed in
    red,
I just hugged her and I kissed her, and to me then she
    said:
"Please, oh, please, oh, do not let me fall,
You're all mine, and I love you best of all;
And you must be my man or I'll have no man at all,
There'll be a hot time in the old town to-night, my
    baby." — *Chorus*

Had a Set of Double Teeth

By HOLMAN F. DAY

Oh, listen while I tell you a truthful little tale
  Of a man whose teeth were double all the solid way
    around;
He could jest as slick as preachin' bite in two a shin-
    gle-nail,
  Or squonch a molded bullet, sah, and ev'ry tooth
    was sound.

I've seen him lift a kag of pork, a-bitin' on the chine,
  And he'd clench a rope and hang there like a puppy
    to a root;
And a feller he could pull and twitch and yank up on
    the line,
  But he couldn't do no business with that double-
    toothed galoot.

He was luggin' up some shingles,—bunch, sah, under-
    neath each arm,—
  The time that he was shinglin' of the Baptist meet-
    in'-house;
The ladder cracked and buckled, but he didn't think
    no harm,
  When all at once she busted, and he started down
    kersouse.

His head, sah, when she busted, it was jest abreast the
    eaves;
  And he nipped, sah, quicker'n lightnin', and he
    gripped there with his teeth,
And he never dropped the shingles, but he hung to
    both the sheaves,
  Though the solid ground was suttenly more'n thirty
    feet beneath.

He held there and he kicked there and he squirmed,
but no one come;
He was workin' on the roof alone—there warn't no
folks around—
He hung like death to niggers till his jaw was set and
numb,
And he reely thought he'd have to drop them shingles on the ground.

But all at once old Skillins come a-toddlin' down the
street;
Old Skil is sort of hump-backed, and he allus looks
straight down;
So he never seed the motions of them number 'leven
feet,
And he went a-amblin' by him—the goramded blind
old clown!

Now this ere part is truthful—ain't a-stretchin' it a
mite,—
When the feller seed that Skillins was a-walkin'
past the place,
Let go his teeth and hollered, but he grabbed back
quick and tight,
'Fore he had a chance to tumble, and hung there by
the face.

And he never dropped the shingles, and he never
missed his grip,
And he stepped out on the ladder when they raised
it underneath;
And up he went a-flukin' with them shingles on his hip,
And there's the satisfaction of havin' double teeth.

✦ ✦ ✦

The Charming Young Widow I Met on the Train

Anonymous

I live in Vermont, and one morning last summer,
  A letter inform'd me my uncle was dead;
And also requested I'd come down to Boston
  As he'd left me a large sum of money, it said.
Of course I determin'd on making the journey,
  And to book myself by the "first class" I was fain
Tho' had I gone "second" I had never encountr'd
  The Charming Young Widow I met on the train.

Yet scarce was I seated within the compartment,
  Before a fresh passenger entered the door;
'Twas a female, a young one, and dressed in deep
    mourning:
  An infant in long clothes she gracefully bore;
A white cap surrounded a face, oh, so lovely!
  I never shall look on one like it again.
I fell deep in love over head in a moment,
  With the Charming Young Widow I met on the
    train.

The widow and I, side by side, sat together,
  The carriage containing ourselves and no more;
When silence was broken by my fair companion,
  Who enquired the time by the watch that I wore;
I, of course, satisfied her, and then conversation
  Was freely indulged in by both, till my brain
Fairly reeled with excitement, I grew so enchanted
  With the Charming Young Widow I met on the
    train.

We became so familiar, I ventured to ask her
  How old was the child that she held at her breast;

"Ah, sir!" she responded, and into tears bursting,
  Her infant still closer convulsively pressed;
"When I think of my child, I am well nigh distracted;
  Its father—my husband—oh, my heart breaks with
    pain."
She, choking with sobs, leaned her head on my waist-
    coat,
  Did the Charming Young Widow I met on the train.

By this time the train arrived at a station
  Within a few miles of the great one in town,
When my charmer exclaimed, as she looked through
    the window:
"Good gracious alive! why, there goes Mr. Brown.
He's my late husband's brother—dear sir, would you
    kindly
  My best beloved child for a moment sustain?"
Of course, I complied; then off on the platform
  Tripped the Charming Young Widow I met on the
    train.

Three minutes elapsed, then the whistle it sounded:
  The train began moving—no widow appeared:
I bawled out, "Stop! stop!" but they paid no atten-
    tion:
  With a snort and a jerk, starting off as I feared;
In the horrid dilemma, I sought for the hour—
  But my watch, ha! where was it? where was my
    chain?
My purse, too, my ticket, gold pencil case, all gone,
  Oh, that Artful Young Widow I met on the train!

While I was my loss so deeply bewailing,
  The train again stopped, and I "Tickets, please,"
    heard;
So I told the conductor, while dandling the infant,
  The loss I'd sustained, but he doubted my word;
He called more officials—a lot gathered round me—

Uncovered the child—oh, how shall I explain?
For behold, 'twas no baby—'twas only a dummy!
  Oh, that Crafty Young Widow I met on the train!

Satisfied I'd been robbed, they allowed my departure,
  Though, of course, I'd settle my fare the next day;
And now I wish to counsel young men from the country
  Lest they should get served in a similar way.
Beware of young widows you meet on the railway,
  Who lean on your shoulder—whose tears fall like rain;
Look out for your pockets—in case they resemble
  The Charming Young Widow I met on the train.

No More Booze

ANONYMOUS

There was a little man and he had a little can,
And he used to rush the growler;
He went to the saloon on a Sunday afternoon,
And you ought to hear the bartender holler:

CHORUS

No more booze, no more booze,
No more booze on Sunday;
No more booze, no more booze,
Got to get your can filled Monday.

She's the only girl I love,
With a face like a horse and buggy.
Leaning up against the lake,
O fireman! save my child!

The chambermaid came to my door,
"Get up, you lazy sinner,
We need those sheets for table-cloths
And it's almost time for dinner." — *Chorus*

When Someone Cares

Anonymous

When you meet some disappointment,
An' you're feelin' kind-o'-blue;
When your plans have all got sidetracked,
Or some friend has proved untrue;
When you're toilin', praying, struggling,
At the bottom of the stairs—
It is like a panacea, just to know that SOMEONE CARES.

It will send a thrill of rapture through the framework
    of the heart;
It will stir the inner bein' till the tear-drops want to
    start;
For this life is worth the livin' when someone your
    sorrow shares—
Life is truly worth the livin' when you know that
    SOMEONE CARES.

Oh! this world is not all sunshine—some days dark
    clouds disclose;
There's a cross for every joy-bell, an' a thorn for
    every rose;
But the cross is not so grievous, not the thorn the
    rosebud wears—
An' the clouds have silver linin's—WHEN SOMEONE
    REALLY CARES.

Swing Low, Sweet Chariot

Anonymous

I looked over Jordan and what did I see,
    Comin' for to carry me home?
A band of angels comin' afteh me,
    Comin' for to carry me home.

Swing low, sweet chariot,
  Comin' for to carry me home;
Swing low, sweet chariot,
  Comin' for to carry me home.

If you get there befo' I do,
  Comin' for to carry me home,
Jus' tell 'em I'm a-comin' too,
  Comin' for to carry me home. — *Chorus*

I ain't been to heb'n, but I been tol',
  Comin' for to carry me home,
De streets in heb'n am paved wid gol';
  Comin' for to carry me home. — *Chorus*

I'm sometimes up and sometimes down,
  Comin' for to carry me home;
But still my soul am hebenly-boun',
  Comin' for to carry me home. — *Chorus*

Black Rock Pork

ANONYMOUS

I shipped aboard a lumber-boat,
  Her name was Charles O'Rourke.
The very first thing they rolled aboard
  Was a barrel of Black Rock pork.

They fried a chunk for breakfast
  And a chunk for luncheon too.
It didn't taste so goody-good,
  And it was hard to chew.

From Buffalo to old New York
  They fed it to dear-old-me;

They boiled the barrel and the rest of the pork,
  And we had it all for tea.

About three days out, we struck a rock
  Of Lackawanna coal.
It gave the boat quite a shock,
  And stove in quite a hole.

So I hollered at the driver
  Who was off a-treadin' dirt;
He jumped aboard and stopped the leak
  With his crumby undershirt.

Now the cook upon this canal boat
  Stood six feet in her socks;
She had a bosom like a box-car,
  And her breath would open the locks.

Now the cook is in the poor-house,
  And the crew is all in jail,
And I'm the only canaller
  That is left to tell the tale.

Polly-Wolly-Doodle

ANONYMOUS

Oh, I went down South for to see my Sal,
Sing Polly-wolly-doodle all the day;
My Sally am a spunky girl,
Sing Polly-wolly-doodle all the day.
Fare thee well, fare thee well,
Fare thee well, my fairy fay,
For I'm going to Louisana
For to see my Susyanna,
Sing Polly-wolly-doodle all the day.

Oh, I came to a river; and I couldn't get across,
Sing Polly-wolly-doodle all the day;

So I jumped on a nigga' an' I thought he was a hoss.
Sing Polly-wolly-doodle all the day.

A grasshopper sitting on a railroad track,
Sing Polly-wolly-doodle all the day;
And picking his teeth with a carpet tack,
Sing Polly-wolly-doodle all the day.

Behind the barn down on my knees,
Sing Polly-wolly-doodle all the day,
I think I heard a chicken sneeze,
Sing Polly-wolly-doodle all the day.

He sneezed so hard with the whooping cough,
Sing Polly-wolly-doodle all the day,
He sneezed his head and tail right off,
Sing Polly-wolly-doodle all the day.

The Boston Burglar

ANONYMOUS

While the hero of this ballad operated on a scale much smaller than that of our moderns, such as the men who staged the multimillion-dollar Brink holdup in Boston, he did do well enough to get a term in Charlestown jail. Needless to say, like all Bostonians—and some burglars—he came from a respectable family.

I came here from Boston, a town you all know well,
Brought up by honest parents, the truth to you I'll tell.
Brought up by honest parents and raised most tenderly,
Until I started roving, when I was twenty-three.

My character I ruined and I was sent to jail,
My friends they did their levellest to get me out on bail;
The twelve men called me guilty, the clerk he wrote it down.

The judge he passed my sentence, to jail in Charlestown.

They put me on the passenger one cold, cold winter's
day.
And every depot that I passed I heard the people say,
"That man's the Boston Burglar, for prison he is
bound,
All for his evil doings he's off to Charlestown."

I thought then of my father, a-pleading at the bar,
Likewise my patient mother, a-pulling out her hair,
A-tearing out her gray locks and tears all streaming
down,
"My darling boy, what have you done to go to Charles-
town?"

And there's the girl in Boston, the one I love so well,
To whom I should be married in peace to live and
dwell,
When I get out of prison, bad company I'll shun,
I'll never touch another card or look upon bad rum.

O people, you in freedom, pray keep so if you can,
Remember that it's evil to break the laws of man;
For sad it is to find yourself in such a fix as me,
A-facing twenty-three years in penitentiary.

✦ ✦ ✦

Frankie and Johnnie

ANONYMOUS

The ballad of Frankie and Johnnie can lay stout claim to being America's Number One favorite. It has inspired novels, plays, and motion pictures, perhaps because it deals with the most basic of human emotions—jealousy. There are many, many variations of it and it comes in many lengths. Its parentage is doubtful, but we are quite sure that while it was born in St. Louis, it grew up all over the country.

Frankie and Johnnie were lovers,
Oh, Lordy, how they could love;
Swore to be true to each other,
Just as true as the stars above.
　　He was her man,
　　But he done her wrong.

Frankie, she was a good woman,
Just like everyone knows,
She'd give her man a hundred dollars,
Just to buy himself some clothes.
　　He was her man,
　　But he done her wrong.

Frankie went to Memphis—
She went on the morning train—
She paid a hundred dollars
For Johnnie a watch and chain.
　　He was her man,
　　But he done her wrong.

Frankie lived down in a crib-house,
Crib-house with only one door,
Gave all her money to Johnnie,
To throw on the parlor-girls' floor.
　　He was her man,
　　But he done her wrong.

Johnnie went down to the corner saloon,
He called for a glass of beer;

Frankie went down in an hour or so,
And said, "Has Johnnie Dean been here?"
  He was her man,
  But he done her wrong.

"I'll not tell you any stories,
I'll not tell you a lie,
Johnnie left here about an hour ago
With a girl called Ella Bly."
  He was her man,
  But he done her wrong.

Frankie went down to the pawn-shop,
She bought herself a little forty-four,
She aimed it at the ceiling,
And shot a big hole in the floor.
  He was her man,
  But he done her wrong.

Frankie went down to the hotel,
She rang that hotel bell,
"Stand back, all you floozies,
Or I'll blow you all to hell!"
  He was her man,
  But he done her wrong.

Frankie looked over the transom,
And there before her eye,
Yes, there on the chair sat Johnnie,
Makin' love to Ella Bly.
  He was her man,
  But he done her wrong.

Frankie threw back her kimono,
She took out her bright forty-four,
Root-a-toot-toot, three times she shot,
Right through that hardwood door.
  She shot her man,
  But he done her wrong.

Johnnie he grabbed off his Stetson,
"O-my-gawd, Frankie, don't shoot!"
But Frankie put her finger on the trigger,
And again it went root-a-toot-toot.
    For he was her man,
    But he done her wrong.

"Roll me over once, doctor,
Roll me over slow,
Roll me onto my right side,
For those bullets hurt me so!"
    She finished her man,
    But he done her wrong.

"Bring on your rubber-tired carriages,
Bring on your rubber-tired hack,
Take my daddy to the cemetery,
But bring his suit and wrist-watch back.
    Best part of my man,
    That has done me wrong."

Thirteen girls dressed in mourning,
Thirteen men dressed in black,
They all went out to the cemetery,
But only twelve of the men came back.
    They left her man,
    That had done her wrong.

"Oh, bring 'round a thousand policemen,
Bring 'em around today,
To lock me in the dungeon,
And throw the key away.
    I shot my man,
    But he done me wrong.

"Yes, put me in that dungeon,
Oh, put me in that cell,
Put me where the north wind blows
From the southeast corner of hell.

I shot my man,
When he done me wrong."

Frankie then said to the warden,
"What are they goin' to do?"
The warden said to Frankie,
"It's a pardon, my girl, for you.
You shot your man,
But he done you wrong."

The sheriff came 'round in the morning,
And said it was all for the best,
He said her lover, Johnnie,
Was nothin' but a gawdam pest.
He was her man,
But he done her wrong.

Now it wasn't any kind of murder,
In either the second or third,
This woman simply dropped her lover,
Like a hunter drops a bird.
He was her man,
But he done her wrong.

Frankie now sits in the parlor,
Underneath an electric fan,
Telling her little sisters
To beware of the gawdam man.
They'll do you wrong,
Yes, they'll do you wrong.

The last time I saw pretty Frankie,
She surely was looking fine,
Diamonds as big as horse birds,
The owner of a big silver mine.
She was minus her man,
That had done her wrong.

This story has no moral,
This story has no end,
This story only goes to show
That there ain't no good in men.
  He was her man,
  But he done her wrong.

John Maynard

By Horatio Alger, Jr.

Horatio Alger's novels at the start of the century inspired many a boy to work to become a hero or a millionaire. This ballad honors the memory of John Maynard, who gave his life to save others on the burning Ocean Queen.

'Twas on Lake Erie's broad expanse
  One bright midsummer day,
The gallant steamer *Ocean Queen*
  Swept proudly on her way.
Bright faces clustered on the deck
  Or leaning o'er the side,
Watched carelessly the feathery foam
  That flecked the rippling tide.

Ah, who beneath that cloudless sky,
  That, smiling, bends serene,
Could dream that danger, awful, vast,
  Impended o'er the scene—
Could dream that ere an hour had sped
  That frame of sturdy oak
Would sink beneath the lake's blue waves,
  Blackened with fire and smoke?

A seaman sought the captain's side,
  A moment whispered low;
The captain's swarthy face grew pale;
  He hurried down below.
Alas, too late! Though quick and sharp

And clear his orders came,
No human efforts could avail
  To quench the insidious flame.

The bad news quickly reached the deck,
  It sped from lip to lip,
And ghastly faces everywhere
  Looked from the doomed ship.
"Is there no hope, no chance of life?"
  A hundred lips implore;
"But one," the captain made reply,
  "To run the ship on shore."

A sailor whose heroic soul
  That hour should yet reveal,
By name John Maynard, Eastern born,
  Stood calmly at the wheel.
"Head her southeast!" the captain shouts
  Above the smothered roar,
"Head her southeast without delay!
  Make for the nearest shore!"

No terror pales the helmsman's cheeks,
  Or clouds his dauntless eye,
As, in a sailor's measured tone,
  His voice responds, "Ay, ay!"
Three hundred souls, the steamer's freight,
  Crowd forward, wild with fear,
While at the stern the dreaded flames
  Above the deck appear.

John Maynard watched the nearing flames,
  But still with steady hand
He grasped the wheel and steadfastly
  He steered the ship to land.
"John Maynard, can you still hold out?"
  He heard the captain cry;

A voice from out the stifling smoke
   Faintly responds, "Ay! ay!"

But half a mile, a hundred hands
   Stretch eagerly to shore;
But half a mile that distance sped,
   Peril shall all be o'er.
But half a mile! Yet stay, the flames
   No longer slowly creep,
But gather round that helmsman bold
   With fierce, impetuous sweep.

"John Maynard!" with an anxious voice
   The captain cries once more.
"Stand by the wheel five minutes yet,
   And we shall reach the shore."
Through flame and smoke that dauntless heart
   Responded firmly still,
Unawed, though face to face with death,
   "With God's good help I will!"

The flames approach with giant strides,
   They scorch his hand and brow;
One arm, disabled, seeks his side,
   Ah! he is conquered now.
But no, his teeth are firmly set,
   He crushes down his pain;
His knee upon the stanchion pressed,
   He guides the ship again.

One moment yet! one moment yet!
   Brave heart, thy task is o'er;
The pebbles grate beneath the keel,
   The steamer touches shore.
Three hundred grateful voices rise
   In praise to God that he
Hath saved them from the fearful fire,
   And from the engulfing sea.

But where is he, the helmsman bold?
  The captain saw him reel;
His nerveless hands released their task;
  He sank beside the wheel.
The wave received his lifeless corse,
  Blackened with smoke and fire.
God rest him! Never hero had
  A nobler funeral pyre!

The Frozen Maid

ANONYMOUS

Charlottie liv'd on a mountain top in a bleak and
  lonely spot,
There were no other dwellings there except her
  father's cot.
And yet, on many a wintry night, young swains were
  gathered there;
Her father kept a social board and she was very fair.

On a New Year's Eve as the sun went down, far looked
  her wishful eye
Out from the frosty window pane as a merry sleigh
  dashed by.
At a village fifteen miles away was to be a ball that
  night,
And though the air was piercing cold her heart was
  warm and light.

How brightly gleamed her laughing eye, as a well
  known voice she heard;
And dashing up to the cottage door her lover's sleigh
  appeared.
"Oh, daughter dear," her mother cried, "this blanket
  round you fold,
Tonight is a dreadful one, you'll get your death of
  cold."

"Oh, nay, oh, nay!" Charlottie cried, as she laughed
  like a gypsy queen,
"To ride in blankets muffled up I never would be
  seen;
My silken cloak is quite enough, you know 'tis lined
  throughout,
And there's my silken scarf to twine my head and
  neck about."

Her bonnet and her gloves were on, she leaped into
  the sleigh,
And swiftly they sped down the mountain side and
  o'er the hills away.
With muffled beat so silently five miles at length were
  passed,
When Charles with a few and shivering words the silence broke at last.

"Such a dreadful night, I never saw, the reins I scarce
  can hold."
Charlottie faintly then replied, "I am exceeding
  cold."
He cracked his whip, he urged his steed much faster
  than before;
And thus five other weary miles in silence were passed
  o'er.

Said Charles: "How fast the shivering ice is gathering
  on my brow,"
And Charlott' then more faintly cried, "I'm growing
  warmer now."
Thus on they rode through frosty air and the glittering cold starlight,
Until at last the village lamps and the ballroom came
  in sight.

They reached the door and Charles sprang out, he
  reached his hand to her,

"Why set you there like a monument that has no
  power to stir?"
He called her once, he called her twice, she answered
  not a word;
He asked her for her hands again, but still she never
  stirred.

He took her hand in his,—'twas cold and hard as any
  stone;
He tore the mantle from her face, the cold stars o'er
  it shone.
Then quickly to the lighted hall her lifeless form he
  bore;
Charlottie's eyes had closed for aye, her voice was
  heard no more.

And there he sat down by her side, while bitter tears
  did flow,
And cried, "My own, my charming bride, 'tis you may
  never know."
He twined his arms around her neck, he kissed her
  marble brow;
His thoughts flew back to where she said, "I'm growing warmer now."

A Drunkard's Ode

ANONYMOUS

How well do I remember, 'twas in the late November,
  I was walking down the street quite full of pride,
My heart was all a-flutter as I slipped down in the
  gutter,
  And a pig came there and laid down by my side;
And as I lay there in the gutter, all too soused to even
  mutter,
  A lady passing by was heard to say:
"One may tell a brute that boozes by the company he
  chooses."
  Hearing this the pig got up and walked away.

The Lily of the West

ANONYMOUS

I just came down from Louisville, some pleasure for
    to find,
A handsome girl from Michigan, so pleasing to my
    mind,
Her rosy cheeks and rolling eyes like arrows pierced
    my breast,
They call her handsome Mary, the Lily of the West.

I courted her for many a day, her love I thought to
    gain,
Too soon, too soon she slighted me which caused me
    grief and pain,
She robbed me of my liberty—deprived me of my rest,
They call her handsome Mary—the Lily of the West.

One evening as I rambled down by yonder shady
    grove,
I met a lord of high degree, conversing with my love;
He sang, he sang so merrily, whilst I was sore op-
    pressed.
He sang for handsome Mary, the Lily of the West.

I rushed up to my rival, a dagger in my hand,
I tore him from my true love, and boldly bade him
    stand;
Being mad to desperation, my dagger pierced his
    breast,
I was betrayed by Mary, the Lily of the West.

Now my trial has come on, and sentenced soon I'll be,
They put me in the criminal box, and there convicted
    me.
She so deceived the Jury, so modestly did dress,
She far outshone bright Venus, the Lily of the West.

Since then I've gained my liberty, I'll rove the coun-
try through,
I'll travel the city over, to find my loved one true,
Although she stole my liberty and deprived me of my
rest,
Still I love my Mary, the Lily of the West.

When Willie Wet the Bed

ATTRIBUTED TO EUGENE FIELD

*This should awaken happy memories in many a loving mother as she
gazes fondly on her stalwart son.*

When Willie was a little boy,
    Not more than five or six,
Right constantly he did annoy
    His mother with his tricks,
Yet not a picayune cared I
    For what he did or said,
Unless, as happened frequently,
    The rascal wet the bed.

Closely he cuddled up to me,
    And put his hands in mine,
Till all at once I seemed to be
    Afloat in seas of brine,
Sabean odors clogged the air
    And filled my soul with dread,
Yet I could only grin and bear
    When Willie wet the bed.

'Tis many times that rascal has
    Soaked all the bed clothes through,
Whereat, I'd feebly light the gas
    And wonder what to do.
Yet there he lay, so peaceful like;
    God bless his curly head;

I quite forgave the little tyke
    For wetting of the bed.

        Ah me, those happy days have flown,
            My boy's a father, too,
        And little Willies of his own
            Do what he used to do.
        And I! Ah, all that's left for me
            Is dreams of pleasures fled;
        Our boys ain't what they used to be
            When Willie wet the bed.

    Had I my choice, no shapely dame
        Should share my couch with me,
    No amorous jade of tarnished fame,
        Nor wench of high degree;
    But I should choose and choose again
        The little curly-head
    Who cuddled close beside me when
        He used to wet the bed.

Virginiana

By Mary Johnston

For the first time this piece is published in a ballad anthology. It will stir the heart of any Virginian or anyone else who reads it.

Slow turns the water by the green marshes,
In Virginia.
Overhead the sea fowl
Make silver flashes, cry harsh as peacocks.
Capes and islands stand,
Ocean thunders,
The lighthouses burn red and gold stars.
In Virginia
Run a hundred rivers.

Published by permission of Miss Elizabeth Johnston, sister of the author.

The dogwood is in blossom,
The pink honeysuckle,
The fringe tree.
My love is the ghostly armed sycamore,
My loves are the yellow pine and the white pine,
My love is the mountain linden,
Mine is the cedar.

Ancient forest,
Hemlock-mantled cliff,
Black cohosh,
Goldenrod, ironweed,
And purple farewell-summer,
Maple red in the autumn,
And plunge of the mountain brook.
The wind bends the wheat ears,
The wind bends the corn,
The wild grape to the vineyard grape
Sends the season's greetings.
Timothy, clover,
Apple, peach!
The blue grass talks to the moss and fern.
Sapphire-shadowed, deep-bosomed, long-limbed,
Mountains lie in the garden of the sky,
Evening is a passion flower, morning is a rose!
Old England sailed to Virginia,
Bold Scotland sailed,
Vine-wreathed France sailed,
And the Rhine sailed,
And Ulster and Cork and Killarney.
Out of Africa—out of Africa!
Guinea Coast, Guinea Coast,
Senegambia, Dahomey—
Now one,
In Virginia.

Pocahontas steals through the forest,
Along the Blue Ridge ride the Knights of the Horse-
shoe,
Young George Washington measures neighbor's land
from neighbor,
In the firelight Thomas Jefferson plays his violin,
Violin, violin!
Patrick Henry speaks loud in Saint John's church,
Andrew Lewis lifts his flintlock—
O Fringed Hunting Shirt, where are you going?
George Rogers Clark takes Kaskaskia and Vincennes.
They tend tobacco
And they hoe corn,
Colored folk singing,
Singing sweetly of heaven
And the Lord Jesus.
Broad are the tobacco leaves,
Narrow are the corn blades,
Little blue morning-glories run through the cornfields.

Sumach, sumach!
Blue-berried cedar,
Persimmon and pawpaw,
Chinquepin.
Have you seen the 'possum?
Have you seen the 'coon?
Have you heard the whippoorwill?
Whippoorwill! Whippoorwill!
Whip-poor-will!

White-top wagons
Rolling westward.
Bearded men
Looking westward.
Women, children,
Gazing westward.
Kentucky!
Ohio!

Halt at eve and build the fire.
Dogs,
Long guns,
Household gear.
'Ware the Indians!
White-top wagons going westward.
Edgar Allan Poe
Walking in the moonlight,
In the woods of Albermarle,
'Neath the trees of Richmond,
Pondering names of women,
Annabel—Annie,
Lenore—Ulalume.

Maury, Maury!
What of Winds and Currents?
Maury, Maury,
Ocean rover!
But when you come to die,
"Carry me through Goshen Pass
When the rhododendron is in bloom!"

Men in gray,
Men in blue,
Very young men,
Meet by a river.
Overhead are fruit trees.
Water—water!
"We will drink, then fight."
"O God, why do we
Fight anyhow?
It's a good swimming hole
And the cherries are ripe!"
Bronze men on bronze horses,
Down the long avenue,
They ride in the sky,

Bronze men.
Stuart cries to Jackson,
Jackson cries to Lee,
Lee to Washington,
Bronze men,
Great soldiers.

The church bells ring,
In Virginia.
Sonorous,
Sweet,
In the sunshine,
In the rain.

Salvation! It is Sunday,
Salvation! It is Sunday,
In Virginia.
Locust trees in bloom,
Long grass in the churchyard,
June bugs zooming round the roses,
First bell, second bell!
All the ladies are in church,
Now the men will follow,
In Virginia,
In Virginia.

Ten Thousand Cattle

BY OWEN WISTER

Here is one of our finest cowboy ballads, written by a Harvard man
from Philadelphia, and sung in the play "The Virginian" in 1904, based
on his famous novel of the same title.

Ten thousand cattle straying,
They quit my range and travel'd away,
And it's sons-of-guns is what I say,
I am dead broke, dead broke this day.

Reprinted by permission of Mrs. Walter Stokes, Owen Wister's daughter.

Dead Broke! In gambling hells delaying,
Dead broke! Ten thousand cattle straying,
And it's sons-of-guns is what I say,
They've rustled my pile, my pile away.

My girl she has gone straying,
She's quit me too and travel'd away,
With a son-of-a-gun from I-o-way,
I'm a lone man, lone man this day. — *Chorus*

So I've took to card playing,
I handle decks but it don't seem to pay,
And it's son-of-a-gunner I get each day,
They've rustled my pile, my pile away. — *Chorus*

Tho' all my luck's gone straying,
Tho' I make no strike by night or day,
It is sons-of-guns I still will say,
I'm in the game to stay, to stay. — *Chorus*

It's Great When You Get In

BY EUGENE O'NEILL

*America's greatest dramatist wrote this in 1912 when he was a promis-
ing cub reporter on the New London, Conn. Telegraph.*

They told me the water was lovely
That I ought to go for a swim,
The air was maybe a trifle cool,
"You won't mind it when you get in."
So I journeyed cheerfully beachward,
And nobody put me wise,
But everyone boosted my courage
With an earful of jovial lies.

*From Barrett H. Clark's "O'Neill, The Man and His Work" Published
by Robert M. McBride & Co., Copyright 1929.*

The Sound looked cold and clammy,
The water seemed chilly and gray,
But I hastened into my bathing suit
And floundered into the spray.
Believe me, the moment I touched it
I realized then and there
That the fretful sea was not meant for me,
But fixed for a Polar bear.
I didn't swim for distance,
I didn't do the crawl.
(They asked me why I failed to reach the raft,
And I told them to hire a hall.)
But I girded my icy garments
Round my quaking limbs, so blue,
And I beat it back to the bathhouse
To warm up for an age or two.
I felt like a frozen mummy
In an icy winding sheet.
It took me over an hour
To calm my chattering teeth.
And I sympathized with Peary,
I wept for Amundsen's woes,
As I tried to awaken some life in
My still unconscious toes.
So be warned by my experience
And shun the flowing sea,
When the chill winds of September
Blow sad and drearily.
Heed not the tempter's chatter,
Pass them the skeptic's grin,
For the greatest bull that a boob can pull
Is "It's great when you get in."

The Mountain Woman

BY DUBOSE HEYWARD

Here is one about a Spartan woman of North Carolina that is worthy of a place in any collection of American ballads.

Among the sullen peaks she stood at bay
And paid life's hard account from her small store,
Knowing the code of mountain wives, she bore
The burden of the days without a sigh;
And, sharp against the somber winter sky,
I saw her drive her steers afield that day.

Hers was the hand that sunk the furrows deep
Across the rocky, grudging southern slope.
At first youth left her face, and later hope;
Yet through each mocking spring and barren fall,
She reared her lusty brood, and gave them all
That gladder wives and mothers love to keep.

And when the sheriff shot her eldest son
Beside his still, so well she knew her part,
She gave no healing tears to ease her heart;
But took the blow upstanding, with her eyes
As drear and bitter as the winter skies.
Seeing her then, I thought that she had won.

But yesterday her man returned too soon
And found her tending, with reverent touch,
One scarlet bloom; and, having drunk too much,
He snatched its flame and quenched it in the dirt.
Then, like a creature with a mortal hurt,
She fell, and wept away the afternoon.

Reprinted by permission of Dorothy Heyward and the Macmillan Co.

✦ ✦ ✦

Mr. Goody's Goat

BY JOSEPH SEAMON COTTER

*This colored boy from Nelson County, Ky., studied nights while labor-
ing at various jobs. He became a schoolteacher and a contributor to
the* Louisville Courier-Journal.

Old Mr. Goody had a goat
That was quiet and genteel;
His mustache started at his chin
And ended at his heel.
This goat thought he was just as smart
As anything could be;
He said no other goat alive
Knew half as much as he.
He knew that corn was made to grow,
And eggs were made to hatch;
But, lo, he never yet had seen
The thing you call a match.
So, one day as he pondered o'er
The many things he knew,
He chanced to see this very thing
Lying plainly in his view.
Said he: "Of all things I have seen
Not one of them I've feared;
So I will take this something up
And hang it on my beard."
Just then a monkey came along,
And sneeringly he spoke:
"The thing that dangles from your beard
Was clearly made to smoke."
"And how?" the goat made quick reply,
The monkey said: "Just so;"
And gave the match a kind of stroke
That monkeys only know.
And in a trice there stood a goat
As beardless as a flea,
And one that thought the smallest thing
Knew just as much as he.

Noah an' Jonah an' Cap'n John Smith

By Don Marquis

I enjoyed appearing in Don Marquis' comedy "Everything's Jake." Don had a gift for expressing profundities in humorous form, as can readily be seen in "The Old Soak" and his famous verse about archy and mehitabel. This ballad is my old friend at his whimsical best and was a great favorite of Franklin D. Roosevelt.

Noah an' Jonah an' Cap'n John Smith,
Mariners, travelers, magazines of myth,
Settin' up in Heaven, chewin, and a-chawin',
Eatin' their terbaccy, talkin' and a-jawin';
Settin' by a crick, spittin' in the worter,
Talkin' tall an' tactless, as saints hadn't orter,
Lollin' in the shade, baitin' hooks and anglin',
Occasionally friendly, occasionally wranglin'.

Noah took his halo from his old bald head
An' swatted of a hoppergrass an' knocked it dead,
An' he baited of his hook, an' he spoke an' said:
"When I was the skipper of the tight leetle Ark
I useter fish fer porpus, useter fish fer shark,
Often I have ketched in a single hour on Monday
Sharks enough to feed the fambly until Sunday—
To feed all the sarpints, the tigers an' donkeys,
To feed all the zebras, the insects an' monkeys,
To feed all the varmints, bears an' gorillars,
To feed all the camels, cats an' armadillers,
To give all the pelicans stews fer their gizzards,
To feel all the owls an' catamounts an' lizards,
To feed all the humans, their babies an' their nusses,

To feed all the houn' dawgs an' hippopotamusses,
To feed all the oxens, feed all the asses,
Feed all the bison an' leetle hoppergrasses—
Always I ketched in half a hour on Monday
All that the fambly could gormandize till Sunday!''

Jonah took his harp, to strum an' to string her,
An' Cap'n John Smith tetched his nose with his finger.
Cap'n John Smith, he hemmed some and hawed some,
An' he bit off a chaw, an' he chewed some an' chawed
    some:—
''When I was to China, when I was to Guinea,
When I was to Javy, an' also in Verginny,
I teached all the natives how to be ambitious,
I learned 'em my trick of ketchin' devilfishes.
I've fitten tigers, I've fitten bears,
I have fitten sarpints an' wolves in their lairs,
I have fit with wild men an' hippopotamusses,
But the periloussest varmints is the bloody octopusses!
I'd rub my forehead with phosphorescent light
An' plunge into the ocean an' seek 'em out at night!
I ketched 'em in grottoes, I ketched 'em in caves,
I used fer to strangle 'em underneath the waves!
When they seen the bright light blazin' on my forehead
They used fer to rush at me, screamin' something hor-
    rid!
Tentacles wavin', teeth white an' gnashin',
Hollerin' an' bellerin', wallerin' an' splashin'!
I useter grab 'em as they rushed from their grots,
Ketch all their legs an' tie 'em into knots!''

Noah looked at Jonah an' said not a word,
But if winks made noises, a wink had been heard.
Jonah took the hook from a mudcat's middle
An' strummed on the strings of his hallelujah fiddle;
Jonah gave his whiskers a backhand wipe
An' cut some plug terbaccer an' crammed it in his
    pipe!

—(Noah an' Jonah an' Cap'n John Smith,
Fishermen an' travelers, narratin' myth,
Settin' up in Heaven all eternity,
Fishin' in the shade, contented as could be!
Spittin' their terbaccer in the little shaded creek,
Stoppin' of their yarns fer ter hear the ripples speak!
I hope fer Heaven, when I think of this—
You folks bound hellward, a lot of fun you'll miss!)
Jonah, he decapitates that mudcat's head,
An' gets his pipe ter drawin'; an' this is what he said:
"Excuse me if yer stories don't excite me much!
Excuse me if I seldom agitate fer such!
You think yer fishermen! I won't argue none!
I won't even tell yer the half o' what I done!
You has careers dangerous an' checkered!
All as I will say is: Go an' read my record!
You think yer fishermen! You think yer great!
All I ask is this: Has one of ye been *bait?*
Cap'n Noah, Cap'n John, I heerd when ye hollered:
What I asks is this: Has one of ye been *swallered?*
It's might purty fishin' with little hooks an' reels,
It's mighty easy fishin' with little rods an' creels,
It's mighty pleasant ketchin' mudcats fer yer dinners,
But here is my challenge fer saints an' fer sinners,
Which one of ye has v'yaged in a varmint's inners?
When I see a big fish, tough as Mathooslum,
I used fer to dive into his oozy-goozlum!
When I see a strong fish, wallopin' like a lummicks,
I uster foller 'em, dive into their stummicks!
I could v'yage an' steer 'em, I could understand 'em,
I uster navigate 'em, I uster land 'em!
Don't you pester *me* with any more narration!
Go git famous! Git a reputation!"

Cap'n John he grinned his hat brim beneath,
Clicked his tongue of silver on his golden teeth;
Noah an' Jonah an' Cap'n John Smith,

Strummin' golden harps, narratin' myth!
Settin' by the shallows forever an' forever,
Swappin' yarns an' fishin' in a little River!

Pasquale Passes

BY T. A. DALY

*This author found subjects for many of his ballads among the Italian
people of Philadelphia. The poetic mind seems to find material everywhere.*

Rosa Beppi she'sa got
Temper dat's so strong an' hot,
Ees no matter w'at you say
W'en she's start for have her way
She's gon' have eet; you can bat
Evra cent you got on dat!
Theenk she gona mind her Pop?
She ain't even 'fraid of cop!
Even devil no could stop
Rosa Beppi w'en she gat
Foolish things eenside her hat.
Dat'sa why her Pop ees scare',
Dat'sa why he growl an' swear
W'en he sees her walkin' out
Weeth Pasquale from da Sout'.

Eef, like Beppi, you are com'
From da countra nort' of Rome,
You would know dat man from Sout'
Ain'ta worth for talks 'bout.
Ees no wondra Beppi swear,
Growl an' grumble like a bear.
W'en da Padre Angelo
Come an' see heem actin' so,
He's su'prise an' wanta know.

Beppi tal him. "Ah!" he say,
"I weell talk weeth her to-day,
So she stoppa walkin' out
Weeth Pasquale from da Sout'."

Beppi shak' hees head an' sigh.
He don't theenk eet's use for try,
But da Padre smile an' say:
"I gon' speak weeth her to-day."
Pretta soon, bimeby, he do—
Only say one word or two—
But so soon as he ees through
You should see da Rosa! My!
Dere's a fire from her eye,
Cutta through you lika knife.
She ees mad, you bat my life!
But no more she's walkin' out
Weeth Pasquale from da Sout'.

Beppi's gladdest man I know
W'en he see how theengsa go.
"My!" he say, "I am su'prise'
Church can be so strong an' wise."
"Yes", say Padre Angelo,
"Church ees always wisa so.
All I say to her ees dees:
'Rosa, I am moocha please'
Dat at las' you gotta beau.
He ain't verra good one, no;
But you need no minda dat
Seence he's best dat you can gat.
So I'm glad for see you out
Weeth Pasquale from da Sout'."

Reprinted from Madrigal: *by T. A. Daly, by permission of Harcourt, Brace & Co.*

Mademoiselle From Armentières

ANONYMOUS

This was an enormously popular ballad with our soldiers during World War 1.

Madamoiselle from Armentiers, parley voo,
Madamoiselle from Armentiers, parley voo,
  Madamoiselle from Armentiers,
  She hasn't been kissed in forty years,
Hinky, dinky, parley voo.

Madamoiselle from Armentiers, parley voo,
Madamoiselle from Armentiers, parley voo,
  She had a form like the back of a hack,
  When she cried the tears ran down her back,
Hinky, dinky, parley voo.

Madamoiselle from Armentiers, parley voo,
Madamoiselle from Armentiers, parley voo,
  She never could hold the love of a man
  'Cause she took her baths in a talcum can,
Hinky, dinky, parley voo.

Madamoiselle from Armentiers, parley voo,
Madamoiselle from Armentiers, parley voo,
 She had four chins, her knees would knock,
 And her face would stop a coo-coo clock.
Hinky, dinky, parley voo.

Madamoiselle from Armentiers, parley voo,
Madamoiselle from Armentiers, parley voo,
 She could guzzle a barrel of sour wine,
 And eat a hog without peeling the rine,
Hinky, dinky, parley voo.

Madamoiselle from Armentiers, parley voo,
Madamoiselle from Armentiers, parley voo,
 She could beg a franc, a drink, a meal,
 But it wasn't because of sex appeal,
Hinky, dinky, parley voo.

The M.P.'s think they won the war, parley voo,
The M.P.'s think they won the war, parley voo,
 The M.P.'s think they won the war
 By standing guard at a cafe door,
Hinky, dinky, parley voo.

The officers get the pie and cake, parley voo,
The officers get the pie and cake, parley voo,
 The officers get the pie and cake,
 And all we get is the bellyache,
Hinky, dinky, parley voo.

The sergeant ought to take a bath, parley voo,
The sergeant ought to take a bath, parley voo,
 If he ever changes his underwear
 The frogs will give him a croix de guerre,
Hinky, dinky, parley voo.

You might forget the gas and shells, parley voo,
You might forget the stinking hells, parley voo,
 You might forget the groans and yells,
 But you'll never forget the madamoiselles,
Hinky, dinky, parley voo.

Madamoiselle from Armentiers, parley voo,
Madamoiselle from Armentiers, parley voo,
Just blow your nose and dry your tears
For we'll be back in a few short years.
Hinky, dinky, parley voo.

Lips That
Touch
Liquor

ANONYMOUS

To kiss a young lady when you had liquor on your breath was considered highly improper in my young days. I have reason to know this. But along came Prohibition, bringing what my friend Heywood Brown called "co-educational drinking."

You are coming to woo me, but not as of yore,
When I hastened to welcome your ring at the door;
For I trusted that he who stood waiting me then
Was the brightest, the truest, the noblest of men.
Your lips on my own when they printed "Farewell"
Had never been soiled by the "beverage of Hell,"
But they come to me now with the bacchanal sign,
And the lips that touch liquor must never touch mine.

I think of that night in the garden alone,
When in whispers you told me your heart was my own,
That your love in the future should faithfully be

Unshared by another, kept only for me.
Oh, sweet to my soul is the memory still
Of the lips which met mine, when they whispered "I
    will";
But now to their pressure they no more incline,
For the lips that touch liquor must never touch mine.

Oh, John! how it crushed me, when first in your face
The pen of the "Rum Fiend" had written "disgrace";
And turned me in silence and tears from that breath
All poisoned and foul from the chalice of death.
It scattered the hopes I had treasured to last;
It darkened the future and clouded the past;
It shattered my idol, and ruined the shrine,
For the lips that touch liquor must never touch mine.

I loved you—Oh, dearer than language can tell,
And you saw it, you proved, you knew it too well!
But the man of my love was far other than he
Who now from the "Tap-room" comes reeling to me;
In manhood and honor so noble and right—
His heart was so true, and his genius so bright—
And his soul was unstained, unpolluted by wine;
But the lips that touch liquor must never touch mine.

You promised reform, but I trusted in vain;
Your pledge was but made to be broken again;
And the lover so false to his promises now,
Will not as a husband be true to his vow.
The word must be spoken that bids you depart—
Though the effort to speak it should shatter my
    heart—
Though in silence, with blighted affection, I pine,
Yet the lips that touch liquor must never touch mine!

If one spark in your bosom of virtue remain,
Go fan it with prayer till it kindles again;
Resolved, with "God helping," in future to be

From wine and its follies unshackled and free!
And when you have conquered this foe of your soul—
In manhood and honor beyond his control—
This heart will again beat responsive to thine,
And the lips free from liquor be welcome to mine.

The Dying Hogger

ANONYMOUS

*In the old railroading days the engi-
neers were called "hoggers"; brakemen
and switchmen were called "snakes"
and "stingers"; the fireman was a
"tallow-pot".*

A hogger on his deathbed lay.
His life was oozing fast away;
The snakes and stingers round him pressed
To hear the hogger's last request.
He said "Before I bid adieu,
One last request I'll make of you;
Before I soar beyond the stars
Just hook me on to ninety cars.

"A marble slab I do not crave;
Just mark the head of my lonely grave
With a draw-bar pointing to the skies,

Showing the spot where this hogger lies.
Oh, just once more before I'm dead
Let me stand the conductor on his head;
Let me see him crawl from under the wreck
With a way-car window-sash around his neck.

"And you, dear friends, I'll have to thank,
If you'll let me die at the water-tank,
Within my ears that old-time sound,
The tallow-pot pulling the tank-spout down.
And when at last in my grave I'm laid,
Let it be in the cool of the water-tank shade.
And put within my cold, still hand
A monkey-wrench and an old oil can."

You Never Miss the Water
Till the Well Runs Dry

ANONYMOUS

When a child I liv'd at Lincoln with my parents at
the farm,
The lessons that my mother taught to me were quite a
charm;
She would often take me on her knee when tir'd of
childish play
And as she pressed me to her breast I've heard my
mother say:

CHORUS

Waste not, want not, is a maxim I would teach.
Let your watchword be despatch, and practice what
you preach;
Do not let your chances like sunbeams pass you by,
For you never miss the water till the well runs dry.

As years roll'd on I grew to be a mischief-making boy.
Destruction seem'd my only sport, it was my only joy.
And well do I remember when ofttimes well chastised,
How father sat beside me then and thus has me advised: — *Chorus*

When I arriv'd at manhood I embark'd in public life,
And found it was a rugged road, bestrewn with care
and strife:
I speculated foolishly, my losses were severe,
But still a tiny little voice ekpt whisp'ring in my ear:
— *Chorus*

Then I studied strict economy and found to my surprise,
My funds instead of sinking very quickly then did
rise:
I grasp'd each chance and always struck the iron
while 'twas hot,
I seiz'd my opportunities and never once forgot:
— *Chorus*

I'm married now and happy. I've a careful little wife.
We live in peace and harmony, devoid of care and
strife:
Fortune smiles upon us, we have little children three.
The lesson that I teach them, as they prattle round
my knee: — *Chorus*

Joshua Ebenezer Fry

ANONYMOUS

> I'm the Constibule of Pumpkinville,
> Jist traded hosses at the mill.
> My name's Joshua
> Ebenezer Fry.

I know a thing or two,
　　Yew bet yer life I do.
Yew cain't fool me
　　'Cause I'm too dern'd sly.

Wal, I swan!
　　I must be gittin' on.
Giddap, Napoleon!
　　It looks like rain.
I'll shoot a hawk!
　　If the critter didn't balk,
I'll lick Jed Hawkins,
　　Sure as Joshua's my name.

I went to the County Fair,
　　Met a city slicker there.
He says: "Gimme two tens
　　Fer a five."
I says: "Ye derned fool,
　　I be the Constibule.
Now you're arrested,
　　Jist as sure as you're alive."

Wal, I swan!
　　I must be gittin' on.
Giddap, Napoleon!
　　It looks like rain.
I'll bet two bits
　　The money's counterfeit,
That city feller gimme
　　Comin' down on the train.

I hitched up the old mare,
　　Druv'er to the County Fair.
Took first prize,

On a load of squash.
I got so derned full,
  I went and sold the red bull,
And give away the cow
  That wore the silver bell.

CHORUS

Wal, I swan!
  I must be gittin' on.
Giddap, Napoleon!
  It looks like rain.
I'll be derned!
  If the butter ain't churned.
Now we'll have some buttermilk,
  Or Josh is not my name.

I got home so derned late,
  Couldn't find the barn gate.
Ma says: "Joshua!
  Is it possible?
Yew air a disgrace.
  Yew ort to go and hide yer face.
I never seed sich actions
  For to be a Constibule."

CHORUS

Wal, I swan!
  I must be gittin' on.
Giddap, Napoleon!
  It looks like rain.
I'll be switched,
  And the hay ain't pitched.
Drap in when yew're
  Over to the farm again.

✦ ✦ ✦

The Old, Old Story

ANONYMOUS

You say I've no place among women,
  You call me a girl of the town.
Well, I am; but I'm what the world made me,
  It is no fault of mine that I'm down.
Your path perhaps was scattered with roses,
  The camelias o'ershadowed my door,
Yet I once had a good and fond mother,
  But our misfortune was we were poor.

Poor and lonely, for years we were honest,
  And worked hard for rent and for bread;
I say we—I mean mother and I—
  For father had long since been dead.
Poor mother, she took in shirt-making,
  For which little enough they would pay;
I clerked in a store for a pittance
  For ten long hours each day.

Girls said that I'd soon catch a lover
  Who would pay for a beautiful wife;
Well, I found one, and he is the cause
  Of my leading a dissolute life.
He was handsome enough as a man goes,
  And his money he spent like a lord;
I gave up my lips to his kisses,
  But of marriage he seldom spoke word.

He told me the days of fond wooing,
  Were always the hey-days of life,
And that when he could claim his large fortune
  'Twould be time for to cherish a wife.
I took all his protests as gospel,
  And gave him my heart in return;
I had scarcely then seen sixteen summers,
  And since found I had plenty to learn.

❧ 341 *❧*

For a year I was supremely happy,
　　The only care that would shadow my brow
Was the thought that perchance I might lose him
　　He was dearer than life to me now.
I lived on his words and his kisses;
　　When his strong arm encircled my waist
The hot blood would rush up to my temples
　　And banish all thoughts that were chaste.

Well, the winter was long and a hard one,
　　I was rugged and could stand the cold blast,
But poor mother got weak and so sickly
　　She was forced to quit sewing at last;
This made our lot very much harder,
　　For the most I could earn at the store
Was so small that I found it not easy
　　To keep the grim wolf from the door.

My Adonis could see I was troubled,
　　And offered to give me right there
Enough money to keep us from starving,
　　He said he had plenty to spare.
In such straits how could I gainsay him?
　　I thought him an angel of grace!
In my worship I gave him my treasure,
　　So would you had you been in my place.

But to shorten a lengthy sad story,
　　Half a year had gone over my head
When poor mother discovered my folly—
　　Next day she lay on her death bed.
For years I had been her sole worship,
　　Her idol, her joy and her pride.
And with tears coursing down her poor wrinkles,
　　She kissed me and blessed me, and died.

Left alone, I implored the protection
　　Of him who had brought me to shame,
But he suddenly fled from our city

With the brand of a criminal's name,
But if he'd return to my bosom,
  Though he hadn't a penny to give,
I'd forget all the sorrow he caused me,
  And love him as long as I live.

But there's no chance of his ever coming,
  Or any one leading the way
To make me a good honest woman,
  So a girl of the town I must stay.
In this world I know I'm a lost one,
  But the last judgment day you may see
That the Saviour who cheered the Magdalene
  Will put in a good word for me.

In the Baggage Car Ahead

By Gussie Davis

On a dark, stormy night as the train rattled on,
  All the passengers had gone to bed,
Except one young man with babe in his arms,
  Who sat there with bowed down head;

The innocent one began crying just then,
  As though its poor heart it would break,
When an angry man said: "Make that child stop its
    noise,
  For it is keeping all of us awake."

"Put it out," said another, "don't keep it in here,
  We have paid for our berths and want rest,"
But never a word said the man with the child,
  As he fondled it close to his breast.

Reprinted by arrangement with the Edward B. Marks Music Corp.

"Where is its mother? Go take it to her,"
  This a lady then softly said.
"I wish that I could," was the man's sad reply,
  "But she's dead in the coach ahead!"

CHORUS

While the train rolled onward, a husband sat in tears,
Thinking of the happiness of just a few short years,
For baby's face brings pictures of a cherished hope
    that's dead,
But baby's cries can't waken her, in the baggage
    coach ahead.

Every eye filled with tears, when his story he told,
  Of a wife that was faithful and true:
He told how he'd saved up his earnings for years,
  Just to build up a home for two;

How when heaven had sent them this sweet little babe,
  Their young happy lives were blessed,
His heart seemed to break when he mentioned her
    name,
  And in tears tried to tell them the rest,

Every woman arose to assist with the child,
  There were mothers and wives on that train;
And soon was the little one sleeping in peace,
  With no thought of sorrow or pain.

Next morn at the station he bade all goodbye,
  "God bless you," he softly said;
Each one had a story to tell in their homes
  Of the baggage coach ahead. — *Chorus*

❊ 344 ❊

Why Are You Weeping, Sister?

ANONYMOUS

Why are you weeping, sister? Why are you sitting
    alone?
I'm old and gray and I've lost my way,
All my to-morrows were yesterday,
I traded them off for a wanton's pay,
I bartered my graces for silks and laces,
My heart I sold for a pot of gold,
Now I'm old.

Why did you do it, sister? Why did you sell your soul?
I was foolish and fair and my form was rare,
I longed for life's baubles and did not care,
When we know not the price to be paid we dare,
I listened when vanity lied to me
And I ate the fruit of the bitter tree,
Now I'm old.

Why are you lonely, sister? Where have your friends
    all gone?
Friends I have none for I went the road

Where women must harvest what men have sowed,
And they never come back when the field is mowed,
They gave the lee of the cup to me,
But I was blinded and would not see,
Now I'm old.

Where are your lovers, sister? Where are your lovers
    now?
My lovers were many but all have run,
I betrayed and deceived them every one,
And they lived to learn what I had done,
A poisoned draught from my lips they quaffed,
But I who knew it was poisoned—laughed,
Now I'm old.

Will they not help you, sister, in the name of your
    common sin?
There is no debt for my lovers bought,
They paid my price for the things I brought,
I made the terms so they owe me naught,
I have no hold for 'twas I who sold,
One offered his heart but mine was cold,
Now I'm old.

Where is that lover, sister? He will come when he
    knows your need
I broke his hope and I stained his pride,
I dragged him down in the undertide,
Alone and forsaken by me he died,
The blood that he shed is on my head,
For all the while I know that he bled,
Now I'm old.

Is there no mercy, sister, for the wanton whose course
    is spent?
When a woman is lovely the world will fawn,
But not when her beauty and grace are gone,
When her face is seamed and her limbs are drawn,

I've had my day and I've had my play,
In my winter of loneliness I must pay,
Now I'm old.

What of the morrow, sister? How shall the morrow
    be?
I must feed to the end upon remorse,
I must falter alone in my self-made course,
I must stagger along with my self-made cross,
For I bartered my graces for silks and laces,
My heart I sold for a pot of gold,
Now I'm old.

A Song of Panama

By ALFRED DAMON RUNYON

Forty years ago I listened to Damon Runyon as we sat in the press box at a game between the Highlanders (now the Yankees) and the White Elephants (now the Athletics.) He told of his first writings for an Army paper in the Philippines, while he was a cavalryman chasing the rebel Aguinaldo. When he became a famous sports writer he dropped the Alfred from his name. "A Song of Panama" was inspired by President Theodore Roosevelt's order to the Canal engineers: "Make the dirt fly!"

"Chuff! chuff! chuff!" An' a mountain bluff
    Is moved by the shovel's song;
"Chuff! chuff! chuff!" Oh, the grade is rough
    A liftin' the landscape along!

We are ants upon a mountain, but we're leavin' of our
    dent,
An' our teeth-marks bitin' scenery they will show the
    way we went;
We're a liftin' half creation, an' we're changin' it
    around,
Just to suit our playful purpose when we're diggin'
    in the ground.

"Chuff! chuff! chuff!" Oh, the grade is rough,
  An' the way to the sea is long;
"Chuff! chuff! chuff!" an' the engines puff
  In tune to the shovel's song!

We're a shiftin' miles like inches, and we grab a for-
    est here
Just to switch it over yonder so's to leave an angle
    clear;
We're a pushin' leagues o' swamps aside so's we can
    hurry by—
An' if we had to do it we would probably switch the
    sky!

"Chuff! chuff! chuff!" Oh, it's hard enough
  When you're changin' a job gone wrong;
"Chuff! chuff! chuff!" an' there's no rebuff
  To the shovel a singin' its song!

You hears it in the mornin' an' you hears it late at
    night—
It's our battery keepin' action with support o' dyna-
    mite;
Oh, you gets it for your dinner, an' the scenery skips
    along
In the movin' panorama to the chargin' shovel's song!

"Chuff! chuff! chuff!" an' it grabs the scruff
  Of a hill an' boots it along;
"Chuff! chuff! chuff!" Oh, the grade is rough,
  But it gives to the shovel's song!

This is a fight that's fightin', an' the battle's to the
    death;
There ain't no stoppin' here to rest or even catch your
    breath;
You ain't no noble hero, an' you leave no gallant
    name—
You're a fightin' Nature's army, an' it ain't no easy
    game!

"Chuff! chuff! chuff!" Oh, the grade is rough,
  An' the way to the end is long,
"Chuff! chuff! chuff!" an' the engines puff
  As we lift the landscape along!

The Shooting of
Dan McGrew

BY ROBERT W. SERVICE

Klondike Mike was a famous old sourdough. On his return from the Yukon, the rumor spread that he had been in at the death of Dan McGrew. Despite his repeated denials, the rumor persisted until finally Mike began to believe it himself.

A bunch of the boys were whooping it up in the Mala-
  mute saloon;
The kid that handles the music-box was hitting a jag-
  time tune;
Back of the bar, in a solo game, sat Dangerous Dan
  McGrew;
And watching his luck was his light-o'-love, the lady
  that's known as Lou.

Reprinted by permission of Dodd, Mead & Company from The Collected Poems of Robert Service.

When out of the night, which was fifty below, and into
the din and the glare,
There stumbled a miner fresh from the creeks, dog-
dirty, and loaded for bear.
He looked like a man with a foot in the grave and
scarcely the strength of a louse,
Yet he tilted a poke of dust on the bar, and he called
for drinks for the house.
There was none could place the stranger's face,
though we searched ourselves for a clue;
But we drank his health, and the last to drink was
Dangerous Dan McGrew.

There's men that somehow just grip your eyes, and
hold them hard like a spell;
And such was he, and he looked to me like a man who
had lived in hell;
With a face most hair, and the dreary stare of a dog
whose day is done,
As he watered the green stuff in his glass, and the
drops fell one by one.
Then I got to figgering who he was, and wondering
what he'd do,
And I turned my head—and there watching him was
the lady that's known as Lou.

His eyes went rubbering round the room, and he
seemed in a kind of daze,
Till at last that old piano fell in the way of his wan-
dering gaze.
The rag-time kid was having a drink: there was no
one else on the stool,
So the stranger stumbles across the room, and flops
down there like a fool.
In a buckskin shirt that was glazed with dirt he sat,
and I saw him sway;
Then he clutched the keys with his talon hands—my
God! but that man could play.

Were you ever out in the Great Alone, when the moon
    was awful clear,
And the icy mountains hemmed you in with a silence
    you most could *hear;*
With only the howl of a timber wolf, and you camped
    there in the cold,
A half-dead thing in a stark, dead world, clean mad
    for the muck called gold;
While high overhead, green, yellow and red, the North
    Lights swept in bars?—
Then you've a hunch what the music meant...hunger
    and night and the stars.

And hunger, not of the belly kind, that's banished
    with bacon and beans,
But the gnawing hunger of lonely men for a home and
    all that it means:
For a fireside far from the cares that are, four walls
    and a roof above;
But oh! so cramful of cozy joy, and crowned with a
    woman's love—
A woman dearer than all the world, and true as Hea-
    ven is true—
(God! how ghastly she looks through her rouge—the
    lady that's known as Lou.)

Then on a sudden the music changed, so soft that you
    scarce could hear;
But you felt that your life had been looted clean of all
    that it once held dear;
That someone had stolen the woman you loved; that
    her love was a devil's lie;
That your guts were gone, and the best for you was to
    crawl away and die.
'Twas the crowning cry of a heart's despair, and it
    thrilled you through and through—
"I guess I'll make it a spread misere," said Danger-
    ous Dan McGrew.

The music almost died away. . .then it burst like a pent-up flood;

And it seemed to say, "Repay, repay," and my eyes were blind with blood.

The thought came back of an ancient wrong, and it stung like a frozen lash,

And the lust awoke to kill, to kill . . .then the music stopped with a crash,

And the stranger turned, and his eyes they burned in a most peculiar way;

In a buckskin shirt that was glazed with dirt he sat, and I saw him sway;

Then his lips went in a kind of grin, and he spoke, and his voice was calm,

And "Boys," says he, "you don't know me, and none of you care a damn;

But I want to state, and my words are straight, and I'll bet my poke they're true,

That one of you is a hound of hell. . .and that one is Dan McGrew."

Then I ducked my head, and the lights went out, and two guns blazed in the dark,

And a woman screamed, and the lights went up, and two men lay stiff and stark.

Pitched on his head, and pumped full of lead, was Dangerous Dan McGrew,

While the man from the creeks lay clutched to the breast of the lady that's known as Lou.

These are the simple facts of the case, and I guess you ought to know.

They say that the stranger was crazed with "hooch," and I'm not denying it's so.

I'm not so wise as the lawyer guys, but strictly between us two—

The woman that kissed him—and pinched his poke— was the lady that's known as Lou.

The Ballad of Yukon Jake

BY EDWARD E. PARAMORE, JR.

Imitation may be the sincerest form of flattery, but in parody is also an implicit tribute to the fame of the original. I think Mr. Paramore has paid Robert Service a high compliment in his masterful parody.

Oh, the North Countree is a hard countree
That mothers a bloody brood;
And its icy arms hold hidden charms
For the greedy, the sinful and lewd.
And strong men rust, from the gold and the lust
That sears the Northland soul,
But the wickedest born, from the Pole to the Horn,
Is the Hermit of Shark-Tooth Shoal.

Now Jacob Kaime was the Hermit's name
In the days of his pious youth,
Ere he cast a smirch on the Baptist church
By betraying a girl named Ruth.
But now men quake at "Yukon Jake,"

The Hermit of Shark-Tooth Shoal,
For that is the name that Jacob Kaime
Is known by from Nome to the Pole.
He was just a boy and the parson's joy
(Ere he fell for the gold and the muck),
And had learned to pray, with the hogs and the hay
On a farm near Keokuk.
But a Service tale of illicit kale,
And whisky and women wild,
Drained the morals clean as a soup tureen
From this poor but honest child.

He longed for the bite of a Yukon night
And the Northern Light's weird flicker,
Or a game of stud in the frozen mud,
And the taste of raw red licker.
He wanted to mush along in the slush,
With a team of husky hounds,
And to fire his gat at a beaver hat
And knock it out of bounds.

So he left his home for the hell-town Nome,
On Alaska's ice-ribbed shores,
And he learned to curse and to drink, and worse,
Till the rum dripped from his pores,
When the boys on a spree were drinking it free
In a Malamute saloon
And Dan Megrew and his dangerous crew
Shot craps with the piebald coon;
When the Kid on his stool banged away like a fool
At a jag-time melody,
An the barkeep vowed, to the hard-boiled crowd,
That he'd cree-mate Sam McGee—

Then Jacob Kaime, who had taken the name
Of Yukon Jake, the Killer,
Would rake the dive with his forty-five
Till the atmosphere grew chiller.

With a sharp command he'd make 'em stand
And deliver their hard-earned dust,
Then drink the bar dry of rum and rye,
As a Klondike bully must.
Without coming to blows he would tweak the nose
Of Dangerous Dan Megrew,
And, becoming bolder, throw over his shoulder
The lady that's known as Lou.

Oh, tough as a steak was Yukon Jake—
Hard-boiled as a picnic egg.
He washed his shirt in the Klondike dirt,
And drank his rum by the keg.
In fear of their lives (or because of their wives)
He was shunned by the best of his pals,
An outcast he, from the comradery
Of all but wild animals.
So he bought him the whole of Shark-Tooth Shoal,
A reef in the Bering Sea,
And he lived by himself on a sea lion's shelf
In lonely iniquity.

But, miles away, in Keokuk, Ia.,
Did a ruined maiden fight
To remove the smirch from the Baptist Church
By bringing the heathen Light;
And the Elders declared that all would be spared
If she carried the holy words
From her Keokuk home to the hell-town Nome
To save those sinful birds.

So, two weeks later, she took a freighter,
For the gold-cursed land near the Pole,
But Heaven ain't made for a lass that's betrayed—
She was wrecked on Shark-Tooth Shoal!
All hands were tossed in the sea, and lost—
All but the maiden Ruth,
Who swam to the edge of the sea lion's ledge

Where abode the love of her youth.
He was hunting a seal for his evening meal
(He handled a mean harpoon)
When he saw at his feet, not something to eat,
But a girl in a frozen swoon,
Whom he dragged to his lair by her dripping hair,
And he rubbed her knees with gin.
To his great surprise, she opened her eyes
And revealed—his Original Sin!

His eight-months beard grew stiff and weird,
And it felt like a chestnut burr,
And he swore by his gizzard and the Artic blizzard
That he'd do right by her.
But the cold sweat froze on the end of her nose
Till it gleamed like a Tecla pearl,
While her bright hair fell, like a flame from hell,
Down the back of the grateful girl.
But a hopeless rake was Yukon Jake,
The Hermit of Shark-Tooth Shoal!
And the dizzy maid he betrayed
And wrecked her immortal soul. . . .
Then he rowed her ashore, with a broken oar,
And he sold her to Dan Megrew
For a husky dog and some hot eggnog,
As rascals are wont to do.

Now ruthless Ruth is a maid uncouth
With scarlet cheeks and lips,
And she sings rough songs to the drunken throngs
That come from the sealing ships.
For a rouge-stained kiss from this infamous miss
They will give a seal's sleek fur,
Or perhaps a sable, if they are able;
It's much the same to her.

Oh, the North Countree is a rough countree,
That mothers a bloody brood;

And its icy arms hold hidden charms
For the greedy, the sinful and lewd.
And strong men rust, from the gold and the lust
That sears the Northland soul,
But the wickedest born from the Pole to the Horn
Was the Hermit of Shark-Tooth Shoal!

The Cremation of Sam McGee

By Robert W. Service

Mr. Service's admirers are divided as to which is his best—this or "The Shooting of Dan McGrew." I wonder how you feel about it.

There are strange things done in the midnight sun
  By the men who moil for gold;
The Arctic trails have their secret tales
  That would make your blood run cold;
The Northern Lights have seen queer sights,
  But the queerest they ever did see
Was that night on the marge of Lake Lebarge
  I cremated Sam McGee.

Reprinted by permission of Dodd, Mead & Company. From The Collected Poems of Robert Service.

Now Sam McGee was from Tennessee, where the cotton
    blooms and blows.
Why he left his home in the South to roam 'round the
    Pole, God only knows.
He was always cold, but the land of gold seemed to
    hold him like a spell;
Though he'd often say in his homely way that "he'd
    sooner live in hell."

On a Christmas Day we were mushing our way over
    the Dawson trail.
Talk of your cold! through the parka's fold it stabbed
    like a driven nail.
If our eyes we'd close, then the lashes froze till some-
    times we couldn't see;
It wasn't much fun, but the only one to whimper was
    Sam McGee.

And that very night, as we lay packed tight in our
    robes beneath the snow,
And the dogs were fed, and the stars o'erhead were
    dancing heel and toe,
He turned to me, and "Cap," says he, "I'll cash in
    this trip, I guess;
And if I do, I'm asking that you won't refuse my last
    request."

Well, he seemed so low that I couldn't say no; then he
    says with a sort of moan:
"It's the cursed cold, and it's got right hold till I'm
    chilled clean through to the bone.
Yet 'tain't being dead—it's my awful dread of the icy
    grave that pains;
So I want you to swear that, foul or fair, you'll cre-
    mate my last remains."

A pal's last need is a thing to heed, so I swore I would
    not fail;

And we started on at the streak of dawn; but God! he
    looked ghastly pale.
He crouched on the sleigh, and he raved all day of his
    home in Tennessee;
And before nightfall a corpse was all that left of Sam
    McGee.

With a corpse half hid that I couldn't get rid, I hur-
    ried, horror-driven,
There wasn't a breath in that land of death, and be-
    cause of a promise given;
It was lashed to the sleigh, and it seemed to say: "You
    may tax your brawn and brains,
But you promised true, and it's up to you to cremate
    those last remains."

Now a promise made is a debt unpaid, and the trail
    has its own stern code.
In the days to come, though my lips were dumb, in
    my heart how I cursed that load.
In the long, long night, by the lone firelight, which the
    huskies, round in a ring,
Howled out their woes to the homeless snows— O God!
    how I loathed the thing.

And every day that quiet clay seemed to heavy and
    heavier grow;
And on I went, though the dogs were spent and the
    grub was getting low;
The trail was bad, and I felt half mad, but I swore I
    would not give in;
And I'd often sing to the hateful thing, and it heark-
    ened with a grin.

Till I came to the marge of Lake Lebarge, and a dere-
    lict there lay;
It was jammed in the ice, but I saw in a trice it was
    called the "Alice May."

And I looked at it, and I thought a bit, and I looked
at my frozen chum;
Then "Here," said I, with a sudden cry, "is my cre-
ma-tor-eum."

Some planks I tore from the cabin floor, and I lit the
boiler fire;
Some coal I found that was lying around, and I heaped
the fuel higher;
The flames just roared, and the furnace roared—such
a blaze you seldom see;
And I burrowed a hole in the glowing coal, and I
stuffed in Sam McGee.

Then I make a hike, for I didn't like to hear him sizzle so;
And the heavens scowled, and the huskies howled, and
the wind began to blow.
It was icy cold, but the hot sweat rolled down my
cheeks, and I don't know why;
And the greasy smoke in an inky cloak went streaking
down the sky.

I do not know how long in the snow I wrestled with
grisly fear;
But the stars came out and they danced about ere
again I ventured near;
I was sick with dread, but I bravely said: "I'll just
take a peep inside.
I guess he's cooked, and it's time I looked"; . . . then
the door I opened wide.

And there sat Sam, looking cool and calm, in the heart
of the furnace roar;
And he wore a smile you could see a mile, and he said:
"Please close that door.
It's fine in here, but I greatly fear you'll let in the cold
and storm—
Since I left Plumtree, down in Tennessee, it's the first
time I've been warm."

There are strange things done in the midnight sun
  By the men who moil for gold;
The Arctic trails have their secret tales
  That would make your blood run cold;
The Northern Lights have seen queer sights,
  But the queerest they ever did see
Was that night on the marge of Lake Lebarge
  I cremated Sam McGee.

Out Where the West Begins ·

By Arthur Chapman

John Chapman, noted drama critic of the New York News, sends me this note on his father's famous verse: "It was in 1912. My father, Arthur Chapman, was conducting a column on the Denver Republican, and in Buffalo there was a convention of state governors. Dad saw a news item about the governors' having got into an argument over just where the West began. So he wrote 'Out where the West Begins.' To my father it was just another piece for the column; but to the linotype operator who set it from the original typewritten copy it seemed better than average, and he asked if he could keep the original. Dad said, 'Sure.' I don't know who the printer was."

Out where the handclasp's a little stronger,
Out where the smile dwells a little longer,
  That's where the West begins;
Out where the sun is a little brighter,
Where the snows that fall are a trifle whiter,
Where the bonds of home are a wee bit tighter,
  That's where the West begins.

Out where the skies are a trifle bluer,
Out where friendship's a little truer,
  That's where the West begins;
Out where a fresher breeze is blowing,
Where there's laughter in every streamlet flowing,
Where there's more of reaping and less of sowing,
  That's where the West begins.

Out where the world is in the making,
Where fewer hearts in despair are aching,
  That's where the West begins;
Where there's more of singing and less of sighing,
Where there's more of giving and less of buying,
And a man makes friends without half trying,
  That's where the West begins.

In Kansas

ANONYMOUS

The hillbillys of old Kansas must have been a hell-roaring, rip-snorting outfit, judging by this ballad. Those were the days when "men wuz men and gals wuz gals." There is a similar ballad with an Arkansas setting.

Oh, they churn the butter well
  In Kansas.
They churn the butter well
  In Kansas.
They churn the butter well
And the buttermilk they sell
And they git as lean as hell
  In Kansas.

Oh, potatoes they grow
  In Kansas.
Potatoes they grow small
  In Kansas.
Oh, potatoes they grow small
And they dig 'em in the fall
And they eat 'em hides and all
  In Kansas.

Oh, they chaw terbaccer thin
  In Kansas.
They chaw terbaccer thin
  In Kansas.

They chaw terbaccer thin
Till it runs down on their chin,
But they lick it up agin
   In Kansas.

Oh, they say that drink's a sin
   In Kansas.
They say that drink's a sin
   In Kansas.
They say that drink's a sin
So they guzzle all they kin,
And they throw it up agin
   In Kansas.

Come all who want to roam
   To Kansas.
Come all who want to roam
   To Kansas.
Come all who want to roam
And find yourself a home
And be happy with your doom
   In Kansas.

The Old Settler's Song

By FRANCIS HENRY

Here is one indigenous to the State of Washington about a philosopher who took many lickings, but never knew defeat.

I'd wandered all over the country
Prospecting and digging for gold—
I'd tunnelled, hydraulicked, and cradled,

And I had been frequently sold.
For one who gets riches by mining,
Perceiving that hundreds grow poor,
I made up my mind to try farming—
The only pursuit that is sure.
So rolling my grub in my blankets,
I left all my tools on the ground,
And started one morning to shank it
For a country they call Puget Sound.
Arriving flat broke is mid-winter,
I found it enveloped in fog,
And covered all over with timber
Thick as hair on the back of the dog.
As I looked on the prospect so gloomy
The tears trickled over my face,
For I felt that my travels had brought me
To the edge of the jumping-off place.
I took up a claim in the forest,
And sat myself down to hard toil ;
For two years I chopped and I niggered,
But I never got down to the soil.
I tried to get out of the country,
But poverty forced me to stay
Until I became an Old Settler—
Then nothing could drive me away.
And now that I'm used to the climate,
I think if a man ever found
A spot to live easy and happy,
That Eden is on Puget Sound.
No longer the slave of ambition,
I laugh at the world and its shams,
As I think of my pleasant condition,
Surrounded by acres of clams.

◆ ◆ ◆

Woman's the Cause of It All

ANONYMOUS

*This is a more or less complete catalogue of the evils women can do.
Supply the rest yourself.*

When a man waxes his mustache and tries to look neat,
  Woman's the cause of it all;
He brushes his clothes from his head to his feet,
  Woman's the cause of it all;
He walks down the street, a young lady he'll meet,
He's caught by her smile, because she looks neat,
But when he feels the effect of her husband's big feet,
  Woman's the cause of it all!

When a man's married a year he loses his brain,
  Woman's the cause of it all;
One year, that's all, and he's fully insane,
  Woman's the cause of it all;
A baby is born, he raved and he swore,
He carries the kid and walks up and down the floor,
One kid is enough, he don't want any more,
  Woman's the cause of it all!

Adam one time the apple did bite,
  Woman's the cause of it all;
He must have done wrong, for he didn't do right,
  Woman's the cause of it all;
Mother Eve made him do it, he wasn't to blame,
And when they got Abel, they started to raise Caine.
And now the whole world is doing the same,
  Woman's the cause of it all!

✦ ✦ ✦

Lydia Pinkham

ANONYMOUS

The fame of this obscure but enterprising woman of New England became nationwide. Her product still marches on.

Let us sing of Lydia Pinkham
And her love for the human race:
How she sells her veg'table compound,
And the papers publish her face.

Mrs. Brown had female weakness;
Couldn't have a child at all,
Till she took some veg'table compound;
Now she has triplets every fall.

Oh, it sells for a dollar a bottle,
Which is very cheap you see,
And if it doesn't cure you
She will sell you six for three.

Now she's dead and gone to Heaven,
Mourned by all the human race;
Still they sell her veg'table compound,
And the papers publish her face.

✦ ✦ ✦

Jersey City Maiden

ANONYMOUS

Originally English, this has several American locales. But, some of my best friends being Jerseyites, I choose this version for sentimental as well as artistic reasons.

In Jersey City where I did dwell,
A bold butcher boy loved me quite well,
'Til there came a girl of ill repute
And the butcher boy became a brute,
Then he ran away from this fair town,
Took him a chair and sat right down,
Took other strange girls upon his knee
And told them things he kept from me.
Now I don't see any reason why
Unless they had more golden eyes:
But gold will melt, silver will fly.
I hope some day they'll become as I.

She went upstairs to fix her bed;
Not a word to her mamma she said.
Mamma went off upstairs saying
"Daughter dear, what is troubling you?"
"Oh, Mamma, Mamma, I dare not tell;
It's the butcher boy I loved so well,
He courted me my heart away
And with me he would not stay."
Her papa came in from work
Saying "where is my daughter so dear,"
Off upstairs he did go
And there found her hanging by a rope.
Upon her breast was a letter found
Saying, "when you find me cut me down—
Go dig my grave both wide and deep;
Place a marble stone at my head and feet;
Upon my breast place a turtle dove,
To show the world I died for love."

How Salvator Won the Race

By Ella Wheeler Wilcox

*This author wrote much about love, but I'm sure she liked to look 'em
over once in a while.*

The gate was thrown open, I rode out alone,
More proud than a monarch who sits on a throne
I am but a jockey, but shout upon shout
Went up from the people who watched me ride out,
And the cheers that rang forth from the warm-hearted
    crowd
Were as earnest as those to which monarch e'er bowed.

My heart thrilled with pleasure, so keen it was pain,
As I patted my Salvator's soft silken mane;
And a sweet shiver shot from his hide to my hand
As we passed by the multitude down to the stand.
The great waves of cheering came billowing back.
As the hoofs of brave Tenny ran swift down the track;
And he stood there beside us, all bone and all muscle,
Our noble opponent, well trained for the tussle
That waited us there on the smooth shining course,
My Salvator, fair to the lovers of horse,
As a beautiful woman is fair to man's sight—
Pure type of the thoroughbred, clean limbed and
    bright,
Stood taking the plaudits as only his due
And nothing at all unexpected or new.

And then, there before us the bright flag is spread,
There's a roar from the grandstand, and Tenny's
    ahead;
At the sound of the voices that shouted 'a go!'
He sprang like an arrow shot straight from the bow
I tighten the reins on Prince Charlie's great son,
He is off like a rocket, the race is begun.

Half way down the furlong, their heads are together,
Scarce room 'twixt their noses to wedge in a feather,
Past grandstand and judges, in neck-to-neck strife,
Ah, Salvator, boy! 'tis the race of your life.

I press my knees closer, I coax him, I urge—
I feel him go with a leap and a surge;
I see him creep on, inch by inch, stride by stride,
While backward, still backward, falls Tenny beside.
We are nearing the turn, the first quarter is passed—
'Twixt leader and chaser the daylight is cast;
The distance elongates, still Tenny sweeps on,
As graceful and free-limbed and swift as a fawn,
His awkwardness vanished, his muscles all strained,
A noble opponent, well born and well trained.

I glanced o'er my shouder, hah, Tenny, the cost
Of that one second's flagging, will be—the race lost.
One second's weak yielding of courage and strength,
And the daylight between us had doubled its length.
The first mile is covered, the race is mine—no!
For the blue blood of Tenny responds to a blow.
He shoots through the air like a ball from a gun,
And the two lengths between us are shortened to one.

My heart is contracted, my throat feels a lump—
For Tenny's long neck is at Salvator's rump;
And now, with new courage, grows bolder and bolder,
I see him once more running shoulder to shoulder.
With knees, hands, and body I press my great steed,
I urge him. I coax him. I pray him to heed!
Oh, Salvator! Salvator! List to my calls.
For the blow of my whip will hurt both if it falls.
There's a roar from the crowd like the ocean in storm,
As close to my saddle leaps Tenny's great form;
One more mighty plunge, and, with knee, limb, and
    hand,

I lift my horse first by a nose past the stand;
We are under the string now—the great race is done—
And Salvator, Salvator, Salvator won!

Cheer, hoar-headed patriarchs; cheer loud, I say,
'Tis the race of the century witnessed to-day!
Though ye live twice the space that's allotted to men,
Ye never will see such a grand race again.
Yet the shouts of the populace roar like the surf,
For Salvator, Salvator, king of the turf!
He has rivalled the record of thirteen long years,
He has won the first place in the vast line of peers;
'Twas a neck-to-neck contest, a grand, honest race,
And even his enemies grant him the place;
Down into the dust let old records be buried,
And hang out 2:05 in the gaze of the world.

Since Hannah Answered "Yes."

By Clarence Hawkes

This blind singer of Goshen, Massachusetts retained his sense of humor despite his affliction.

I 'low a change has come my way,
The wind has kind o' shifted,
Life didn't hardly seem to pay
Afore the shadow lifted.
The farm wuz all a-runnin' down,
The craps wuz gittin' bad
There wa'n't no market in the town
For anything I had;
The pigs looked runty, an' the cows
Were all a goin' dry,
There wa'n't much clover in the mows,
An' provender wuz high;
An' somehow, too, the dear ole sky

Looked duller ev'ry day,—
Perhaps 'twas somethin' in my eye
That made it seem that way.
But one dark night there came a change—
There! now, I've let it out;
It seemed ter me so very strange
That it should come about.
This night I saw the dear girl hum;
Nor dreamed that she would bless
My lonely life, yet told her all,
An' Hannah answered "Yes."
Why! what a change came over things!
The pigs began ter fat!
The hens laid eggs enough each day
Ter more than fill my hat.
The weeds got scurser, an' the craps
Began ter grow like mad,
An' ev'ry day was bright enough
Ter make a stunwall glad!
All Nater seemed ter jine right in!
Perhaps you'll think it chaff,
But true's I'm born, that very night
Ole Brindle hed a calf!

A Soiled Little Girl and a Cop

BY KENNETH C. BEATON (K.C.B.)

Who doesn't remember this author's unique style of comment on the little, everyday acts of kindness he observed?

SITTING DOWN.
IN AN automobile.
WAITING FOR someone.
I SAW a girl.
A VERY small girl.
AND WHETHER it was.

SHE'D BEEN in swimming.
AND DIDN'T know how.
TO DRESS herself.
OR HAD a fight.
WITH SOME tough little girl.
I COULDN'T tell.
BUT SHE came along.
WITH FREQUENT stops.
AND VAIN attempts.
TO MAKE herself.
MORE PRESENTABLE.
AND AS she neared.
MY WAITING place.
IT WAS plain to see.
SHE HAD been crying.
FOR HER little eyes.
WERE VERY red.
AND HER face was soiled.
WHERE IT had been rubbed.
WITH DIRTY hands.
AND I didn't know.
WHAT I should do.
FOR I don't know much.

BUT I had a feeling.
I SHOULD do something.
AND HAD determined.
TO OFFER aid.
WHEN THERE appeared.
AROUND THE corner.
A BIG policeman.
AND HE looked at her.
AND SPOKE to her.
AND PICKED her up.
AND STOOD her.
ON A concrete wall.
BEFORE A lawn.

AND LOOKED her over.
AND FUSSED around.
FOR A little while.
AND TOOK from a pocket.
A HANDKERCHIEF.
AND UNFOLDED it.
AND DAMPENED it.
AT A nearby hydrant.
AND WASHED her face.
AND PUT her down.
AND SHE ran away.
AS FAST as she could.
AND NEVER once.
DID THE big cop smile.
HE JUST fixed her up.
AND WENT his way.
AND A few minutes later.
I SAW him again.
HERDING THE children.
ACROSS THE street.
AT A nearby school.
AND I know women.
WHO FRIGHTEN their children.
BY THREATENING them.
THEY'LL call a policeman.
I THANK YOU.

◆ ◆ ◆

Yut Ho

By Wallace Irwin

Most American ballads come from the wide-open spaces, but here is a superb piece out of the Chinese district of the biggest city in the world.

Ghosts, yu ask, in Chinytown? Say ther ain't no moon
    to-night,
An' the alley here is dark—let's move over to the light.
Did yu see 'er? No, the one wit' the blossom in 'er
    hair—
Kind o' sidle t'rough the crowd, kind o' fade up yon-
    der stair
Wit' 'er flat eyes showin' white, on 'er lips a bloody
    stain—
Yes, I've been a-smokin' hop and the devil's in me
    brain—
But the Chinee ghosts is out, and I seen 'er, seen 'er
    plain!

'Twas a shadder? Yes, perhaps. I have orfen seen 'em
    so,
And the little one that passed was the shadder of Yut
    Ho,

Reprinted from Chinatown Ballads by permission of the author.

Her that was a Christian slave, daughter of the merchant, Kwan,
Sam Up boss, who ruled the roost till he dropped 'is wealth at *fan*
Died in pious peace and left 'is fat widow fer to pay
Fer cold storage on 'is bones w'en they shipped the box away
To be planted in the tombs w'ere 'is dads and granddads lay.

Now the mother, Luey Sing wit' 'er little porky eyes
Figgered up the girl, Yut Ho, as a piece o' merchandise,
Thinkin' how the cash on hand to be netted on the same
Would pay off the honest debts Kwan had left behind the game.
So she made a sing-song talk wit' the dealer, Wong Tin Gay,
Till he promised on 'is joss he would call around next day
Wit' a thousand dollars cash, jest to take the girl away.

Yut Ho, squattin' in 'er room, seen the dealer come, and heard
All the chin-chin down below—understood it every word;
And she gathered what she owned in a green silk handkerchief,
Raised the skylight of 'er room and crept quiet as a thief
T'rough the frame, along the tiles, 'cross the roof wit' padded feet,
Found a ladder to the ground w'ere she glided down, then fleet
As a bird she sought the door o' the Mission up the street.

So the Mission Lady came and she found 'er at the
door
Bobbin' like a j'inted doll till 'er *saam* sleeves touched
the floor,
Sayin' over as she dipped, like a lesson, very slow,
All the English words she knew: "Melly Clistmas—me
Yut Ho."
Then her green silk handkerchief she untied and
brought to view
What she owned: a ring o' jade and a pitcher fer *sam
shu*,
And a little candy heart stamped in English, "I Love
You."

Well, the Lady understood and the Mission took 'er in;
But the mother, Luey Sing, bein' old in years and sin,
Vowed to git 'er daughter back, even if she had to
raise
All the Eight Immortal Ones and the High Six Com-
panies,
So she offered Yung Ho-eng, blackmail expert, Hop
Sing man,
Half the value of the girl if he'd smoke 'er up a plan,
Somp'n smooth—and that's the time that the tunnel-
work began.

Two years passed, a deal o' time w'en a girl is seventeen
(Courtin' time for any girl, be she yeller, white or
green);
So the Mission Lady looked for a decent Chinee lad
As would take 'er to 'is home and as wouldn't treat 'er
bad—
Two years! what the hell are *they* to the yeller race—
as cold
As the idols that they feed wit' their rice-cakes and
ther gold
To appease their wooden hearts, shriveled tight—and
oh, how old!

Yut Ho, bein' trained and taught, was a-gittin' civil-
ized,
Learnin' white folks' customs, too, in a manner Chris-
tianized,
Half-believed the Bible-talks and the pious hymns, I
think
(Which is plenty more sincere than the average Chris-
tian Chink);
Called the Mission school 'er home, never pinin' for
the lack
Of 'er early heathen ways—always dreadin' to go back
To the slav'ry and the sin of 'er Bartlett Alley shack.

'Bout this time ther come a Chink to the Mission Sun-
day-school,
Pie-faced barber, name Min Hop, godly as the Golden
Rule.
He was just a pig-tailed saint—nothin' less—in all 'is
acts,
Seemed to eat the very ink off the gospel books and
tracts,
Talked religion t'rough 'is hat till 'is teachers felt so
free
That they smiled a happy smile w'en he calls and says,
says he,
"Me heep Clistian China boy—likee Yut Ho mally
me."

Sure the Mission Lady t'ought that Min Hop was jest
the stuff—
Yut Ho also seen the boy and she liked 'im well
enough,
Though she had 'er own mistrusts, fer she hesitated
some
W'en he asked an early date fer the weddin'-day to
come.
After that Min called wit' flowers Thursday evenin'
onct a week,

Sat there purrin' like a cat, somp'n wonderful how
 meek,
Yut Ho doin' fancy-work, much too proper-like to
 speak.

No one knows how it occurred—it was jest the Chinee
 way—
Min the barber and Yut Ho left the Mission school one
 day.
Yes, I seen 'em hand in hand shufflin' on wit' padded
 feet
T'rough the little painted lane leadin' into Jackson
 Street,
Wit' her green silk handkerchief holdin' all the wealt'
 she knew—
Jest a finger-ring o' jade and a pitcher fer *sam shu,*
And a little candy heart marked in English "I Love
 You."

Bartlett Alley, number twelve—see the workin' of the
 plan?—
Wit' a brace o' handy pals stood Ho-eng, the Hop
 Sing man,
Lookin' up and down the lane from the corner of 'is
 eye.
Min Hop leadin' of the girl, nudged 'im soft as he went
 by,
And the shadders drew in close, choked 'er, dragged 'er
 'er up a stair—
Someone shuffled down the hall and an iron door
 banged in there—
Chinytown, a-passin' by, seen and smiled and didn't
 care.

Bartlett Alley, number twelve—in a cellar-room behind
There's an opium-smokin' j'int buried where the cops
 can't find.

Yes, I've been there off and on—mostly *on* I guess of late,
Fer the "black smoke" draws and draws till yu love the things yu hate;
Love the brown molasses string as yu pull it frum the shell,
As it bulbs above the lamp wit' its sickish, peanut smell
Till yu drink and drink the smoke, tastin' heaven in its hell.

On a brown bench 'long o' mine, poppy-dead, a smoker lay
Wit' 'is open eyes all glazed like the lacquer on a tray.
At 'is desk (way off it looked), the proprietor, Ah Ying,
Sat a-countin' of 'is cash, passin' beads upon a string;
Now the room seemed long and long, and the light was like a spark;
Ying seemed threadin' colored stars on to moonbeams t'rough the dark,
Catchin' comets by their tails—Hello! *What's that racket?—Hark!*

In a room above me head I could hear a moanin' high
Like a woman in distress callin' China-fashion, "Ai-i-i-i!"
Full an hour it seemed to wail all around me—then was still
Till the silence creepin' in struck me clammy-like and chill.
Som'ers in me dopy brain I could hear a small voice say:
"That was *her,* and that was *her* that you seen 'em steal to-day!"
Then the smoke clumb to me head and I tumbled clean away.

W'en I woke and looked around, middle daylight, gray and wide,
Filtered t'rough a greasy pane from a greasy court outside.
Wit' the stable drug in me brain and me senses all awhirl
Comes the memory of a sound—'twas the night-cry of the girl
I had heard—then wit' the thrills, pins and needles in me hair.
From the reekin' j'int I reeled, staggered to the open air—
Bartlett Alley, number twelve, up the narrow, windin' stair.

Down the long, dark passageway, gropin, wit' me hands I steered
To a gratin' in the wall w'ere a square o' lamplight leered.
Peepin' t'rough the prison-hole all the inside room I seen:
China lilies in a bowl, teak-wood tables, brown and clean,
Hangin' prayer-scrolls—as I looked a black shadder seemed to fall
Stark and straight and human-like, up and down across the wall—
(Shadders! ah, the shapes they take, and I guess I've seen 'em all!)

Peerin' closer I could see to the beam above me head
Yut Ho hangin' by 'er neck from 'er silken waist-sash —dead.
Right before me near the lamp—could o' touched 'em wit' me hand—
Was 'er green silk handkerchief spread out careful on a stand

Where she'd laid wit' lovin' care all the treasures that
    she knew—
Jest a finger-ring o' jade and a pitcher fer *sam shu*
And a little candy heart stamped in English "I Love
    You."

Ghosts in Chinytown? O Gawd! if the risin' spooks
    begin
Comin' in their proper shapes wit' a ghost fer every
    sin,
What a beastly lot would swarm from the cellars over
    there,
Spotted, dragon-headed worms wit' ther queues o'
    human hair—
But *she* doesn't come that way when she flutters from
    the grave,
Fades and flickers like the breath of the little life she
    gave
As a heathen sacrifice with a Christian soul to save!

Scum o' the Earth

BY ROBERT HAVEN SCHAUFFLER

*This ballad should give us pause when we stand at highly-polished bars
or sit at abundant dinner tables giving vent to our opinions of people
we know so little about.*

I

At the gate of the West I stand,
On the island where nations throng.
We call the "scum o' the earth;"

Stay, are we doing you wrong,
Young fellow from Socrates' land?—

You, like Hermes so lithe and strong
Fresh from the master Praxiteles' hand?
So you're of Spartan birth?
Descended, perhaps, from one of the band—
Deathless in story and song—
Who combed their long hair at Thermopylae's
    pass? ....
Ah, I forget what straits (alas!),
More tragic than theirs, more compassion-worth,
Have doomed you to march in our "immigrant class"
Where you're nothing but "scum o' the earth."

II

You Pole with the child on your knee,
What dower have you to the land of the free?
Hark! does she croon
The sad little tune
Chopin once mined from the Polish air
And mounted in gold for us to wear?
Now a ragged young fiddler answers
In wild Czech melody
That Dvorak took whole from the dancers.
And the heavy faces bloom
In the wonderful Slavic way;
The dull little eyes, the foreheads' gloom,
Are suddenly fair and gay,
While, watching these folk and their mystery,
I forget that we,
In our scournful mirth
Brand them as "Polacks"—and "scum o' the earth."

III

Genoese boy of the level brow,
Lad of the lustrous, dreamy eyes
Agaze at Manhattan's pinnacles now
In the first, glad shock of a hushed surprise;
Within your far-rapt seer's eyes
I catch the glow of the wild surmise

That played on the *Santa Maria's* prow
In that still gray dawn,
Four centuries gone,
When a world from the wave began to rise.
Oh, who shall foretell what high emprise
Is the goal that gleams
When Italy's dreams
Spread wing and sweep into the skies?
Caesar dreamed him a world ruled well;
Dante dreamed Heaven out of Hell;
Angels brought us there to dwell;
And you, are you of a different birth?—
You're only a "dago,"—"scum o' the earth!"

IV

Stay, are we doing you wrong
Calling you "scum o' the earth,"
Man of the sorrow-bowed head,
Of the features tender yet strong,—
Man of the eyes full of wisdom and mystery
Mingled with patience and dread?
Have not I known you in history,
Sorrow-bowed head?
Were you the poet-king, worth
Treasures of Ophir unpriced?
Or were you the prophet, whose art
Foretold how the rabble would mock
That shepherd of spirits, ere long,
Who should gather the lambs to his heart
And tenderly feed his flock?
Man—lift that sorrow-bowed head. . . .
Behold, the face of the Christ!
The vision dies at its birth.
You're merely a butt for our mirth.
You're a "sheeny"—and therefore despised
And rejected as "scum o' the earth."

Countrymen, bend and invoke
Mercy for us blasphemers,
For that we spat on these marvelous folk,
Nations of darers and dreamers,
Scions of singers and seers,
Our peers, and more than our peers.
"Rabble and refuse," we name them
And "scum o' the earth," to shame them.
Mercy for us of the few, young years,
Of the culture so callow and crude,
Of the hands so grasping and rude,
The lips so ready for sneers,
At the sons of our ancient more-than-peers.
Mercy for us who dare despise
Men in whose loins our Homer lies;
Mothers of men who shall bring to us
The glory of Titian, the grandeur of Huss;
Children in whose frail arms may rest
Prophets and singers and saints of the West.
Newcomers all from the eastern seas,
Help us incarnate dreams like these.
Forgive and forget that we did you wrong.
Help us to father a nation strong
In the comradeship of an equal birth,
In the wealth of the richest bloods of earth.

The Conqueror

BY GRANTLAND RICE

You will find much food for thought in this piece by one of America's greatest sports writers.

I am the conqueror of clown and king,
Of prince and pauper in this shaking world.

I rule the race, as to the field I bring
Power that leaves so many banners furled.

I grip the young and old, and drive them back
From heights they might have gained, except for me.
I am the ghost which haunts each open track
By vale or mountain or by plain and sea.

I am the barrier that wrecks a dream.
I am the fog from which the cautious steer.
I take from life its color and its gleam.
I am the master—and my name is Fear.

From Only The Brave, *Published by A. S. Barnes & Co.*

Old Soldiers Never Die

Anonymous

From an old English ballad book. This is the version introduced at West Point by General Summerall in the early '90s. Like all the others, this is derived from "Kind Words Never Die", written by the Hutchinson family in England and published in this country in 1858.

Old Soldiers never die,
  Never die,
  Never die;
Old Soldiers never die—
They simply fade away.

Old Soldiers never die,
  Never die,
  Never die;
Old Soldiers never die,
Young ones wish they would.

This rain will never stop,
  Never stop,
  Never stop;
This rain will never stop,
No, oh! no, no, no.

Index of First Lines

INDEX OF FIRST LINES